Korean
phrase book

Berlitz Publishing Company, Inc.

Princeton   Mexico City   Dublin   Eschborn   Singapore

Developed and produced for Berlitz Publishing Company by:
G&W Publishing Services, Oxfordshire, U.K.
Korean edition: Dr. Heejin Lee, Dr. Jaehoon Yeon, and Bong-Nye Shin.

Contents

Stores & Services 129

Health 161

English--Korean dictionary & index 169
Korean–English glossary 208

Reference 216

Pronunciation

This section is designed to familiarize you with the sounds of Korean using our simplified phonetic transcription. You'll find the pronunciation of the Korean sounds explained below, together with their "imitated" equivalents. This system is used throughout the phrase book. When you see a word spelled phonetically, simply read the pronunciation as though it were English, noting any special rules.

The Korean language

Korean has an affinity with Chinese and Japanese. It is related in writing and, to a certain extent, in vocabulary to Chinese. The structure of Korean sentences is similar to those of Japanese. The Koreans have adopted a great number of Chinese words and characters. These often have a polite, scientific or cultural bearing, in the same way as words of French (Latin) origin in English generally have a more lofty meaning than those of Anglo-Saxon origin. They are not normally those used in everyday language by the man in the street. Also Korean is undergoing steady change and is developing as time goes on. Words disappear and new ones are picked up, just as the English spoken today is no longer that of Shakespeare's day.

Korean has a certain number of dialects; someone from the north of the country may be incapable of understanding a man from the south. However, when they get together they will generally make themselves understood by using the dialect of Seoul which is accepted as being the leading version of Korean.

Written Korean

The unique Korean alphabetic system, **hangul**, was devised after many years of study by King Sejong and his scholars, and was introduced in 1446 during his reign. It originally consisted of 28 letters, but this number has been reduced to 24. These are used for writing native Korean words. Before **hangul** was devised, there was no adequate way of depicting Korean thought and language in written form. The only method available was through the use of Chinese characters. However, Korean and Chinese were unrelated languages, and hence the system was completely unsatisfactory. **Hangul** is an ingenious system, and is remarkably simple to learn (➤ 8–9). King Sejong boasted that a clever person could learn **hangul** in a morning, and even a foolish person could understand it after only ten days of study! Koreans are proud of **hangul**, and King Sejong is widely respected. October 9th is celebrated as *Hangul Day* in Korea.

In addition to **hangul**, written Korean also uses Chinese characters, known as **hanja**. There is a basic list of 1,800 approved **hanja**, but there are many more identified in Korean dictionaries. However, nowadays very few Koreans, whether from the north or south, could be described as being functionally literate in **hanja**. In South Korea, Chinese characters are usually restricted to maps, limited use in newspapers, restaurant signs, and occasionally for writing names on name cards.

Korean Sounds

Hangul is composed less of vowels and consonants than of syllables, consisting of a consonant and a vowel. Single consonants do occur at the end of words and there are double and complex consonant groups, but generally the pattern you will find is one of consonant and vowel, consonant and vowel.

Consonants

Letter	Approximate pronunciation	Symbol	Example	Pronunciation
ㄱ	g as in get	g	감	gam
ㄴ	n as in no	n	나	na
ㄷ	d as in duck	d	돈	dawn
ㄹ	1. between English r and l 2. pronounced n after m, n, or ng	r/l	나라	nara
ㅁ	m as in moon	m	물	mool
ㅂ	b as in book	b	불	bool
ㅅ	1. s as in sip 2. sh as in ship	s/sh	산	san
ㅇ	ng as in thing	ng	양	yang
ㅈ	j as in jam	j	줄	jool
ㅊ	ch as in chicken	ch	춤	choom
ㅋ	k as in kill	k	콩	kawng
ㅌ	t as in table	t	탈	tal
ㅍ	p as in park	p	팔	pal
ㅎ	h as in hill	h	혼	hawn

Vowels

Letter	Approximate pronunciation	Symbol	Example	Pronunciation
ㅏ	*a* as in *a*rm	a	안	*an*
ㅑ	*ya* as in *y*ard	ya	야구	*yagoo*
ㅓ	*u* as in f*u*r	o	엄지	*omjee*
ㅕ	*aw* as in l*aw*	yo	여자	*yoja*
ㅗ	*o* as in n*o*	aw	오전	*awjon*
ㅛ	*yo* as in *yo*ga	yo	요금	*yogum*
ㅜ	*oo* as in b*oo*t	oo	우산	*oosan*
ㅠ	like the word *you*	yoo	유산	*yoosan*
ㅡ	*e* as in brok*e*n	u	어른	*orun*
ㅣ	*ee* as in f*ee*t	**ee**	비	*bee*

These are the main sounds connected with each letter, but they can vary and this is reflected in the imitated pronunciation for individual phrases.

The Korean alphabet and word formation

The **hangul** alphabet forms words in a very different way to Western alphabets. The emphasis is more on putting vowels and consonant together in blocks so that they rather resemble a Chinese character. In this way for example the first syllable of the word "hangul" itself is made up by an '**h**' in the top left corner, an '**a**' in the top right corner, and an '**n**' at the bottom, with the grouping having a distinct resemblance to a Chinese character. These syllabic groupings are then strung together to form words.

Traditionally the language was written from top to bottom and from right to left as in Chinese. However, now the Western practice of writing horizontally from left to right is standard.

Some basic Korean words

Below you can see some examples of how words are formed in the **hangul** script. Instead of writing the letters one after the other in a straight line, they are written in a square, starting at the top, left-hand corner. So the first word below is **san** (mountain), which consists of the letters ㅅ (**s**), ㅏ (**a**), and ㄴ (**n**). These letters are written in a square to form the word **san**: 산.

산   *san* (mountain)
(ㅅ+ㅏ+ㄴ)

물   *mool* (water)
(ㅁ+ㅜ+ㄹ)

밥   *bap* (rice)
(ㅂ+ㅏ+ㅂ)

공   *kawng* (ball)
(ㄱ+ㅗ+ㅇ)

돈   *don* (money)
(ㄷ+ㅗ+ㄴ)

Basic Expressions

ESSENTIAL

Yes/No.	네/아니요. ne/a-neeyo
Okay.	좋습니다. chaw-ssumneeda
Please.	부탁합니다. pootak-hamneeda
Thank you (very much).	(정말) 감사합니다. (chong-mal) kamsa-hamneeda

Greetings/Apologies 인사/사과

Hello!/Hi!	안녕하세요.	an-nyong haseyo
Good morning/afternoon.	안녕하세요.	an-nyong haseyo
Good evening.	안녕하세요.	an-nyong haseyo
Good night.	안녕히 주무세요.	an-nyong-ee choomoo-seyo
Good-bye. (if you're leaving)	안녕히 계세요.	an-nyong-ee keseyo
Good-bye. (to someone leaving)	안녕히 가세요.	an-nyong-ee kaseyo
Excuse me! (getting attention)	여보세요!	yobaw-seyo
Excuse me. (May I get past?)	실례합니다.	seelle-hamneeda
Sorry!	미안합니다!	meean-hamneeda
Don't mention it. _it's OKay_	천만에요.	chon-maneyo
Never mind.	괜찮습니다.	kwen-chan-ssumneeda

Communication difficulties
의사소통의 어려움

Do you speak English?	영어 하세요? *yong-o haseyo*
Does anyone here speak English?	여기 영어 하시는 분 계십니까? *yogee yong-o hasee-nun poon ke-seemneekka*
I don't speak (much) Korean.	저는 한국어 (잘) 못 합니다. *cho-nun han-googo (chal) mawt-ham-needa*
Could you speak more slowly?	더 천천히 말씀해 주시겠습니까? *to chon-chonee malssume chooseege-ssumneekka*
Could you repeat that?	다시 말씀해 주시겠습니까? *tasee malssume chooseege-ssumeekka*
Excuse me? [Pardon?]	뭐라 하셨습니까? *moo-o-ra hasyo-ssumeekka*
Please write it down.	써 주십시오 *sso chooseep-seeyo*
Can you translate this for me?	이걸 번역해 주시겠습니까? *eegol pon-yoke chooseege-ssumeekka*
What does this/that mean?	이건/그건 무슨 뜻입니까? *eegon/kugon moosun dut-eem-neekka*
Please point to the phrase in the book.	이 책에서 그 구절을 가리켜 주십시오. *ee cheg-eso ku koojo-rul karee-kyo jooseep-seeyo*
I understand.	알겠습니다. *alge-ssumneeda*
I don't understand.	모르겠습니다. *mawruge-ssumneeda*
Do you understand?	아시겠습니까? *aseege-ssumneekka*

– *aw-chon-won eemneeda.*
– *mawruge-ssumneeda.*
– *aw-chon-won eemneeda.*
– *sso chooseep-seeyo. ... ah, "5000 won."*

Questions 질문

To form simple questions you change the **-da** ending of the statement into the **-kka** question ending and add rising intonation.

Peter-ka sine-e kam-nee-da.   Peter is going to town.
Peter-ka sine-e kam-nee-kka?   Is Peter going to town?

Where? 어디? _ODEE_

Where is it?	어디에 있습니까? _odee-e ee-ssumneekka_
Where are you going?	어디 가십니까? _odee ka-seemneekka_
at the meeting place [point]	만남의 장소에서 manna-me chang-saw-eso
downstairs	아래층 are-chung
from the U.S.	미국에서 mee-goog-eso
here (to here)	여기 (여기로) yogee (yogee-raw)
in the car	차 안에 cha-ane
in Korea	한국에 han-googe
inside	안에 ane
near the bank	은행 근처에 unheng kuncho-e
next to the apples	사과 바로 옆에 sagwa paraw yope
opposite the market	시장 맞은 편 seejang majun-pyon
on the left/on the right	왼쪽에 / 오른쪽에 wen-zawge/awrun-zawge
there (to there)	거기 (거기로) kogee (kogee-raw)
to the hotel	호텔로 hawtel-law
towards Pusan	부산으로 pusan-uraw
outside the café	카페 밖에 kape pakge
up to the traffic lights	저 교통 신호등까지 cho kyo-tawng seenhaw-dung-gajee
upstairs	위층 wee-chung

When? 언제?

When does the museum open? ONDE	박물관 몇시에 엽니까? *pang-mool-gwan myo-ssee-e yom-neekka*
When does the train arrive?	기차 언제 도착합니까? *keecha onje tawchak ham-neekka*
10 minutes ago	십분 전 *seep-boon jon*
after lunch	점심 후 *chomseem hoo*
always	항상 *hang-sang*
around midnight	자정 쯤 *chajong zum*
at 7 o'clock	일곱시에 *eelgawp-see-e*
before Friday	금요일 전에 *kum-yo-eel jone*
by tomorrow	내일까지 *ne-eel-gajee*
early	일찍 *eelzeek*
every week	매 주 *me choo*
for 2 hours	두시간 동안 *too-seegan tawng-an*
from 9 a.m. to 6 p.m.	오전 아홉시부터 오후 여섯시까지 *awjon ahawp-see booto awhoo yosot-see gajee*
immediately	즉시 *chuk-see*
in 20 minutes	이십분 지나서 *eeseep-boon cheenaso*
never	단 한번도 *tan hanbon-daw*
not yet	아직 *ajeek*
now	지금 *jee-gum*
often	종종 *chawng-jawng*
on March 8	삼월 팔일에 *samwol pal-eere*
on weekdays	주중에 *choo-joong-e*
sometimes	가끔 *kakgum*
soon	곧 *kawt*
then	그때 *kutde*
within 2 days	이일 안에 *ee-eel ane*

What sort of ...?

I'd like something ...	... 주십시요. *chooseep-seeyo*
It's beautiful/ugly.	예쁩니다./밉습니다. *yepbum-needa/meep-ssumneeda*
It's big/small.	큽니다/작습니다. *kum-needa/chak-ssumneeda*
It's cheap/expensive.	쌉니다/비쌉니다. *ssam-needa/pee-ssam-needa*
It's clean/dirty.	깨끗합니다/더럽습니다. *gegut-hamneeda/torop-ssumneeda*
It's dark/light.	어둡습니다/밝습니다. *odoop-ssumneeda/pal-ssumneeda*
It's easy/difficult.	쉽습니다/어렵습니다. *sweep-ssumneeda/oryop-ssumneeda*
It's good/bad.	좋습니다/나쁩니다. *chaw-ssumneeda/napbum-needa*
It's heavy/light.	무겁습니다/가볍습니다. *moogop-ssumneeda/kabyop-ssumneeda*
It's hot/cold.	뜨겁습니다/참니다. *dugop-ssumneeda/cham-needa*
It's narrow/wide.	좁습니다/넓습니다. *chawp-ssumneeda/ nol-ssumneeda*
It's old/new.	낡았습니다/새것입니다. *nalga-ssumneeda/sego-seemneeda*
It's open/shut.	열려 있습니다/닫혀 있습니다. *yollyo-ee-ssumneeda/tacho-ee-ssumneeda*
It's quick/slow.	빠릅니다/느립니다. *barum-needa/nureem-needa*
It's right/wrong.	맞습니다/틀립니다. *ma-ssum-needa/ tulleem-needa*
It's tall/short.	깁니다/짧습니다. *keem-needa/ zal-ssumneeda*
He's young/old.	그 사람은 젊습니다/늙었습니다. *ku sara-mun chom-sumneeda/ nulgo-ssumneeda*

Korean nouns have no articles (a, an, the) and no plural forms. Whether the noun is singular or plural is judged from the context, or by a number modifying the noun.

Adjectives are usually placed in front of nouns, as in English: **cha** (a car); **chaw-un cha** (a nice car).

Korean verb forms do not vary between singular and plural, but change depending on who you are talking to and their status (➤ 169).

How much/many? 얼마/몇개? *ALMA*

How much is that?	그거 얼마입니까? *kugo olma eemneekka*
How many are there?	몇개 있습니까? *myotge ee-ssumneekka*
1/2/3	일/이/삼 *eel/ee/sam*
4/5	사/오 *sa/aw*
none	하나도 없습니다. *hanado op-ssumneeda*
about 1, 000 Won	약 천원 *yak chon-won*
a little	조금 *chaw-gum*
a lot of milk	우유 많이 *oo-yoo manee*
enough	충분히 *choong-boon-ee*
few/a few of them	조금 *chaw-gum*
more than that	그것보다 많이 *kugo-bawda manee*
less than that	그것보다 적게 *kugo-bawda chokge*
much more	훨씬 더 많이 *hwol-sseen to manee*
There is nothing else.	더 없습니다. *to op-ssumneeda*
too much	너무 많이 *nomoo manee*

Why? 왜? *weh*

Why is that?	왜 그럽니까? *we kurom-neekka*
Why not?	왜 안됩니까? *we an-dwem-neekka*
It's because of the weather.	날씨때문입니다. *nalssee demoon-eemneeda*
Because I'm in a hurry.	바쁘기 때문입니다. *papboo-gee demoon-eemneeda*
I don't know why.	이유를 모릅니다. *eeyoorul mawrum-needa*

Who?/Which? 누구?/어떤?

Who's there?	누구세요? *noogoo-seyo*
It's me!	접니다! *chom-needa*
It's us!	우립니다! *ooreem-needa*
someone	어떤 사람 *otdon saram*
no one	아무도 *a-moodaw*
Which one do you want?	어느 것으로 하시겠습니까? *onu kosuraw haseege-ssumneekka*
this one/that one	이것/그것 *eegot/kugot*
one like that	그와 같은 것 *kuwa-gatun got*
not that one	그게 아니고 *kuge aneego*
something	무언가 *moo-on-ga*
nothing	아무것도 *amoo-got-daw*
none	아무것도 *amoo-got-daw*

Whose? 누구 것?

Whose is that?	그것은 누구 것입니까? *kugo-sun noo-goo got-eemneekka*
It's mine/ours/yours.	내 것/우리 것/당신 것입니다. *ne got/ooree got/tangseen got eemneeda*
It's his/hers/theirs.	그 남자 것/그 여자 것/그 사람들 것입니다. *ku namja got/ku yoja got/ku saramdul got eemneeda*
It's ... turn.	... 차례입니다. *... chare-eemneeda*
my/our/your	제/우리의/당신의 *che/ooree-e/tangseen-e*
his/her/their	그 남자의/그 여자의/그 사람들의 *ku namja-e/ku yoja-e/ku saram-dure*

GRAMMAR

The order of words in a Korean sentence is different from English. The basic rule is subject – object – verb, whereas in English it is usually subject – verb – object. Subordinate clauses, or additional information, come last in the sentence. For example, in English we say "My wife wore a new dress when she came home," but in Korean the word order would be "My wife home came when, [and] she wore a new dress."

How? 어떻게?

How would you like to pay?	어떻게 계산하시겠습니까?
otdoke	*otdoke kesan-haseege-ssumneekka*
I'll pay by credit card.	신용 카드로 하겠습니다.
	seen-yong kadu-raw hage-ssumneeda
I'll pay by cash.	현금으로 하겠습니다.
	hyon-gum-uraw hage-ssumneeda
How are you getting here?	어떻게 여기 오셨습니까?
	otdoke yogee awsyo-ssumneekka
I'm getting here …	… (여기) 왔습니다.
	… (yogee) wa-ssumneeda
by car/by bus/by train	차로/버스로/기차로
	cha-raw/posu-raw/keecha-raw
on foot	걸어서 *koroso*
quickly	빨리 *ballee*
slowly	천천히 *chon-chonee*

Is it …?/Are there …? … 입니까?/있습니까?

Is it …?	… 입니까? *… eemneekka*
Is it free of charge?	공짜입니까? *kawng-za-eemneekka*
It isn't ready.	준비가 안됐습니다.
	choonbee-ga an-dwe-ssumneeda
Is there …?	… 있습니까? *… ee-ssumneekka*
Are there …?	… 있습니까? *… ee-ssumneekka*
Is there a shower in the room?	방에 샤워 있습니까?
	pang-e syawo ee-ssumneekka
Are there buses into town?	시내로 가는 버스 있습니까?
	seene-raw ganun posu ee-ssumneekka
There aren't any towels in my room.	제 방에 수건이 한 장도 없습니다.
	che pang-e soogon-ee han-chang-daw op-sumneeda
Here it is/they are.	여기 있습니다. *yogee ee-ssumneeda*
There it is/they are.	저기 있습니다. *chogee ee-ssumneeda*

Can/May?
할 수있습니까?/해주시겠습니까?

Can I/we have …?	… 해주시겠습니까?
	he chooseege-ssumneekka
May I speak to …?	… 씨 계십니까?
(over the telephone)	… *ssee keseemneekka*
Can you tell me …?	… 제게 말씀해 주시겠습니까?
	jege malssume chooseege-ssumneekka
Can you help me?	도와주시겠습니까?
	taw-wa chooseege-ssumneekka
Can you direct me to …?	… 로 어떻게 갑니까?
	… *raw otdoke kamneeda*
I'm sorry, but I can't.	죄송합니다만 할 수 없습니다. *chwe-sawng-*
	ham-needa-man hal-soo op-sumneeda

What do you want? 뭘 하시겠습니까?

I'd/We'd like a(n) …	… 주십시요. … *chooseep-seeyo*
I'd/We'd like to …	… 하고 싶습니다.
	… *hagaw seep-sumneeda*
Could I have …?	… 주시겠습니까?
	… *chooseege-ssumneekka*
Give me …	… 주세요. … *chooseyo*
I'm looking for …	저는 … 찾고 있습니다.
	cho-nun … chatgo ee-ssumneeda
I need to find …	저는 … 찾아야 합니다.
	cho-nun … chajaya hamneeda
I need to see …	저는 … 봐야 합니다.
	cho-nun … paw-aya hamneeda
I need to speak to …	저는 … 얘기해야 합니다.
	cho-nun … yegee-heya hamneeda

– *seelle-hamneeda.*
– *ne?*
– *chonun meesuto keem gwa yegee hagaw*
  seep-ssumneeda.
– *cham-ganman kee-daryo chooseep-seeyo.*

18

Other useful words
기타 유용한 표현

fortunately	다행히도 *taheng-eedaw*
hopefully	바라건대 *para-gonde*
of course	물론 *mool-lawn*
perhaps/possibly	아마 *ama*
probably	어쩌면 *ozo-myon*
unfortunately	불행히도 *poolheng-eedaw*

Exclamations 감탄문

At last!	드디어! *tu-dee-o*
Go on.	계속하세요 *kesawk-haseyo*
Goodness!	맙소사! *map-sawsa*
I don't mind.	상관 없습니다. *sang-gwan op-ssumneeda*
Really?	정말입니까? *chong-mal-eemneekka*
Nonsense.	말도 안되는 소리. *maldaw an-dwenun sawree*
That's enough.	됐습니다. *dwe-ssumneeda*
That's true.	사실입니다. *saseel-eemneeda*
You're joking!	농담이지요! *nawng-dam eejeeyo*
How are things?	요즘 어떻습니까? *yojum otdo-ssumneekka*
Fine, thank you.	잘 지냅니다. *chal cheenem-needa*
great/terrific	근사합니다 *kunsa-hamneeda*
very good	아주 좋습니다 *ajoo chaw-ssumneeda*
fine	좋습니다 *chaw-sumneeda*
not bad	나쁘지 않습니다 *napbujee an-ssumneeda*
okay	괜찮습니다 *kwen-chan-ssumneeda*
not good	좋지 않습니다 *chaw-chee an-ssumneeda*
terrible	엉망입니다 *ong-mang eemneeda*

Accommodations

Making reservations ahead of time is essential in most major tourist centers during the high season (May to November). If you are stuck without a room, the Korean National Tourism Organization (**han-gook kwan-gwang hyop-hwe**) can help you find one. In South Korea, there is a wide range of accommodation to choose from, from luxury Western-style hotels to government-run campsites. In North Korea, foreigners must stay in Western-style tourist hotels which are modern but expensive.

호텔 hawtel
Western-style hotels. There are many Western-style hotels in South Korea, and their standards are comparable to equivalent hotels in Europe and the United States. All top-end hotels and many mid-range ones will charge an extra 10% tax plus 10% service charge.

여관 yogwan
Korean-style inns. These are cheaper than Western-style hotels, and give you the opportunity to get to know Korean people and culture. Bathrooms usually have to be shared, although some rooms have private facilities. **Chang**-type inns are more upmarket and have private baths in all rooms.

민박 meenbak
Home-stay system. These are rooms in private houses, and facilities are usually shared with the family. In some rural areas, this may be the only type of accommodation available. You can find out about **meenbak** at tourist information centers or in stores and restaurants.

산장/대피소 sanjang/tepeesaw
Mountain huts and shelters. These can be found in many national parks, are very basic (no private facilities), and are only open during the summer season.

유스호스텔 yoosu-hawsutel
Youth hostels. There are only 10 youth hostels in South Korea, but they are large, modern, and usually have restaurants. You can book them through the Korean Youth Hostel Association (KYHA) in Seoul, ☎ 02 725 3031.

Reservations 예약

In advance 사전 예약

Can you recommend a
hotel in ...?

... 에 좋은 호텔 뭐 있습
니까?
*... e chaw-un hawtel moo-o
ee-ssumneekka*

Is it near the center of town?

시내 근처에 있습니까?
seene kuncho-e ee-ssumneekka

How much is it per night?

하룻밤에 얼마입니까?
haroop-bame olma-eemneekka

Is there anything cheaper?

더 싼 거 있습니까?
to ssan go ee-ssumneekka

Could you reserve me
a room there, please?

거기 방 하나 예약해 주시겠습니까?
*kogee pang hana yeyake
chooseege-ssumneekka*

At the hotel 호텔에서

Do you have any vacancies?

빈 방 있습니까?
peen pang ee-ssumneekka

Is there another hotel nearby?

근처에 다른 호텔 있습니까?
kuncho-e tarun hawtel ee-ssumneekka

I'd like a single/double room.

저는 일인용 방을/이인용 방을 원합니다.
*cho-nun eereen-nyong pang-ul/
ee-een-nyong pang-ul won-hameeda*

Can I see the room, please?

방을 볼 수 있겠습니까?
pang-ul pawl soo eetge-ssumneekka

I'd like a room with ...

...가 있는 방을 주십시요.
...ka een-nun pang-ul chooseep-seeyo

twin beds/a double bed

일인용 침대 두개/이인용 침대 *eereen-
nyong cheemde tooke/ee-een-nyong cheemde*

a bath/shower

욕조/샤워 *yokzaw/syawo*

- chonun ee-een-nyong pang-ul won-hamneeda.
- chwe-sawng hameeda, mawdoo gwak cha-ssumneeda.
- kuncho-e tarun hawtel ee-ssumneekka?
- ne, chawson hawte-ree paraw
kuncho-e ee-ssumneeda.

Reception 프론트

I have a reservation. 저는 예약했습니다.
cho-nun yeyak he-ssumneeda

My name is ... 제 이름은 ... 입니다.
che eeru-mun ... emneeda

We've reserved a double and 우리는 이인용 방과 일인용 방을
a single room. 예약했습니다. *ooree-nun ee-een-nyong pang-gwa eereen-nyong pang-ul yeyak he-ssumneeda*

I confirmed my reservation 편지로 예약을 확인했습니다.
by mail. *pyon-jee-raw yeya-gul hwag-een he-ssumneeda*

Could we have adjoining rooms? 붙어있는 방으로 주시겠습니까?
pooto-eennun pang-uraw chooseege-ssumneekka

Amenities and facilities 시설

Is there (a/an) ... in the room? 그 방에 ... 있습니까?
ku pang-e ... ee-ssumneekka

air conditioning 에어컨 *eokon*

TV/telephone 텔레비전/전화
tele-beejon/chon-hwa

Does the hotel have a(n) ...? 호텔에 ... 있습니까?
hawtere ... ee-ssumneekka

cable TV 유선 방송 *yooson pang-sawng*

laundry service 세탁 서비스 *setak sobeesu*

solarium 일광욕실 *eel-gwang-yok-seel*

swimming pool 수영장 *sooyong-jang*

Could you put ... in the room? 방에 ... 넣어주시겠습니까?
pang-e ... no-o chooseege-ssumneekka

an extra bed 보조 침대 *pawchaw cheemde*

a crib [a child's cot] 아기용 침대 *agee-yong cheemde*

Do you have facilities for 어린이용/장애 자용 시설이 있습니까?
children/the disabled? *oreenee-yong/chang-eja-yong seesoree ee-ssumneekka*

How long ...? 얼마나 ...?

We'll be staying ...	우리는 ... 묵을 것입니다. *ooree-nun ... moogul ko-seemneeda*
one night only	하룻밤만 *haroop-bam-man*
a few days	며칠간 *myo-cheel-gan*
a week (at least)	(적어도) 일주일간 *(cho-godaw) eelzoo-eelgan*
I don't know yet.	아직 모르겠습니다. *ajeek mawruge-ssumneeda*
I'd like to stay an extra night.	하룻밤 더 묵고 싶습니다. *haroop-bam to mookgaw seep-sumneeda*
What does this mean?	이게 무슨 뜻입니까? *eege moosun du-seemneekka*

– an-nyong haseyo. che eerumun
John Newton-eemneeda.
– an-nyong haseyo, Newton-ssee.
– ooree-nun myo-cheel-gan moogul ko-seemneeda.
– chaw-ssumneeda. ee yong-jee-rul chaksong-he
chooseep-seeyo.

여권을 보여주시겠습니까?	May I see your passport, please?
이 용지를 작성해주십시요.	Please fill in this form.
선생님 자동차 번호가 어떻게 됩니까?	What is your car registration number?

방만 ... 원	room only ... Won
아침식사 포함	breakfast included
식사 됩니다	meals available
이름	name/first name
주소	home address
국적/직업	nationality/profession
생년월일/출생지	date/place of birth
여권 번호	passport number
자동차 번호	car registration number
서명	signature

Price 가격

How much is it ...?	... 얼마입니까? *... olma-eemneekka*
per night/week	하룻밤에/일주일에 *haroop-bame/eelzoo-ee-re*
for bed and breakfast	아침식사 포함해서 *acheem-seeksa paw-ham-heso*
excluding meals	식사 제외하고 *seeksa chewe-ha-gaw*
for American Plan (A.P.) [full board]	하루 세 끼 포함해서 *haroo sekgee paw-ham-heso*
for Modified American Plan (M.A.P.) [half board]	아침 저녁 포함해서 *acheem cho-nyok paw-ham-heso*
Does the price include ...?	가격에 ... 포함돼 있습니까? *kagyo-ge ... paw-ham-dwe ee-ssumneekka*
breakfast	아침식사 *acheem-seeksa*
sales tax [VAT]	부가가치세 *pooga gachee-se*
Do I have to pay a deposit?	보증금 내야 합니까? *pawjung-gum neya hamneekka*
Is there a discount for children?	어린이 할인 있습니까? *oreenee hareen ee-ssumneekka*

Decision 결정

May I see the room?	그 방 볼 수 있습니까? *ku pang pawl soo ee-ssumneekka*
That's fine. I'll take it.	좋습니다. 이걸로 하겠습니다. *chaw-ssumneeda. eegol-law hage-ssumneeda*
It's too dark/small.	너무 어둡습니다/작습니다. *nomoo odoop-sumneeda/chak-ssumneeda*
It's too noisy.	너무 시끄럽습니다. *nomoo seekgurop-sumneeda*
Do you have a(n) ... room?	... 방 있습니까? *... pang ee-ssumneekka*
bigger/cheaper	더 큰/더 싼 *to kun/to ssan*
quieter/lighter	더 조용한/더 밝은 *to chaw-yong-han/to palgun*
No, I won't take it.	아니요, 이건 안하겠습니다. *aneeyo, eegon anhage-ssumneeda*

Problems and complaints
문제와 불만사항

The … doesn't work.	… 고장입니다. … *kawjang-eemneeda*
air conditioning	에어컨 *eokon*
fan	선풍기 *sonpoong-gee*
light	전등 *chondung*
I can't turn the heat [heating] on/off.	난방을 켤 수가／끌 수가 없습니다. *nambang-ul kyol soo-ga/gul soo-ga op-sumneeda*
There is no hot water.	더운 물이 나오지 않습니다 *do-oon mooree na-awjee an-ssumneeda*
There is no toilet paper.	화장실 휴지가 없습니다. *hwajang-seel hyoo-jee-ga op-sumneeda*
The faucet [tap] is dripping.	수도꼭지에서 물이 계속 샙니다. *soodaw gawk-zee-eso mooree gesawk semneeda*
The sink/toilet is blocked.	세면대가／화장실이 막혔습니다. *se-myonde-ga/hwajang-see-ree makyo-ssumneeda*
The window/door is jammed.	창문이／문이 열리지 않습니다. *changmoo-nee/moo-nee yol-leejee an-ssumneeda*
My room has not been made up.	방청소가 안 돼있습니다. *pang chong-saw-ga an-dwe-eessumneeda*
The … is broken.	… 고장나 있습니다. … *kawjang-na ee-ssumneeda*
blind/lamp	차양／전등 *chayang/chondung*
lock/switch	자물쇠／스위치 *chamool-swe/suwee-chee*

Action 행동

Could you have that seen to?	그것을 고쳐 주시겠습니까? *kugo-sul kawcho chooseege-ssumneekka*
I'd like to move to another room.	다른 방으로 옮기고 싶습니다. *tarun pang-uraw awm-geegaw seep-sumneeda*
I'd like to speak to the manager.	지배인과 얘기하고 싶습니다. *cheebe-een-gwa yegee-hagaw seepsumneeda*

General requirements
일반 요구사항

Both 110V (U.S.-style: 2 flat pins) and 220V (2 round pins) are common; new tourist hotels tend to have 200V outlets.

About the hotel 호텔에 관하여

Where's the …?	… 어디 있습니까? … odee ee-ssumneekka
bar	바 pa
bathroom [toilet]	화장실 hwajang-seel
dining room	식당 seek-dang
elevator [lift]	엘리베이터 ellee-be-eeto
parking lot [car park]	주차장 choocha-jang
sauna	사우나 sa-oona
shower	샤워실 syawo-seel
swimming pool	수영장 sooyong-jang
tour operator's bulletin board	여행사 안내판 yoheng-sa anne-pan
Where are the bathrooms [toilets]?	화장실 어디 있습니까? hwajang-seel odee ee-ssumneekka
What time is the front door locked?	몇시에 정문을 잠급니까? myossee-e chong-moonul cham-gum-neekka
What time is breakfast served?	몇시에 아침을 줍니까? myossee-e acheemul choomneekka
Is there room service?	룸 서비스 있습니까? loom sobeesu ee-ssumneekka

면도기만 사용가능	razors [shavers] only
비상구	emergency exit
방화문	fire door
방해 하지 마시오	do not disturb
외부 전화는 … 누르세요.	dial … for an outside line

Personal needs 개인적 요구

If you are staying in a Korean house on a bed and breakfast basis (**meenbak**), remember to remove your shoes before you enter and leave them outside.

The key to room ..., please.	... 호 열쇠 주십시오. ... *haw yol-swe chooseep-sseeaw*
I've lost my key.	열쇠를 잃어버렸습니다. *yol-swerul eero-boryo-ssumneeda*
I've locked myself out of my room.	열쇠를 방안에 둔 채 문을 잠갔습니다. *yol-swerul pang-ane toon-che moo-nul cham-go-ssumneeda*
Could you wake me at ...?	... 시에 깨워주시겠습니까? ... *see-e gewo jooseege-ssumneekka*
I'd like breakfast in my room.	방에서 아침을 먹고 싶습니다. *pang-eso acheemul mokgaw seep-sumneeda*
Can I leave this in the safe?	이걸 금고에 보관해 주시겠습니까? *eegol kumgaw-e paw-gwanhe chooseege-ssumneekka*
Could I have my things from the safe?	금고에서 물건을 찾을 수 있겠습니까? *kumgaw-eso moolgonul chajul-soo eetge-ssumneekka*
Where is our tour guide?	우리 가이드는 어디 있습니까? *ooree gaeedu-nun odee ee-ssumneekka*
May I have (a/an) extra ...?	... 하나 더 주시겠습니까? ... *hana to chooseege-ssumneekka*
bath towel/blanket	욕실 수건/담요 *yokseel soogon/tam-nyo*
hangers/pillow	옷걸이/베개 *awtgoree/pege*
soap	비누 *peenoo*
Is there any mail for me?	제게 온 편지 있습니까? *che-ge awn pyonjee ee-ssumneekka*
Are there any messages for me?	제게 연락 온 것 있습니까? *che-ge yollak awn-go ee-ssumneekka*

BREAKFAST ➤ 43; CHANGING MONEY ➤ 138

Renting 임대

We've reserved an apartment/cottage in the name of ...	우리는 ... 이름으로 아파트를/집을 예약했습니다. *ooree-nun ... erum-uraw apaturul/cheebul yoyak he-ssumneeda*
Where do we pick up the keys?	열쇠를 어디서 받습니까? *yol-swerul odeeso passumneekka*
Where is the ...?	... 어디 있습니까? *... odee ee-ssumneekka*
electricity meter	전기 계량기 *chon-gee ke-ryang-gee*
fuse box	휴즈함 *hooju-ham*
valve [stopcock]	차단밸브 *chadan-belbu*
water heater	온수기 *awnsoo-gee*
Are there any spare ...?	... 여분 있습니까? *... yoboon ee-ssumneekka*
fuses	휴즈 *hooju*
gas bottles	가스통 *kasu-tawng*
sheets	이불 *eebool*
Which day does the maid come?	청소부 무슨 요일에 옵니까? *chong-saw-boo moosun yo-eere awmneekka*
When do I put out the trash [rubbish]?	쓰레기 언제 내놓습니까? *ssuregee onje nenaw-ssumneekka*

Problems 문제거리

Where can I contact you?	선생님께 어떻게 연락할 수 있습니까? *sonseng-neem-ge otdoke yollak-hal soo ee-ssumneekka*
The ... is/are dirty.	... 더럽습니다. *... torop-sumneeda*
The ... has broken down.	... 고장났습니다. *... kawjang-na-ssumneeda*
We accidentally broke/lost ...	실수로 ... 고장냈습니다/잃어버렸습니다. *seelssoo-raw ... kawjang-ne-ssumneeda/ eero-boryo-ssumneeda*
That was already damaged when we arrived.	우리가 도착했을 때 이미 망가져 있었습니다. *ooree-ga tawchak-hessul-de eemee mang-gajo eesso-ssumneeda*

Useful terms 유용한 단어

boiler	보일러 *paw-eel-lo*
crockery	그릇 *kurut*
cutlery (knives and forks)	나이프와 포크 *naeepu-wa pawku*
spoon and chopstick set	수저 *soojo*
frying pan	후라이팬 *hoora-eepen*
kettle	주전자 *choojon-ja*
lamp	전등 *chondung*
refrigerator / freezer	냉장고/냉동고 *neng-jang-gaw/neng-dawng-gaw*
saucepan	냄비 *nembee*
stove [cooker]	난로/조리기구 *nallaw/chawree-gee-goo*
toilet paper	화장실 휴지 *hwajang-seel hyoo-jee*
washing machine	세탁기 *setakgee*

Rooms 방

balcony	발코니 *pal-kawnee*
bathroom	욕실 *yokseel*
bedroom	침실 *cheem-seel*
dining room	식당 *seek-dang*
kitchen	부엌 *poo-ok*
living room	거실 *koseel*
toilet	화장실 *hwajang-seel*

Youth hostel 유스호스텔

Do you have any places left for tonight?	오늘 밤 빈 방 있습니까? *awnul pam peen pang ee-ssumneekka*
Do you rent out bedding?	침구를 빌려줍니까? *cheem-goo-rul peellyo-joomneekka*
What time are the doors locked?	문은 몇시에 잠급니까? *moo-nun myossee-e cham-gum-neekka*
I have an International Student Card.	국제학생증을 갖고 있습니다. *kookze hakseng-zung-ul katgo ee-ssumneeda*

REQUIREMENTS ➤ 26; CAMPING ➤ 30

Camping 캠핑

Camping is very popular in South Korea (weather permitting), and all national parks have campsites. Many are free and where you do pay you are able to use hot showers and flushing toilets.

Reservations 예약

Is there a campsite near here?	근처에 캠핑장 있습니까? *kuncho -e kempeeng-jang ee-ssumneekka*
Do you have space for a tent/trailer [caravan]?	텐트/카라반 자리 있습니까? *tentu/karaban charee ee-ssumneekka*
What is the charge ...?	... 요금은 얼마입니까? *... yogumun olma-ee-mneekka*
per day/week	하루에/일주일에 *haroo-e/eeljoo-eere*
for a tent/a car	텐트 하나에/차 한대에 *tentu hana-e/cha hande-e*
for a trailer [caravan]	카라반 한대에 *karaban hande-e*

Facilities 시설

Are there cooking facilities?	조리시설 있습니까? *chawree-seesol ee-ssumneekka*
Are there any electrical outlets [power points]?	전기 콘센트 있습니까? *chon-gee kawnsentu ee-ssumneekka*
Where is/are the ...?	... 어디 있습니까? *... odee ee-ssumneekka*
drinking water	식수 *seeksoo*
laundry facilities	세탁 시설 *setak seesol*
showers	샤워기 *syawo-gee*
trash cans [dustbins]	쓰레기통 *ssuregee-tawng*
Where can I get some butane gas?	부탄가스 어디서 살 수 있습니까? *pootan-gasu odee-so salsoo eessumneekka*

캠핑 금지	no camping
식수	drinking water
불피지 마시오/취사금지	no fires/no cooking

Complaints 불만사항

It's too sunny/shady/ crowded here.	여기는 너무 햇살이 강합니다/그늘졌습니다/ 혼잡합니다. *yogee-nun nomoo hessa-ree kang-hamneeda/kunul-jossumneeda/ hawnjap-hamneeda*
The ground's too hard/uneven.	바닥이 너무 딱딱합니다/ 울퉁불퉁합니다. *padak-ee nomoo dakdak-hamneeda/ooltoong-booltoong-hamneeda*
Do you have a more level spot?	더 평평한 곳이 있습니까? *to pyong-pyong-han kaw-see ee-ssumneekka*
You can't camp here.	여기서는 캠핑할 수 없습니다. *yogeeso-nun kempeeng-hal soo op-sumneeda*

Camping equipment 캠핑 기구

butane gas	부탄 가스 *pootan-gasu*
campbed	캠핑용 침대 *kempeeng-yong cheemde*
charcoal	숯 *soot*
flashlight [torch]	후레시 *hooresee*
groundcloth [groundsheet]	방수깔개 *pangsoo-galge*
guy rope	밧줄 *pazool*
hammer	망치 *mang-chee*
kerosene stove	휴대용 석유 난로 *hyoode-yong sog-yoo nallaw*
mallet	나무망치 *namoo-mang-chee*
matches	성냥 *song-nyang*
(air) mattress	(공기) 매트리스 *(kawng-gee) metureesu*
paraffin	파라핀 *parapeen*
penknife	주머니칼 *choo-monee-kal*
knapsack	배낭 *penang*
sleeping bag	침낭 *cheem-nang*
tent	텐트 *tentu*
tent pegs	텐트용 쐐기 *tentu-yong sswegee*
tent pole	텐트용 폴 *tentu-yong pawl*

Checking out 체크아웃

What time do we need to vacate the room?	몇시에 방을 비워야 합니까? *myossee-e pang-ul peewoya hamneekka*
Could we leave our baggage here until ... p.m.?	여기에 오후 ... 시까지 짐을 놔둘 수 있습니까? *yogee-e awhoo ... see-gajee chee-mul nwadool soo ee-ssumneekka*
I'm leaving now.	지금 떠납니다. *chee-gum donam-needa*
Could you order me a taxi, please?	택시 불러 주시겠습니까? *teksee poollo chooseege-ssumneekka*
We've had a very enjoyable stay.	아주 잘 묵었습니다. *ajoo chal moogo-sumneeda*

Paying 계산

Although it is not customary to tip in Korea, people do appreciate it. Porters at the airport charge a set fee. And at hotels and restaurants a 10% service charge is normally added to the bill. Tip the porter when he brings the bags to your room, the bellboy if he runs errands, and the taxi driver if he performs a special service like helping with the baggage. However, in nightclubs and other similar venues generous tipping is the order of the day.

May I have my bill, please?	계산서 주시겠습니까? *kesanso chooseege-ssumneekka*
I think there's a mistake in this bill.	계산서에 실수가 있는 것 같습니다. *kesanso-e seelssoo-ga een-nun got kassumneeda*
I've made ... telephone calls.	저는 전화를 ... 통 했습니다. *cho-nun chonhwa-rul ... tawng he-ssumneeda*
I've taken ... from the mini-bar.	저는 미니바에서 ... 꺼내 먹었습니다. *cho-nun meenee-ba-eso ... gone mogo-ssumneeda*
Can I have an itemized bill?	계산서 주시겠습니까? *kesanso chooseege-ssumneekka*
Could I have a receipt, please?	영수증 주시겠습니까? *yong-soojung chooseege-ssumneekka*

TIME ➤ 220

Eating Out

Restaurants 레스토랑

South Korea has many types of eating and drinking establishments. You will find excellent Korean, Chinese, Japanese, and Western-style cuisine. Korean food is usually very spicy and hot, and garlic is a common ingredient. The cuisine is based on meat, poultry, and fish which can pose a problem for vegetarians. Korean food is not served in courses; instead, all the dishes are served at the same time. The standard meal is called **pek-ban** and consists of rice, soup, meat, and a couple of vegetable side dishes (**keem-chee, na-mool** ➤ 43). Koreans eat with spoons (rice and soup) and chopsticks (for side dishes) made of wood, plastic, or metal.

In North Korea, your guide will order you Western-style food in your hotel unless you specifically ask for Korean food. Outside of tourist hotels it is very difficult to find places to eat and drink.

레스토랑 resu-tawrang
These restaurants serve Koreanized Western-style food.

한식집 han-seek jeep
Restaurants specializing in Korean-style food. There are generally two types: those that are large and luxurious and offer entertainment, private rooms, and hostess service – and those that just serve food at ordinary prices.

중국집 choong-gook jeep
Chinese restaurants, which are popular and can be cheap.

분식집 *poon-seek jeep*

Reasonably-priced fast-food restaurants, generally found around universities and other places where young people tend to congregate in large numbers.

다방 *ta-bang*

Coffee shops where coffee and soft drinks are served. They all have music and are very popular throughout South Korea.

술집 *sool-jeep*

A generic term for bars or drinking houses, which are very popular with Koreans.

바 *pa*

Bar where drinks and snacks (**anjoo**) are served. Most bars have hostesses, and you'll have to pay for their drinks, too.

맥주집 *mek-joo jeep*

Beer hall. Serves beer and snacks. Some also offer live entertainment.

룸싸롱 *loom-ssa-rawng*

Literally "room salon." They are like **sool-jeep** and have private rooms and hostesses. They are also very expensive.

포장마차 *paw-jang ma-cha*

Tents which are set up in the evenings and serve drinks and food. These are very popular with Koreans.

Table manners

In Korean homes and restaurants you will find chairs and tables as well as the traditional **awndawl** (heated floor) where you sit on cushions. You will be expected to take off your shoes when entering an **awndawl** dining room. Bare feet, however, may be offensive to older people. Koreans respect their elders, so wait for them to start eating – and do not leave the table before they do.

Korean food can be very hot and spicy, but remember not to blow your nose at the dinner table as this may cause offence. Also, do not leave your spoon or chopsticks in the rice bowl. When you use the spoon, put the chopsticks on the table, and vice versa.

Meal times

Breakfast (**acheem**) 아침   usually served until 9 a.m.
Lunch (**chomseem**) 점심   from noon to 2 p.m.
Dinner (**cho-nyok**) 저녁   from 6 p.m.to 9 p.m.

A table for ..., please.	... 자리 부탁합니다.
	... charee pootak-hamneeda
1/2/3/4	한 사람 /두 사람 /세 사람 /
	네 사람 han saram/too saram/
	se saram/ne saram
Thank you.	감사합니다. kamsa-hamneeda
I'd like to pay.	제가 계산하겠습니다.
	chega kesan hage-ssumneeda

Finding a place to eat 음식점 찾기

Can you recommend a good restaurant?	좋은 음식점 뭐 있습니까? chawun umseek-zom mwo ee-ssumneekka
Is there a ... restaurant near here?	근처에 ... 음식점 있습니까? kunchoe ... umseek-zom ee-ssumneekka
traditional local	전통 한국 chontawng han-gook
Chinese	중국 choong-gook
fish	생선요리 sengson-yoree
Italian	이태리 eeteree
inexpensive	싼 ssan
Japanese	일본 eelbawn
vegetarian	채식 음식점 cheseek umseek-zom
Where can I find a(n) ...?	... 어디 있습니까? ... odee ees-umneekka
burger stand	햄버거집 hembogo-jeep
café/restaurant	카페/레스토랑 kape/resu-tawrang
with a beer garden	비어가든이 있는 beeo-gadunee eennun
fast food restaurant	패스트푸드 음식점 pest-poodu umseek-zom
ice-cream parlor	아이스크림 가게 aeesu-kureem kage
pizzeria	피자 가게 peeja kage
steak house	스테이크 집 sute-eeku jeep

DIRECTIONS ➤ 94

Reservations 식당 예약

I'd like to reserve a table for 2.	두 사람 자리를 예약하고 싶습니다. *too saram charee-rul yeyakagaw seep-sumneeda*
For this evening/tomorrow at ...	오늘 저녁/내일 ... 시 *aw-nul cho-nyok/ne-eel ... see*
We'll come at 8:00.	여덟시에 가겠습니다. *yodol-see-e kage-ssumneeda*
A table for 2, please.	두 사람 자리, 부탁합니다. *too saram charee, bootak-hamneeda*
We have a reservation.	예약했습니다. *yeyak-hessumneeda*

이름이 어떻게 되십니까?	What's the name, please?
죄송합니다. 만원입니다.	I'm sorry. We're very busy/full up.
... 분 후에 자리가 납니다.	We'll have a free table in ... minutes.
... 분 후에 다시 오십시오.	Please come back in ... minutes.

Where to sit 자리

Could we sit ...?	앉을 수 있습니까? *anjul soo ee-ssumneekka*
over there	저기 *cho-gee*
outside	밖에 *pakge*
in a non-smoking area	금연 구역에 *kumyon kooyo-ge*
by the window	창가에 *chang-ga-e*
Smoking or non-smoking?	흡연석 원하십니까, 금연석 원하십니까? *hubyon-sok wonha-seemneekka kumyonsok wonha-seemneekka*

– aw-nul cho-nyok charee-rul yeyakagaw seep-sumneeda.
– myotboon ee-seemneekka?
– ne saram-eemneeda.
– myotsee-e awseel komneekka?
– yodol-see-e kage-ssumneeda.
– eeru-mee otdoke dwe-seemneekka?
– Smith eemneeda.
– alge-ssumneeda. kutde bwep-ge-ssumneeda.

TIME ➤ 220; NUMBERS ➤ 216

Ordering 주문

Waiter!/Waitress!	여보세요! *yobaw-seyo*
May I see the wine list, please?	포도주 리스트를 볼 수 있습니까? *pawdaw-joo leesutu-rul* *bawl soo ee-ssumneekka*
Do you have a set menu?	세트 메뉴 있습니까? *setu me-nyoo ee-ssumneekka*
Can you recommend some typical local dishes?	이 지방 대표 음식으로 무엇이 있습니까? *ee chee-bang depyo* *umseeg-uraw moo-o-see ee-ssumneekka*
Could you tell me what ... is?	... 무언지 말씀해 주시겠습니까? *... moo-onjee malssume* *chooseege-ssumneekka*
What kind of ... do you have?	어떤 종류 ... 있습니까? *otdon chawng-nyoo ... ee-ssumneekka*
I'd like a(n) ...	... 주십시오. *... chooseep-seeaw*
I'll have ...	... 하겠습니다. *... hage-ssumneeda*
a bottle/glass of ...	... 한병/한잔 *... han-byong/han-jan*

주문하시겠습니까?	Are you ready to order?
뭘 드시겠습니까?	What would you like?
음료수 먼저 주문하시겠습니까?	Would you like to order drinks first?
... 추천합니다.	I recommend ...
... 없습니다.	We don't have ...
... 분 걸립니다.	That will take ... minutes.
맛있게 드세요.	Enjoy your meal.

> – *choo-moon haseege-ssumneekka?*
> – *ee chee-bang depyo umseeg-uraw*
>   *moo-o-see ee-ssumneekka?*
> – *ne. Kalbeetang-ee chaw-ssumneeda.*
> – *kuromyon kugo-suraw hage-ssumneeda.*
> – *um-nyosoo-nun moo-ol*
>   *haseege-ssumneekka?*
> – *waeen han-byong chooseep-seeaw.*
> – *alge-ssumneeda.*

DRINKS ➤ *50; MENU READER* ➤ *52*

Side dishes 반찬

Could I have ... without the starter?	전식없이 ... 먹을 수 있습니까? chonseek-opsee ... mogul soo ee-ssumneekka
With a side order of ...	... 반찬으로 ... panchan-uraw
Could I have soup instead of vegetables, please?	야채 대신 국으로 할 수 있습니까? yache teseen koo-guraw hal soo ee-ssumneekka
Does the meal come with vegetables/potatoes?	식사가 야채와/감자와 같이 나옵니까? seeksa-ga yache-wa/kamja-wa kachee na-awmneekka
What sauces do you have?	어떤 소스가 있습니까? otdon sawsu-ga ee-ssumneekka
Would you like ... with that?	그것과 같이 ... 드시겠습니까? kugotgwa kachee ... duseege-ssumneekka
vegetables/salad	야채/샐러드 yache/sellodu
potatoes/fries	감자/감자튀김 kamja/kamja-tweegeem
sauce	소스 sawsu
ice	얼음 orum
May I have some ...?	... 약간 주시겠습니까? ... yakgan chooseege-ssumneekka
bread	빵 bang
butter	버터 poto
lemon	레몬 le-mawn
mustard	겨자 kyoja
pepper	후추 hoochoo
salt	소금 saw-gum
seasoning	양념 yang-nyom
sugar	설탕 soltang
artificial sweetener	감미료 kam-meeryo
vinaigrette [French dressing]	비너그레트/프렌치 드레싱 beeno-guretu/puren-chee dureseeng

General questions 일반적인 질문

Could I/we have (a) clean ..., please? | 깨끗한 ...주시겠습니까? getgutan ... chooseege-ssumneekka

cup/glass | 컵/유리잔 kop/yooree-jan

fork/knife | 포크/나이프 pawku/naeepu

napkin [serviette]/ashtray | 냅킨/재떨이 nepkeen/chetdoree

plate/spoon | 접시/숟가락 chopsee/sootgarak

I'd like some more ..., please. | ... 좀 더 주십시오. ... chawm to chooseep-seeaw

Nothing more, thanks. | 됐습니다. 감사합니다. dwe-ssumneeda. kamsa-hamneeda

Where are the bathrooms [toilets]? | 화장실 어디 있습니까? hwajang-seel odee ee-ssumneekka

Special requirements 특수한 요구사항

I mustn't eat food containing ... | 저는 ... 있는 음식을 먹어서는 안됩니다. cho-nun ... eennun umsee-gul mogo-sonun an-dwem-needa

flour/fat | 밀가루/지방 meel-garoo/cheebang

salt/sugar | 소금/설탕 saw-gum/soltang

Do you have meals/drinks for diabetics? | 당뇨병 환자를 위한 식사/음료수 있습니까? tang-nyo-byong hwanja-rul weehan seeksa/um-nyo-soo eessumneekka

Do you have vegetarian dishes? | 채식 식단이 있습니까? cheseek seekdanee ee-ssumneekka

For the children 어린이용

Do you do meals for children? | 어린이용 식사 있습니까? oreenee-yong seeksa ee-ssumneekka

Could we have a child's seat, please? | 어린이용 의자 있습니까? oreenee-yong ueeja ee-ssumneekka

Where can I feed/change the baby? | 어디서 아기 젖먹일 수/기저귀 갈 수 있습니까? odeeso agee chon-mogeel soo/keejo-gee kal soo eessumneekka

CHILDREN ➤ 113

Fast food/Café 패스트 푸드/카페

Everywhere you go in towns and cities in South Korea you will see a large variety of fast-food outlets, many of which are internationally known. They serve the usual burgers and fries, hot dogs, pizzas, etc.

Something to drink 음료수

I'd like a cup of ...	... 주십시오. ... chooseep-seeaw
tea/coffee	차/커피 cha/kopee
black/with milk	블랙으로/우유 넣어서 pulleg-guraw/ooyoo no-oso
I'd like a ... of red/white wine.	레드/화이트 와인 한 ... 주십시오. redu/hwa-eetu waeen han ... chooseep-seeaw
glass/bottle	잔/병 chan/pyong
Do you have beer?	맥주 있습니까? mekjoo ee-ssumneekka
bottled/draft [draught]	병맥주/생맥주 pyong-mekjoo/seng-mekjoo

And to eat ... 또 먹을 것

A piece of ..., please.	... 하나 주십시오. ... hana chooseep-seeaw
I'd like two of those.	그것 두개 주십시오. kugot tooge chooseep-seeaw
fries/burger	감자튀김/햄버거 kamja-tweegeem/hembogo
omelet	오물릿 aw-moolleet
sandwich/cake	샌드위치/케이크 sendu-weechee/ke-eeku
ice cream	아이스크림 aeesu-kureem
pizza	피자 peeja
A small/medium/large portion, please.	작은 걸로/중간으로/큰 걸로 주십시오. chagun-gollaw/choong-ganuraw/kun-gollaw chooseep-seeaw
It's to go [take away].	싸주세요. ssa-jooseyo
That's all, thanks.	됐습니다. 감사합니다. dwe-ssumneeda. kamsa-hamneeda

Complaints 불만사항

I have no knife/fork/spoon/chopsticks.	나이프/포크/숟가락/젓가락 없습니다. *naeepu/pawku/sootgarak/chotgarak op-sumneeda*
There must be some mistake.	무언가 잘못됐습니다. *moo-on-ga jalmawt dwe-ssumneeda*
That's not what I ordered.	그것은 제가 주문한 것이 아닙니다. *kugo-sun che-ga choomoon-han ko-see aneem-needa*
I asked for ...	저는 ... 시켰습니다. *cho-nun ... seekyo-ssumneeda*
I can't eat this.	저는 이것을 먹을 수 없습니다. *cho-nun eego-sul mogul soo op-sumneeda*
The meat is ...	이 고기는 ... *ee kaw-gee-nun ...*
overdone/underdone	너무 익었습니다/덜 익었습니다 *nomoo eego-ssumneeda/tol eego-ssumneeda*
too tough	너무 질깁니다 *nomoo cheel-geemneeda*
This is too ...	이것은 너무 ... *eegosun nomoo ...*
bitter/sour	씁니다/십니다 *ssum-needa/seem-needa*
The food is cold.	음식이 식었습니다. *umsee-gee seego-ssumneeda*
This isn't fresh/clean.	이거 싱싱하지/깨끗하지 않습니다. *eego seeng-seeng-hajee/getgutajee an-ssumneeda*
How much longer will our food be?	음식이 얼마나 더 걸립니까? *umsee-gee olmana to kolleem-neekka*
I'd like to speak to the manager.	지배인과 얘기하고 싶습니다. *cheebe-een-gwa yegee-hagaw seep-sumneeda*

41

Paying 계산

A service charge of 10% is normally added to the
restaurant bill. Tipping is optional but appreciated.

The bill, please.	계산서 주십시오. *kesanso chooseepseeaw*
We'd like to pay separately.	따로 계산하고 싶습니다. *daraw kesan-hagaw seep-sumneeda*

It's all together, please.
함께 계산해 주십시오.
hamge kesanhe chooseep-seeaw

I think there's a mistake in
this bill.
이 계산서에 잘못이 있는 것같습니다.
*ee kesanso-e jalmawsee eennun-go
ga-ssumneeda*

What is this amount for?
이 금액은 무엇입니까?
ee kumegun moo-o-seemneekka

I didn't have that. I had …
저는 그것을 먹지 않았습니다. …
먹었습니다. *cho-nun kugo-sul mok-zee
ana-ssumneeda. … mogo-ssumneeda*

Is service included?
봉사료가 포함돼 있습니까?
*pawng-saryo-ga pawham-dwe
ee-ssumneekka*

Can I pay with this credit card?
이 신용카드로 계산할 수 있습니까?
*ee seen-yong kadu-raw kesan hal-soo
ee-ssumneekka*

I've forgotten my wallet.
지갑을 두고 왔습니다.
cheega-bul toogaw wa-ssumneeda

I don't have enough money.
돈이 모자랍니다. *tawnee mawja-ramneeda*

Could I have a receipt, please?
영수증 주십시오.
yong-soojung chooseep-seeaw

That was a very good meal.
아주 잘 먹었습니다.
ajoo chal mogo-ssumneeda

– yobaw-seyo! kesanso chooseepseeaw.
– *alge-ssumneeda. yogee ee-ssumneeda.*
– pawng-saryo-ga pawham-dwe ee-ssumneekka?
– *ne, kuro-ssumneeda.*
– ee seen-yong kadu-raw kesan hal-soo ee-ssumneekka?
– *moollawn-eemneeda.*
– kamsa-hamneeda. ajoo chal mogo-ssumneeda.

Course by course 정식

Breakfast 아침식사

Western-style breakfast (cereal, toast, coffee) is becoming more popular and is available in most hotels. Large Western-style hotels offer Korean, American, or English breakfast.

A typical Korean breakfast often consists of a bowl of rice, soup, and a couple of side dishes, similar to a Korean dinner.

I'd like	... 주십시오. ... *chooseep-seeaw*
bread/butter	빵/버터 *bang/poto*
a boiled egg	삶은 계란 *salmun keran*
fried eggs/scrambled eggs	계란후라이/계란 스크램블 *keran hooraee/keran sukurembul*
fruit juice	과일 쥬스 *kwa-eel choosu*
orange/grapefruit	오렌지/자몽 *awrenjee/cha-mawng*
honey/jam	꿀/잼 *gool/jem*
milk	우유 *ooyoo*
rolls	롤빵 *rawl-bang*
toast	토스트 *tawsutu*

Appetizers/Starters 전식

A traditional Korean meal (**pekpan**) usually consists of rice, soup, and various side dishes containing vegetables and meats, all served together. If you want to eat course by course, you may want to start with the following typically Korean side dishes:

김치 *keem-chee*
No meal is complete without this side dish made of pickled, preserved vegetables (often Chinese leaves). It is usually very hot and spicy.

나물 *na-mool*
Side-dishes served with Korean meals, consisting of seasoned vegetables (fresh or dried), herbs, and roots.

생선구이 *seng-son ku-ee*
A collective name for dishes of seasoned broiled fish.

만두 *mandu*
Dumplings made of meat, vegetables, and sometimes soybean curd, steamed, fried, or boiled in a broth.

Soups 국

ginseng chicken soup	삼계탕	samge-tang (main dish)
beef rib soup with onions and ginger	갈비탕	kalbee-tang (main dish)
rice in a beef and bone stew	설렁탕	sol-long-tang (main dish)
beef and turnip soup	곰국	kawm-gook (main dish)
vegetable soup	야채국	yache-gook
seaweed soup	미역국	meeyok-gook
spinach soup	시금치국	see-gumchee-gook
soybean paste soup	된장국	dwenjang-gook

Always part of a traditional meal. A small portion of light soup is served simultaneously with the rest of the dishes. A large portion of heavy soup with rice in it comprises a main dish on its own in an ordinary meal. In Western-style restaurants you can find Western-style soups.

Rice 밥

In a Korean meal rice (**bap**) is served separately in an individual bowl. It is a medium grain version, slightly sticky, and is perhaps the most important part of the meal. It is never salted, and Koreans sometimes add various ingredients to it like barley, millet, peas, beans, etc.

비빔밥 pee-beem-bap
Rice topped with parboiled fern bracken, bluebell root, soybean sprouts, spinach, and fried egg, mixed with red pepper sauce to taste. Dried, salted seaweed is sometimes added, too.

팥밥 pat-bap
Rice with red-beans.

콩나물밥 kawng-namool-bap
Rice cooked with bean sprouts.

Noodles 국수/면

Noodle dishes (**kook-soo/myon**) are very popular as are the noodle shops where they are served.

물냉면 mool-neng-myon
Cold buckwheat noodles in broth, garnished with boiled beef, hard-boiled eggs, Korean radish, and mustard.

비빔냉면 *peebeem neng-myon*
Buckwheat noodles with hard-boiled eggs, various vegetables, including Korean radish, mixed with red pepper paste.

잡채 *chap-che*
Stir-fried vermicelli noodles with vegetables and meat.

비빔국수 *peebeem gooksoo*
Cold noodles with vegetables and red pepper paste.

라면 *la-myon*
Instant noodles in instant broth.

우동 *oo-dawng*
Long, wide wheat noodles with onions, fried soybean curd, red pepper powder, and egg.

Fish and seafood 생선과 해산물

In coastal areas take advantage of the wonderful variety of fresh fish and seafood which come in various styles, such as grilled, barbecued, salted, dried, raw, and pickled.

cod	대구	*tegoo*
mackerel	고등어	*kawdung-o*
mussels	홍합	*hawng-hap*
octopus	문어	*moon-o*
oysters	굴	*kool*
shrimp [prawns]	새우	*seoo*
squid	오징어	*awjeeng-o*
tuna	참치	*chamchee*
whitebait	뱅어	*peng-o*
eel	장어	*chang-o*
pufferfish	복어	*pawgo*
lobster	바닷가재	*padatgaje*
clam	조개	*chawge*
pollack	명태	*myongte*
monkfish	아구	*agoo*
croaker	조기	*chawgee*

생선회 *seng-son hwe*
Sliced, fresh, raw fish served with a dip of red pepper sauce or soy sauce.

해물잡탕 *hemool-japtang*
Mixed seafood stew.

모듬회 *mawdum hwe*
Array of various raw fishes.

장어구이 *chang-o-koo-ee*
Seasoned broiled eel.

낙지볶음 *nak-jee-bawk-gum*
Stir-fried baby octopus.

북어찜 *pook-o-zeem*
Seasoned steamed pollack.

게장 *ke-jang*
Crabs preserved in soy sauce.

복어매운탕 *pawgo me-oon-tang*
Pufferfish pepper-hot stew.

멸치볶음 *myol-chee bawkgum*
Broiled anchovy.

Egg/Beancurd dishes 계란/두부 요리

계란찜 *keran-zeem*
Steamed egg with hashed vegetables.

계란반숙 *keran-bansook*
Soft-boiled egg.

두부지짐 *tooboo cheejeem*
Pan-fried beancurd served with soy sauce.

순두부 *soon-dooboo*
Uncurdled beancurd.

두부김치 *tooboo keemchee*
Tofu served with kimchi.

Meat 고기

I'd like some ...	... 주십시오.	... chooseep-seeaw
beef	소고기	saw-gaw-gee
pork	돼지고기	dwejee gaw-gee
steak	스테이크	sute-eeku
liver	간	kan
ham	햄	hem
duck	오리고기	awree gaw-gee
turkey	칠면조고기	cheel-myon-jaw gaw-gee
chicken	닭고기	tak-gaw-gee
kidneys	염통	yom-tawng
sausages	소세지	sawsejee
bacon	베이컨	pe-ee-kon

Meat cuts 고기 부위

fillet steak	필레 스테이크	peelle sute-eeku
sirloin steak	설로인 스테이크	sollaw-een sute-eeku
rump steak	럼프스테이크	lompu sute-eeku
T-bone steak	티 본 스테이크	tee-bawn sute-eeku
rib of beef	갈비	kalbee
sirloin (joint)	등심	tung-seem
brisket of beef	차돌박이	chadawl-bagee
neck of pork	목살	mawksal
rib of pork	삼겹살	samgyop-sal
chops	국거리용	kook-goree-yong
leg	다리	taree

불고기 *pool-gaw-gee*
Barbecued beef dishes. Strips of beef marinated in soy sauce, sesame oil, garlic, black pepper, green onions, and toasted sesame seeds, and then grilled or broiled.

전골 chon-gawl
Meat or seafood-based stew made with beancurd and/or vegetables, cooked at the table over a burner.

신선로 seen-sol-law
Casserole cooked in a **seen-sol-law** pot and kept warm with charcoal. It can consist of vegetables, strips of meat, fish, pine nuts, gingko nuts, and quail eggs.

갈비찜 kalbee zeem
Beef-rib stew. Short ribs of beef, turnips, chestnuts, and mushrooms marinated and cooked slowly for a few hours.

곱창전골 kawp-chang jon-gawl
Tripe cooked with mushrooms, onions, garlic, salt, and black and red pepper in a beef broth with noodles and vegetables added.

닭찜 tak zeem
Chicken stewed with onions, carrots, garlic, black and red pepper, salt or soy sauce, and other spices.

Vegetables 야채

cabbage	양배추	yang-bechoo
carrots	당근	tang-gun
Chinese cabbage	배추	pe-choo
eggplant [aubergine]	가지	kajee
green beans	녹두콩	nawk-too-kawng
lettuce	상추	sangchoo
mushrooms	버섯	posot
onions	양파	yang-pa
peas	완두콩	wan-doo-kawng
potatoes	감자	kamja
sweet red peppers	빨간 피망	balgan pee-mang

It is not easy to find vegetarian choices in Korea (▶ 33). However, here are a couple of options:

감자전 kamja-jon
Potato cakes with onions and other vegetables.

두부김치 tooboo-keemchee
Tofu kimchi (steamed tofu served with fried kimchi).

Salad 샐러드

Western-style salad isn't part of traditional Korean cuisine. Pickled vegetables are a Korean equivalent. However, in Western-style restaurants you can find a variety of salads and dressings, and some Korean restaurants offer salad, too.

Cheese 치즈

There is no Korean cheese, but imported cheese is available in some outlets.

Dessert 후식

Koreans seldom finish their meals with sweets or cakes, but often have fruit or fruit punch. On special occasions, however, they do enjoy sweets.

떡 *dok*
A generic term for Korean cakes such as the following:

인절미 *een-jol-mee*
A square cake made from glutinous rice coated with bean flour.

경단 *kyong-dan*
A rice cake dumpling.

약식 *yak-seek*
Sweet spiced rice flavored with nuts and raisins.

식혜 seek-he
Sweet rice drink.

수정과
Refreshing fruit punch containing dried persimmons.

Fruit 과일

apple	사과	*sa-gwa*
banana	바나나	*panana*
cherries	체리	*cheree*
grapefruit	자몽	*cha-mawng*
grapes	포도	*paw-daw*
orange	오렌지	*aw-renjee*
peach	복숭아	*pawk-soong-a*
pear	배	*pe*
strawberries	딸기	*dalgee*

Drinks 음료수

Koreans, especially men, like to drink – and there are drinking houses (**sool-jeep**) on every street corner.

Spirits and liqueurs 독한 술

These are some of the local spirits.

소주 *saw-joo*
Clear liquor, distilled from grains. This popular alcoholic beverage is enjoyed with dishes like barbecued pork and hot peppery fish soup.

막걸리 *mak-gollee*
Unrefined, rough, milky-white beverage brewed from rice; traditionally popular among working farmers.

인삼주 *eensam-joo*
Ginseng liquor.

Beer 맥주

There are two brands of popular Korean-brewed beers: **Hite** and **Ice**. Draft beer is **seng-mek-joo**. The Korean beer goes very well with the local food.

There are also several foreign beers available that are brewed under licence, e.g., Heineken and Budweiser.

Wine 포도주

Grape wines were introduced from abroad relatively recently. The Oriental Brewery Co. produces a Riesling called **Majuang** which is a favorite at better-class restaurants. There are however some interesting rice wines you may want to try:

법주 *pop-joo*
High-quality rice wine sold in traditional local restaurants.

동동주 *tawng-dawng-joo*
Popular country rice wine.

정종 *chong-chawng*
Korean-type **sake** (rice wine), often served warm.

Other alcoholic drinks
기타 알코올 음료

South Korea imports a lot of whisky, but it's worth trying a
few of the home-produced blends such as Valley 9,
VIP, and Gilbert.

위스키	*wee-sukee*	whisky
진	*cheen*	gin
브랜디	*purendee*	brandy
럼	*lom*	rum
보드카	*pawduka*	vodka

Non-alcoholic drinks 비알코올 음료

There are some excellent teas (**cha**) and fruit drinks available in Korea.
Here are some of the most popular ones.

녹차	*nok-cha*	green tea
보리차	*pawree-cha*	barley tea
인삼차	*eensam cha*	ginseng tea
생강차	*seng-gang cha*	ginger tea
수정과	*soojong-gwa*	persimmon punch
식혜	*seek-he*	rice drink

I'd like a/an ...	... 주십시오. ... *chooseep-seeaw*
(hot) chocolate	(핫)초콜랫 *(hat) chaw-kaw-let*
cola/lemonade	콜라/레모네이드 *kawlla/lemaw-ne-eedu*
milkshake	밀크쉐이크 *meelku-swe-eeku*
mineral water	생수 *seng-soo*
carbonated/still water	탄산수/보통물 *tansan-soo/pawtawng-mool*
tonic water	토닉워터 *tawneek-woto*

Menu Reader

This Menu Reader gives listings of certain common food items and dishes under main food group headings. The Korean words are shown in large type to help you to identify, from a menu that has no English, at least the basic ingredients making up a dish.

Meat, fish and poultry

고기	gaw-gee	meat (general)
소고기	saw-gaw-gee	beef
양고기	yang-gaw-gee	lamb
돼지고기	dwejee gaw-gee	pork
개고기	ke-gaw-gee	dog
닭고기	tak-gaw-gee	chicken
오리고기	awree gaw-gee	duck
생선	seng-son	fish (general)
해산물	hesan-mool	seafood (general)
새우	se-oo	shrimp [prawns]
오징어	aw-jeeng-o	squid
장어	chang-o	eel
계란	keran	eggs

Vegetables

채소	*chesaw*	vegetable(s) (general)
콩	*kawng*	beans
콩나물	*kawng-na-mool*	bean sprouts
시금치	*see-gum-chee*	spinach
고구마	*kaw-goo-ma*	sweet potatoes
감자	*kamja*	tomatoes
상추	*sang-choo*	lettuce
오이	*aw-ee*	cucumber
배추	*pechoo*	Chinese leaves
무	*moo*	Korean radish
김, 미역	*keem, mee-yok*	seaweed
양배추	*yang-bechoo*	cabbage
파	*pa*	spring onions
버섯	*posot*	mushrooms
피망	*peemang*	green peppers
고추	*kawchoo*	red chili pepper
마늘	*manul*	garlic

Fruit

Korean	Romanization	English
과일	kwa-eel	fruit (general)
사과	sa-gwa	apple
귤	kyool	mandarin
바나나	panana	banana
참외	chamwe	melon *Korean melons are yellow and small*
배	pe	pear *Korean pears are brown, thick-skinned, round, and sweet.*
복숭아	pawk-soong-a	peach
딸기	dalgee	strawberries
감	kam	persimmon *also known as Sharon fruit*
곶감	kawt-gam	dried persimmon
수박	soobak	watermelon
밤	pam	chestnut
체리62	cheree	cherries
포도	pawdaw	grapes
자몽	cha-mawng	grapefruit

Staples: bread, rice, pasta, etc.

밥	bap	boiled, sticky rice
죽	chook	porridge *rice boiled into a paste*
국수, 면	kooksoo, myon	noodles
메밀국수	me-meel gooksoo	buckwheat noodles
스파게티	supa-getee	spaghetti
빵	bang	bread

Basics

소금	saw-gum	salt
후추	hoochoo	pepper
설탕	soltang	sugar
된장	dwen-jang	soybean paste
간장	kan-jang	soy sauce
고추장	kawchoo-jang	red chili pepper paste (an essential seasoning)
참기름	cham-geerum	sesame oil
깨	ge	dried sesame

구운	koo-oon	baked
볶은	pawk-gun	fried
삶은	salmun	boiled
불에 구운	pure koo-oon	grilled
(열에) 구운	(yore) koo-oon	roasted
살짝 데친	salzak te-cheen	poached
절인	choreen	marinated
훈제한	hoonjehan	smoked
매운	meoon	spicy
찐	zeen	steamed
약한 불로 익힌	yakan poollaw eekeen	stewed
빵가루를 입힌	bang-garoo-rul eepeen	breaded
기름에 튀긴	keeru-me twee-geen	deep-fried
조림	chawreem	food boiled down in soy sauce
볶음	pawkgum	stir-fried or braised
구이	koo-ee	barbecued
전	chon	batter-fried

Classic dishes

불고기	*(pulgogi)* *pool-gaw-gee*	marinated barbecued beef
갈비구이 / 불갈비	*kalbee-goo-ee/ pool-gal-bee*	barbecued short ribs
등심구이	*tung-seem-goo-ee*	Korean-style barbecued sirloin
버섯전골	*posot-chon-gawl*	a pot stew with mushrooms
신선로	*(shinsollo)* *seen-sol-law*	meat, fish, and vegetables prepared in a pot
해물잡탕	*hemool-japtang*	mixed seafood stew
구절판	*Koo-jol-pan*	nine-sectioned lacquerware dish with meat, fish, and vegetables
회	*hwe*	sliced raw fish with red pepper sauce
모듬회	*mawdum hwe*	various raw fish
갈비찜	*kalbee-zeem*	braised short ribs in soy sauce
편육	*pyon-yook*	boiled pressed brisket of beef

닭도리탕	tak-dawree-tang	spicy chicken stew
된장찌개	dwen-jang-zeege	soybean paste pot stew
김치찌개	keemchee-zeege	pot stew containing kimchi as its main ingredient
비빔밥	peebeembap	mixed rice with vegetables and eggs
오징어볶음	aw-jeeng-o-bawk-gum	stir-fried squid
잡채	chap-che	stir-fried vermicelli noodles with vegetables
수육	soo-yook	sliced steamed beef
곱창전골	kawp-chang-jon-gawl	tripe cooked with mushrooms and noodles in a broth
김치볶음밥	keemchee-bawkgum-bap	fried rice with kimchi
김초밥	keem-cho-bap	vinegared rice rolled in a sheet of laver
제육보쌈	jeyook-bawssam	pork chops in a cabbage leaf

Alcoholic drinks

맥주	*mek-joo*	beer
생맥주	*seng-mek-joo*	draft [draught] beer
포도주	*pawdaw-joo*	wine
위스키	*wee-sukee*	whisky
인삼주	*eensam-joo*	ginseng liquor
정종	*chong-jawng*	refined rice wine
동동주	*tawng-dawng-joo*	country rice wine
소주	*(soju)sawjoo*	clear liquor, distilled from grain
막걸리	*mak-gollee*	unrefined drink brewed from rice
매실주	*meseel-joo*	local brandy
법주	*pop-joo*	country rice wine
브랜디	*purendee*	brandy
진	*cheen*	gin
럼	*lom*	rum

물	mool	water
우유	oo-yoo	milk
차	cha	tea (generic term)
인삼차	eensam-cha	ginseng tea
생강차	seng-gang-cha	ginger tea
녹차	nawk-cha	traditional Korean green leaf tea
커피/냉커피	kopee/neng-kopee	coffee/iced coffee
수정과	soo-jong-gwa	refreshing fruit punch containing dried persimmons
화채	hwa-che	fruit punch
식혜	seek-he	sweet rice drink
과일쥬스	kwa-eel joosu	(fruit) juice
오렌지쥬스	aw-renjee joosu	orange juice
레모네이드	lemaw-ne-eedu	lemonade
콜라	kawlla	Cola
토닉워터	tawneek-woto	tonic water
밀크쉐이크	meelku-swe-eeku	milkshake
생수	seng-soo	mineral water

Snacks

프렌치프라이	*puren-chee pura-ee*	chips
햄버거	*hembogo*	hamburger
과자	*kwaja*	cookies [biscuits]
케이크	*ke-ee-ku*	cake
샌드위치	*sendu-weechee*	sandwich
땅콩	*dang-kawng*	peanuts
마른오징어	*marun aw-jeeng-o*	roasted, dried squid
라면	*lamyon*	instant noodles

Side dishes

빈대떡	*peen-det-dok*	mung-bean pancake
파전	*pajon*	spring onion pancake
김치	*kimchi (keemchee)*	popular side dish containing pickled vegetables. *There are over 100 different types of kimchi.*
나물	*na-mool*	side dish of seasoned vegetables, herbs, and roots

국, 탕	kook, tang	soup (general)
조개탕	chawge-tang	clam soup
미역국	meeyok-gook	seaweed soup
갈비탕	kalbee-tang	beef rib soup served with a bowl of rice
설렁탕	sol-long-tang	beef and rice soup
곰국	kawm-gook	beef and turnip soup
매운탕	me-oon-tang	hot fish soup
삼계탕	samge-tang	chicken soup with ginseng, glutinous rice and chestnuts, etc.
육개장	yook-ge-jang	spicy beef soup with rice
만두국	man-doo-gook	meat dumplings in broth
시금치국	see-gumchee-gook	spinach soup
야채국	yache-gook	vegetable soup
된장국	dwen-jang-gook	soybean paste soup
북어국	pook-o-gook	pollack soup
콩나물국	kawng-namool gook	bean sprout soup

Dairy and soy products

치즈	cheeju	cheese
요구르트	yo-goo-rutu	yogurt
크림	kureem	cream
버터	poto	butter
우유	oo-yoo	milk
두부	too-boo	tofu

Noodles

물냉면	mool-neng-myon	cold buckwheat noodles in broth, garnished with boiled beef and pears
비빔냉면	peebeem-neng-myon	cold buckwheat noodles mixed with vegetables and chili sauce
회냉면	hwe-neng-myon	cold buckwheat noodles with raw fish and vegetables
칼국수	kal-gook-soo	thick noodles in chicken broth
수제비	soo-je-bee	clear soup with dough flakes

떡	*dok*	a generic term for Korean cakes
인절미	*een-jol-mee*	square cake made from glutinous rice coated with bean flour
경단	*kyong-dan*	rice-cake dumpling
화전	*hwajon*	sweet fried rice cakes
약식	*yak-seek*	sweet spiced rice flavored with nuts and raisins
한과	*han-gwa*	a generic term for Korean sweets
약과	*yak-gwa*	little honey cakes
깨강정	*gegang-jong*	sesame cakes
송편	*sawng-pyon*	steamed half-moon rice cakes, stuffed with chestnuts or sesame seeds
아이스크림	*a-ee-su-ku-reem*	ice cream
수정과	*soo-jong-gwa*	refreshing fruit punch containing dried persimmons
식혜	*seek-he*	sweet rice drink

Travel

ESSENTIAL

1/2/3 ticket(s) to …, please.	… 표 한장/두장/세장 주십시오. … pyo han-jang/too-jang/se-jang chooseep-seeaw
one way [single]	편도 pyon-daw
round-trip [return]	왕복 wang-bawk
How much …?	… 얼마입니까? … olma-eemneekka

In South Korea, public transportation is cheap, fast and safe, offering excellent rail and bus connections. It is best to reserve train and bus tickets in advance as they can get crowded on non-working days. In North Korea public transportation between cities is almost non-existent, apart from a few trains which have separate cars for foreigners. Foreigners usually have to use drivers and guides to get around.

Safety 안전

Would you accompany me …?	… 같이 가 주시겠습니까? … kachee ka chooseege-ssumneekka
to the bus stop	버스 정거장까지 posu chong-gojang-gajee
to my hotel	제 호텔까지 che hawtel-gajee
I don't feel safe here.	여기는 안전한 것 같지 않습니다. yogee-nun anjon-han kot kat-chee an-ssumneeda

Arrival 도착

To enter South Korea you will need a valid passport, and you will have to fill out an embarkation/disembarkation card. Most visitors can stay for up to 15 days without a visa.

Nationals from the UK, Ireland, and New Zealand can get a 90-day permit, those from Canada a 180-day permit. All other visitors need visas for stays longer than 15 days. For North Korea, it is easier to get business visas than tourist visas, and as most foreigners will enter North Korea via China, it is advisable to get a dual visa for China.

Duty free into:	Cigarettes	Cigars	Tobacco	Spirits	Wine
Korea	200 or	50 or	25g	1 bottle of either	
Australia	200 or	250g or	250g	1L or	1L
Canada	200 and	50 and	900g	1.1L or	1.1L
Ireland	200 or	50 or	250g	1L or	2L
New Zealand	200 or	50 or	250g	1.1L and	4.5L
South Africa	400 and	50 and	250g	1L and	2L
U.K.	200 or	50 or	250g	1L and	2L
U.S.	200 and	100 and	discretionary	1L or	1L

Passport control 입국심사

We have a joint passport.	우리는 공동여권을 갖고 있습니다. *ooree-nun kawng-dawng yokgwo-nul kat-gaw ee-ssumneeda*
The children are on this passport.	아이들은 이 여권에 있습니다. *a-ee-durun ee yokgwo-ne ee-ssumneeda*
I'm here on vacation [holiday]/business.	휴가로/사업상 왔습니다. *hyooga-raw/saob-sang wa-ssumneeda*
I'm just passing through.	통과여객입니다. *tawng-gwa yogeg eemneeda*
I'm going to ...	... 갑니다. ... *kamneeda*
I'm ...	저는 ... *cho-nun ...*
on my own	혼자입니다. *hawn-ja eemneeda*
with my family	가족과 동행하고 있습니다. *kajawk-gwa tawng-heng hagaw-eessumneeda*
with a group	일행이 있습니다. *eelheng-ee eessumneeda*

WHO ARE YOU WITH? ➤ 120

Customs 세관

I have only the normal allowances.

허용한도만을 갖고 있습니다
hoyong-handaw-manul katgaw ee-ssumneeda

It's a gift.

그것은 선물입니다.
kugo-sun sonmool-eemneeda

It's for my personal use.

그것은 제 개인 물건입니다.
kugo-sun che ke-een moolgon-eemneeda

신고하실 물건 있습니까?	Do you have anything to declare?
이것은 관세를 내야 합니다.	You must pay duty on this.
이것을 어디서 사셨습니까?	Where did you buy this?
이 가방을 열어 주십시오.	Please open this bag.
또 다른 짐 있습니까?	Do you have any more luggage?

I would like to declare ...

... 신고하고 싶습니다.
... seen-gaw-hagaw seep-sumneeda

I don't understand.

무슨 말인지 모르겠습니다.
moosun mareenjee mawruge-ssumneeda

Does anyone here speak English?

여기 누구 영어 하십니까?
yo-gee noo-goo yong-o ha-seemneekka

입국심사	passport control
세관	customs
면세	nothing to declare
자진신고	goods to declare
면세품	duty-free goods

Duty-free shopping 면세 쇼핑

What currency is this in?

이것은 어느 나라 돈입니까?
eegosun onu nara tawn-eemneekka

Can I pay ...?

... 계산할 수 있습니까?
... kesan hal-soo ee-ssumneekka

in dollars

달라로 *dalla-raw*

in pounds

파운드로 *pa-oondu-raw*

in Won

원으로 *won-uraw*

Plane 비행기

Kimpo International Airport in Seoul is the principal port of entry for South Korea. Other international airports are in Pusan and Cheju. The domestic airlines are Korean Air and Asiana. North Korea's international airport, Sunan, is 30 km west of Pyongyang. The national airline, Koryo Air, offers no regular domestic flights.

Tickets and reservations 표와 예약

When is the ... flight to Pusan?	부산행 ... 비행기 언제 있습니까? *poosan-heng ... peeheng-gee onje ee-ssumneekka*
first/next/last	첫/다음/마지막 *chot/taum/majee-mak*
I'd like 2 ... tickets to Pusan.	부산행 ... 표 두장 주십시오. *poosan-heng ... pyo too-jang chooseep-seeaw*
one-way [single]	편도 *pyon-daw*
round-trip [return]	왕복 *wang-bawk*
first class	일등석 *eeldung-sok*
business class	비지니스석 *beejee-neesu-sok*
economy class	이코노미석 *eekaw-nawmee-sok*
How much is a flight to ... ?	... 행 비행기 표 얼마입니까? *... heng peeheng-gee pyo olma ee-mneekka*
I'd like to ... my reservation for flight number 123.	123호기 예약을 ... 싶습니다. *123 haw-gee yeyagul ... seep-sumneeda*
cancel/change/confirm	취소하고/변경하고/확인하고 *chwee-saw-hagaw/pyon-gyong-hagaw/ hwag-een-hagaw*

Inquiries about the flight 비행에 관한 문의

How long is the flight?	얼마나 걸립니까? *olmana kolleem-neekka*
What time does the plane leave?	몇시에 떠납니까? *myossee-e donam-neekka*
What time will we arrive?	몇시에 도착합니까? *myossee-e tawchak-hamneekka*
What time do I have to check in?	몇시에 탑승수속해야 합니까? *myossee-e tapsung-soosawk-heya hamneekka*

NUMBERS ➤ 216; TIME ➤ 220

Checking in 탑승수속

Where is the check-in desk for flight ... ?

... 행 탑승수속대가 어디입니까?
... *heng tapsung-soosawk-de-ga odee-eemneekka*

I have ...

... 있습니다. ... *ee-ssumneeda*

3 cases to check in

탑승수속할 가방 세개
tapsung-soosawk-hal gabang sege

2 pieces of hand luggage

손가방 두개
sawn-gabang tooge

표/여권 주십시오.	Your ticket/passport, please.
창쪽 자리 원하십니까, 복도쪽 자리 원하십니까?	Would you like a window or an aisle seat?
흡연석 원하십니까, 금연석 원하십니까?	Smoking or non-smoking?
출발 라운지로 가 주십시오.	Please go through to the departure lounge.
짐이 몇 개입니까?	How many pieces of baggage do you have?
짐이 초과되었습니다.	You have excess baggage.
추가로 ... 원을 내야 합니다.	You'll have to pay a supplement of ... Won.
그것은 들고 가기에 너무 무겁습니다/큽니다.	That's too heavy/large for hand baggage.
이 가방들을 직접 싸셨습니까?	Did you pack these bags yourself?
날카로운 물건이나 전자 제품이 들어 있습니까?	Do they contain any sharp or electronic items?

도착	arrivals
출발	departures
보안검색	security check

BAGGAGE ➤ 71

Information 안내

Is there any delay on flight ... ?	... 비행기가 지연되고 있습니까? *... peeheng-gee-ga chee-yon dwe-gaw ee-ssumneekka*
How late will it be?	얼마나 늦습니까? *olmana nu-ssumneekka*
Has the flight from ... landed?	...발 비행기가 도착했습니까? *... pal peeheng-gee-ga dawchak-he-ssumneekka*
Which gate does flight ... leave from?	... 비행기 몇번 탑승구에서 떠납니까? *... peeheng-gee myot-bon tapsung-goo-eso donam-neekka*

Boarding/In-flight 탑승

Your boarding card, please.	보딩 카드 주십시오. *pawdeeng kadu chooseep-seeaw*
Could I have a drink/ something to eat, please?	음료수/먹을 것 주십시오. *um-nyosoo/ mogul kot chooseep-seeaw*
Please wake me for the meal.	식사시간에 깨워 주십시오. *seeksa-seega-ne gewo chooseep-seeaw*
What time will we arrive?	몇시에 도착합니까? *myossee-e tawcha-kamneekka*
An air sickness bag, please.	구토 봉지 주십시오. *kootaw pawng-jee chooseep-seeaw*

Arrival 도착

Where is/are the ... ?	... 어디 있습니까? *... odee ee-ssumneekka*
currency exchange	환전소 *hwan-jon-saw*
buses	버스 *posu*
car rental [hire]	차렌트 *cha-rentu*
taxis	택시 *tek-ssee*
Is there a bus into town?	시내 가는 버스 있습니까? *seene kanun posu ee-ssumneekka*
How do I get to the ... Hotel?	... 호텔까지 어떻게 갑니까? *... hawtel-gajee otdoke kamneekka*

BAGGAGE▶ 71; CUSTOMS ▶ 67

Baggage 짐

Tipping: Porters at airports and stations charge a set fee.

Porter! Excuse me!	포터! 여보세요! *pawto. yobawseyo*
Could you take my luggage to ... ?	짐을 ... 까지 운반해 주십시오. *chee-mul ... gajee oonbanhe chooseep-seeaw*
a taxi/bus	택시/버스 *tekssee/posu*
Where is/are the ... ?	... 어디 있습니까? *... odee ee-ssumneekka*
luggage carts [trolleys]	손수레 *sawn-soore*
luggage lockers	짐보관함 *cheem baw-gwan-ham*
baggage check [left-luggage office]	짐보관소 *cheem baw-gwan-saw*
baggage reclaim	짐 찾는 곳 *cheem channun-kawt*

Loss, damage, and theft 분실, 손상, 도난

I've lost my luggage.	짐을 잃어버렸습니다. *chee-mul eero-boryo-ssumneeda*
My luggage has been stolen.	짐을 도난당했습니다. *chee-mul tawnan-danghe-ssumneeda*
My suitcase was damaged.	제 여행가방이 손상되었습니다. *che yoheng-gabang-ee sawnsang-dwe-ssumneeda*
Our luggage has not arrived.	우리 짐이 도착하지 않았습니다. *ooree chee-mee tawcha-kajee ana-ssumneeda*

가방이 어떻게 생겼습니까?	What does your luggage look like?
짐표 있으십니까?	Do you have the claim check [reclaim tag]?
선생님 짐은 ...	Your luggage ...
... 쪽으로 보내진 것 같습니다.	may have been sent to ...
오늘 늦게 도착할것 같습니다.	may arrive later today
내일 다시 와 주십시오.	Please come back tomorrow.
짐이 도착했는지 확인하려면 이 번호로 전화 주십시오.	Call this number to check if your luggage has arrived.

POLICE ➤ 152; COLORS ➤ 143

Train 기차

The reliable South Korean rail network covers all major cities. However, English signs are only displayed in some of the larger stations where you may also find special ticket windows for foreigners. The Korean National Tourism Organization (**KNTO**), travel agencies (**yoheng-sa**), and hotels will be able to provide more information about reservations and times. Trains can be very crowded during holidays and on weekends so it is advisable to buy tickets in advance.

You can get snacks and drinks in the buffet car and in the dining car when it isn't being used for main meals. On express trains, waitresses come round with sweets, snacks, and drinks. They also sell lunch boxes (**taw-see-rak**) containing a typical Korean lunch (boiled rice, beans boiled in soy sauce, cooked eggs, fish, and seasoned vegetables). This lunch box can also be bought on other types of trains.

There are four types of train sevice in South Korea:

비둘기호 *pee-dool-gee-haw*
Slow, local trains which stop at each station – 4th class only.

통일호 *tawng-eel-haw*
Limited express trains with reserved seats available and occasionally a dining car.

무궁화호 *moo-goong-hwa-haw*
Express, air-conditioned trains.

새마을호 *se-ma-ul-haw*
Luxury, air-conditioned super-express trains with a dining car.

Children up to the age of 6 travel free; 6–12 year olds pay half fare.

In North Korea there are often trains (non air-conditioned) just for foreigners. Your guide will give you the information you need.

To the station 기차역으로

How do I get to the main train station?	중앙 기차역에 어떻게 갑니까? *choong-ang keecha-yoge otdoke kamneekka*
Do trains to Pusan leave from ... Station?	부산가는 기차 ...역에서 떠납니까? *poosan-ganun keecha ... yogeso donam-neekka*
How far is it?	얼마나 멉니까? *olmana mom-neekka*
Can I leave my car there?	거기에 차 세워놓을 수 있습니까? *ko-gee-e cha se-wo naw-ul soo ee-ssumneekka*

At the station 기차역에서

Where is/are the ... ?	... 어디 있습니까? *... odee eessumneekka*
currency exchange office	환전소 *hwan-jon-saw*
information desk	안내 *anne*
baggage check [left-luggage office]	짐보관소 *cheem baw-gwan-saw*
lost and found [lost property office]	분실물 신고 *poon-seel-mool seen-gaw*
luggage lockers	짐보관함 *cheem baw-gwan-ham*
platforms	플랫폼 *plepawm*
snack bar	간이 식당 *kanee seektang*
ticket office	매표소 *me-pyo-saw*
waiting room	대합실 *tehapseel*

입구	entrance
출구	exit
승강장으로	to the platforms
안내	information
예매	reservations
도착	arrivals
출발	departures

DIRECTIONS ➤ 94

73

Tickets and reservations 표와 예약

Some larger stations have special ticket windows for
foreigners. You can also buy tickets in advance from KNTO
(Korean National Tourism Organization) or through your hotel.

I'd like a ... ticket to Pusan	부산행 ... 표 한 장 주십시요. *poosan-heng ... pyo han-jang chooseep-seeyo*
one-way [single]	편도 *pyon-daw*
round-trip [return]	왕복 *wang-bawk*
first/second class	특실/일반실 *tuk-seel/eelban-seel*
concessionary	할인표 *hareen-pyo*
I'd like to reserve a seat.	좌석 하나 예약하고 싶습니다. *chwa-sok hana yeyakagaw seep-ssumneeda*
aisle seat	복도쪽 자리 *pawk-taw-zawk charee*
window seat	창쪽 자리 *chang-zawk charee*
Is there a sleeper/sleeping car?	침대차 있습니까? *cheemde-cha ee-ssumneekka*
I'd like a ... berth.	... 침대 하나 주십시요. *... cheemde hana chooseep-seeyo*
upper/lower	위칸/아래칸 *weekan/arekan*

Price 가격

How much is that?	얼마입니까? *olma-eemneekka*
Is there a discount for ... ?	... 할인 있습니까? *... hareen ee-ssumneekka*
children/families	어린이/가족 *oreenee/kajawk*
senior citizens	노인 *naw-een*
students	학생 *hakseng*
Do you offer a cheap same-day round-trip [return]?	싼 당일 왕복표 있습니까? *ssan tang-eel wang-bak pyo ee-ssumneekka*

Queries 문의

Do I have to change trains?	기차를 갈아 타야 합니까? *keecha-rul kara-taya* *hamneekka*
Is it a direct train?	그것은 직행 기차입니까? *kugosun cheekeng keecha-eemneekka*
You have to change at …	…에서 갈아 타야 합니다. *…-eso kara-taya hamneeda*
How long is this ticket valid for?	얼마 동안 이 표가 유효합니까? *olma tawng-an ee pyo-ga yoohyo-* *hamneekka*
Can I take my bicycle on to the train?	기차에 자전거를 실을 수 있습니까? *keecha-e chajon-go-rul seerul soo* *ee-ssumneekka*
Can I return on the same ticket?	같은 표로 돌아 올 수 있습니까? *katun pyoraw tawra awl-soo ee-ssumneekka*
In which car [coach] is my seat?	제 자리는 몇번 차량에 있습니까? *che charee-nun myotbon char-yang-e* *ee-ssumneekka*
Is there a dining car on the train?	기차에 식당차 있습니까? *keecha-e seektang-cha ee-ssumneekka*

> – Pawhang-heng pyo han-jang chooseep-seeyo.
> – *pyon-daw eemneekka? wang-bawg eemneekka?*
> – wang-bawg-uraw chooseep-seeyo.
> – *samman-won eemneeda.*
> – keecha-rul kara-taya hamneekka?
> – *ne, Tegoo-eso kara-taya hamneeda.*
> – kamsa-hamneeda. an-nyong-ee keseep-seeyo.

Train times 기차 시간

Could I have a timetable, please?	시간표 하나 주십시오. *seegan-pyo hana chooseep-seeyo*
When is the … train to Tegoo?	대구가는 … 기차 언제 있습니까? *tegoo-ganun … keecha onje* *ee-ssumneekka*
first/next/last	첫/다음/마지막 *chot/daum/majee-mak*

How frequent are the trains to … ?	… 행 기차가 얼마나 자주 있습니까? … heng keecha-ga olmana chajoo ee-ssumneekka
once/twice a day	하루에 한번/두번 haroo-e hanbon/toobon
5 times a day	하루에 다섯번 haroo-e tasot-bon
every hour	매시간마다 me-seegan-mada
What time do they leave?	몇시에 출발합니까? myossee-e choolbal-hamneekka
on the hour	매시 정각에 mesee chong-ga-ge
20 minutes past the hour	매시 이십분에 mesee eeseep-boo-ne
What time does the train stop at … ?	몇시에 …에 정착합니까? myossee-e …e chong-chak-hamneekka
What time does the train arrive in … ?	몇시에 …에 도착합니까? myossee-e …e tawchak-hamneekka
How long is the trip?	얼마나 걸립니까? olmana kolleem-neekka
Is the train on time?	기차가 정시에 있습니까? keecha-ga chong-see-e ee-ssumneekka

Departures 출발

Which platform does the train to … leave from?	어느 플랫폼에서 …행 기차가 출발합니까? onu plepawm-eso … heng keecha-ga choolbal-hamneekka
Where is platform 4?	사번 플랫폼 어디 있습니까? sa-bon plepawm odee ee-ssumneekka
over there	저쪽입니다. cho-zawg eemneeda
on the left/right	왼쪽/오른쪽 입니다. wen-zawk/awrun-zawk eemneeda
Where do I change for … ?	… 가려면 어디서 갈아탑니까? … karyo-moyn odeeso kara tamneekka
How long will I have to wait for a connection?	갈아타는 기차를 얼마나 기다려야 합니까? kara-tanun keecha-rul olmana keeda-ryoya hamneekka

Boarding 승차

Is this the right platform for the train to … ?	…가는 기차 이 플랫폼에서 탑니까? … *ganun keecha ee plepawm-eso tam-neekka*
Is this the train to … ?	이 기차 … 갑니까? *ee keecha … kam-neekka*
Is this seat taken?	이 자리 임자 있습니까? *ee charee eemja ee-ssumneekka*
I think that's my seat.	제 자리인 것 같습니다. *che charee-een kot ka-ssumneeda*
Here's my reservation.	제 예약표 여기 있습니다. *che yeyak-pyo yo-gee ee-sumneeda*
Are there any seats/ berths available?	남는 자리/침대 있습니까? *namnun charee/cheemde ee-ssumneekka*
Do you mind if … ?	… 되겠습니까? … *dwe-ge-ssumneekka*
I sit here	여기 앉아도 *yo-gee anjadaw*
I open the window	창문 열어도 *chang-moon yorodaw*

On the journey 여행 도중

How long are we stopping here for?	얼마동안 여기 섭니까? *olma tawng-an yo-gee somneekka*
When do we get to … ?	언제 …에 도착합니까? *onje …e tawchak-hamneekka*
Have we passed … ?	… 지났습니까? … *cheena-ssumneekka*
Where is the dining/ sleeping car?	식당차/침대차 어디 있습니까? *seektang-cha/cheemde-cha odee ee-ssumneekka*
Where is my berth?	제 침대 어디 있습니까? *che cheemde odee ee-ssumneekka*
I've lost my ticket.	표를 잃어 버렸습니다. *pyo-rul eero-poryo-ssumneeda*

비상 제동 장치	emergency brake
비상벨	alarm
자동문	automatic doors

TIME ➤ 220

Long-distance bus [Coach]
장거리버스

Bus travel in South Korea is frequent, fast, and smoke-free. Inter-city express buses (**kawsawk posu**) can be first (**oodung**) or second (**eelban**) class. Local buses (**seewe posu**) are third class and can be crowded. It is best to get a ticket in advance, especially when traveling during holidays and on weekends. In North Korea there are very few public buses. Tourists usually travel by car or chartered bus with a guide.

Where is the bus [coach] station?	고속버스터미날 어디 있습니까? *kawsawk-posu tomeenal odee ee-ssumneekka*
When's the next bus [coach] to … ?	… 가는 다음 버스 언제 있습니까? *… kanun taum posu onje ee-ssumneekka*
Does the bus [coach] stop at … ?	그 버스 … 에서 섭니까? *ku posu … eso somneekka*
How long does it take to … ?	… 까지 얼마나 걸립니까? *… gajee olmana kolleem-neekka*

Bus 시내버스

In cities and suburbs, there are two types of buses: oridnary buses (**eelban**) which are cheaper but crowded at peak times, and special buses (**chwasok**, which means "seats"). However, at peak times, seats are not guaranteed even in special buses. Also, destinations and route numbers are not in English.

For ordinary buses it is best to buy a token or an electronic bus card (**posu kadu**) at a kiosk (located near bus stops) before boarding. When you get on, put a token in the designated box or scan your electronic card in the scanner. For special buses, you pay cash when you get on.

Where can I get a bus to … ?	… 가는 버스 어디서 탑니까? *… kanun posu odeeso tamneekka*

… 번 버스를 타십시오.	You need bus number …
… 에서 버스를 갈아 타야 합니다.	You must change buses at …

버스정류장	bus stop
금연	no smoking
비상구	(emergency) exit

Buying tickets 버스표 사기

Tokens (**tawkun**) are widely used in South Korea. Fares for each type of bus are the same regardless of the distance you travel. You can buy the tokens in any units you want, and they have no time limits. Increasingly, however, the electronic bus card is used.

Where can I buy tickets?	어디서 버스표 삽니까? *odeeso posu-pyo samneekka*
A token, please.	토큰 하나 주십시오. *tawkun hana chooseep-seeaw*
An (eletronic) bus card, please.	버스 카드 하나 주십시오. *pusu kadu hana chooseep-seeaw*
Can you add ... Won to this card ?	이 카드에 ... 원 어치 넣어 주십시오. *ee kadu-e ... won ochee no-o chooseep-seeaw.*

Traveling 차 안에서

Is this the right bus to ... ?	... 가는 버스 맞습니까? *... kanun posu ma-ssumneekka*
Could you tell me when to get off?	어디서 내리는지 말씀해 주시겠습니까? *odee-so nereenun-jee malssume chooseege-ssumneekka*
Do I have to change buses?	버스를 갈아 타야 합니까? *posu-rul kara-taya hamneekka*
How many stops are there ... to ... ?	... 까지 몇 정거장 남았습니까? *... gajee myot chong-gojang nama-ssumneekka*
Next stop, please!	다음 정거장에 세워 주세요. *taum chong-gojang-e sewo chooseyo*

카드를 여기 대주세요   scan your ticket here

– seelle-hamneeda. seechong-kanun
posu ma-ssumneekka?
– *ne, palbon ma-ssumneeda.*
– odee-so nereenun-jee malssume
chooseege-ssumneekka?
– *yo-gee-booto ne ponze chong-gojang-eemneeda.*

NUMBERS ➤ 216; *DIRECTIONS* ➤ 94

Subway [Metro] 지하철

In South Korea, Seoul and Pusan have efficient subways, but they can get very crowded at peak times. Fares depend on distance and you can buy multiple-use tickets to save money on frequent journeys. In North Korea, only Pyongyang has a subway system.

General inquiries 일반 문의사항

Where's the nearest subway [metro] station?	가장 가까운 지하철 역 어디 있습니까? *kajang katgaoon cheeha-chol yok odee ee-ssumneekka*
Where do I buy a ticket?	표 어디서 삽니까? *pyo odeeso sam-neekka*
Could I have a map of the subway [metro]?	지하철 노선도 하나 주십시오. *cheeha-chol nawson-daw hana chooseep-seeaw*

Traveling 차 안에서

Which line should I take for … ?	… 가려면 몇번 선을 타야합니까? *… karyo-myon myotbon sonul taya-hamneekka*
Is this the right train for … ?	… 가는 지하철 맞습니까? *… kanun cheeha-chol ma-ssumneekka*
Which stop is it for … ?	… 가려면 어디서 내려야 합니까? *… karyo-myon odee-so ne-ryo-ya hamneekka*
How many stops are there to … ?	… 까지 몇 정거장 남았습니까? *… gajee myot chong-gojang nama-ssumneekka*
Is the next stop … ?	다음이 … 입니까? *taum-ee … ee-mneekka*
Where are we?	여기가 어디 입니까? *yogee-ga odee ee-mneekka*
Where do I change for … ?	… 가려면 어디서 갈아 탑니까? *… karyo-myon odee-so kara tam-neekka*
What time is the last train to … ?	… 가는 막차가 몇시입니까? *… kanun makcha-ga myossee-eemneekka*

⊖	다른 노선	to other lines	⊘

NUMBERS ➤ 216; *BUYING TICKETS* ➤ 74, 79

Ferry 여객선

There are numerous ferry and boat services operating out of Mokpo, Wando, and Pusan to the South Korean islands. There is also a ferry connecting Wando and Mokpo (7 hours) and a hydrofoil service between Pusan and Yosu (3 hours), which goes through Hallyo Haesang National Park. During the summer months you can also take ferries from Pohang, Sokcho and Tonghae to the island of Ullung-do, a popular holiday destination with Koreans.

When is the … car ferry to Cheju?	제주가는 … 카페리 언제 있습니까? *chejoo kanun … kaperee onje ee-ssumneekka*
first/next/last	첫/다음/마지막 *chot/taum/majee-mak*
hovercraft/ship	쾌속정/배 *kwe-sawk-chong/pe*
A round-trip [return] ticket for …, please.	… 가는 왕복표 하나 주십시오. *… kanun wang-bawk pyo hana chooseep-seeaw*
2 adults and 3 children	어른 둘, 아이 셋 *orun tool, a-ee set*
I want to reserve a … cabin.	… 선실 하나 예약하고 싶습니다. *… sonseel hana yeyakagaw seep-sumneeda*
single/double	일인용/이인용 *eereen-yong/ee-een-yong*

구명보트	life boat
구명조끼	life preserver/life belt
비상시 집합장소	muster station

Boat trips 보트관광

Is there a …?	… 있습니까? *… ee-ssumneekka*
boat trip	보트관광 *bawtu kwan-gwang*
river cruise	강유람선 *kang yooram-son*
What time does it leave/return?	몇시에 떠납니까?/돌아옵니까? *myossee-e donamneekka/ tawra-awm-neekka*
Where can we buy tickets?	표를 어디서 삽니까? *pyo-rul odeeso sam-neekka*

TIME ➤ 220; BUYING TICKETS ➤ 74, 79

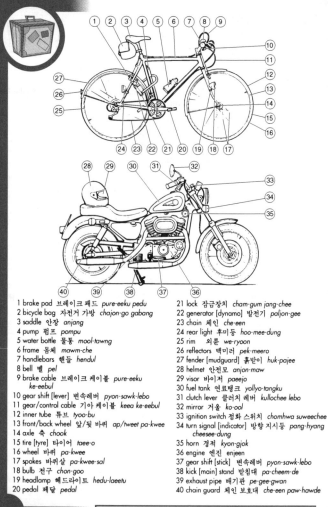

1 brake pad 브레이크 패드 pure-eeku pedu
2 bicycle bag 자전거 가방 chajon-go gabang
3 saddle 안장 anjang
4 pump 펌프 pompu
5 water bottle 물통 mool-tawng
6 frame 몸체 mawm-che
7 handlebars 핸들 hendul
8 bell 벨 pel
9 brake cable 브레이크 케이블 pure-eeku ke-eebul
10 gear shift [lever] 변속레버 pyon-sawk-lebo
11 gear/control cable 기아 케이블 keea ke-eebul
12 inner tube 튜브 tyoo-bu
13 front/back wheel 앞/뒷 바퀴 ap/tweet pa-kwee
14 axle 축 chook
15 tire [tyre] 타이어 taee-o
16 wheel 바퀴 pa-kwee
17 spokes 바퀴살 pa-kwee-sal
18 bulb 전구 chon-goo
19 headlamp 헤드라이트 hedu-laeetu
20 pedal 페달 pedal

21 lock 잠금장치 cham-gum jang-chee
22 generator [dynamo] 발전기 paljon-gee
23 chain 체인 che-een
24 rear light 후미등 hoo-mee-dung
25 rim 외륜 we-ryoon
26 reflectors 백미러 pek-meero
27 fender [mudguard] 흙받이 huk-pajee
28 helmet 안전모 anjon-maw
29 visor 바이저 paeejo
30 fuel tank 연료탱크 yollyo-tangku
31 clutch lever 클러치 레버 kullochee lebo
32 mirror 거울 ko-ool
33 ignition switch 점화 스위치 chomhwa suweechee
34 turn signal [indicator] 방향 지시등 pang-hyang cheesee-dung
35 horn 경적 kyon-gjok
36 engine 엔진 enjeen
37 gear shift [stick] 변속레버 pyon-sawk-lebo
38 kick [main] stand 받침대 pa-cheem-de
39 exhaust pipe 배기관 pe-gee-gwan
40 chain guard 체인 보호대 che-een paw-hawde

82

Bicycle/Motorbike
자전거/소형오토바이

Getting around by bicycle is not recommended in Seoul, but the Korean National Tourism Organization can give you the address of a rental firm if you're determined. You cannot rent bikes/mopeds in North Korea.

I'd like to rent a ...
... 한 대 빌리고 싶습니다.
... hande peellee-gaw seep-sumneeda

3-/10-speed bicycle
삼단 기아/십단 기아 자전거
samdam keea/seepdan keea chajon-go

moped/motorbike
소형 오토바이 *saw-hyong awtaw-ba-ee*

How much does it cost per day/week?
하루에/일주일에 얼마입니까?
haroo-e/eeljooee-re olma-eemneekka

Do I have to pay a deposit?
보증금을 내야합니까?
pawjung-gumul neya-hamneekka

The brakes don't work.
브레이크가 작동하지 않습니다.
pure-eeku-ga chakdawng-hajee an-ssumneeda

There are no lights.
불이 들어오지 않습니다.
pooree turo-awjee an-ssumneeda

The front/rear tire [tyre] has a flat [puncture].
앞/뒤 타이어가 펑크났습니다.
ap/dwee taeeo-ga pong-ku na-ssumneeda

Hitchhiking 히치하이킹

Hitchhiking is not customary and the meaning of an outstretched thumb is not generally known.

I'm heading for ....
저는 ... 로 갑니다.
cho-nun ... raw kamneeda

Is that on the way to ...?
그곳은 ... 가는 길에 있습니까?
kugaw-sun ... kanun keere ee-ssumneekka

Could you drop me off ...?
... 내려 주시겠습니까?
... neryo chooseege-ssumneekka

here
여기서 *yogeeso*

downtown
시내에서 *seene-eso*

Thanks for giving me a lift.
태워주셔서 감사합니다.
te-wo joo-syoso kamsa-hamneeda

DIRECTIONS ➤ 94; NUMBERS ➤ 216

Taxi/Cab 택시

There are two types of taxi in South Korea, ordinary (**eelban teksee**) and black deluxe (**mawbom teksee** – marked "Deluxe Taxi"). They are all metered. Ordinary taxis can be quite difficult to get hold of, and you may have to share with other passengers. In North Korea, taxis can only be booked from tourist hotels.

Where can I get a taxi?	택시 어디서 잡습니까? *teksee odeeso chap-sumneekka*
Do you have the number for a taxi?	콜택시 전화번호 있습니까? *kawl-teksee chonhwa-bonhaw ee-ssumneekka*
I'd like a taxi	... 택시를 불러 주십시요. *... teksee-rul poollo chooseep-seeyo*
now	지금 *chee-gum*
in an hour	한시간 후에 *han-seegan hoo-e*
for tomorrow at 9:00	내일 아침 아홉시에 *ne-eel acheem ahawp-see-e*
The address is .... I'm going to ...	주소는 ...입니다. ... 갑니다. *choosaw-nun ...eemneeda. ... kamneeda*

⊘ 빈차	for hire ⊘
Please take me to (the)	... 가주십시오. *... ka-jooseep-seeaw*
airport	공항 *kawng-hang*
train station	기차역 *keecha-yok*
this address	이 주소 *ee choosaw*
How much is that?	얼마입니까? *olma-eemneekka*
You said ... Won.	아까 ... 원이라고 말했습니다. *atga ... won eeragaw mal-hessumneeda*
Keep the change.	거스름돈은 가지세요. *kosurum-dawn-un kajeeseyo*

- keecha-yok-uraw ka-chooseep-seeyo.
  - *alge-ssumneeda.*
  - olma-eemneekka?
    - *awchon-won eemneeda. ta wa-ssumneeda.*
- kamsa-hamneeda. kosurum-dawn-un kajeeseyo.

Car/Automobile 자동차

There are no realistic opportunities for driving in North Korea as you will be traveling in specially-arranged transportation accompanied by your guide.

Driving in South Korea is not for the fainthearted, especially in cities and towns. Speed limits vary and are not always indicated. International road signs are used throughout South Korea but signposting in cities and towns is not always clear to the Western traveler. So before you head out it is best to obtain bilingual road maps from the tourist office.

Koreans drive on the right-hand side of the road and front seat passengers must wear seat belts.

You will need a passport, an international insurance certificate (green card), and an international driver's license to drive in Korea. If you plan to bring your own car, you will also need to display a nationality sticker and to carry a red warning triangle. However, you should check exact requirements with the Korean consulate or embassy before leaving home.

Road network

kaw-sawk-taw-raw

Expressway/tollway [motorway]. A toll is charged according to the size of the car and the distance traveled. The speed limit is 100 km/h.

kook-taw

Main highways. The speed limit 80 km/h.

Conversion chart

km	1	10	20	30	40	50	60	70	80	90	100	110	120	130
miles	0.62	6	12	19	25	31	37	44	50	56	62	68	74	81

Car rental 차렌트

You will need an international driver's license, a passport, one year's driving experience, and must be at least 21 to rent a car in South Korea.

Where can I rent a car?	차 어디서 빌릴 수 있습니까? *cha odeeso peelleel soo ee-ssumneekka*
I'd like to rent a(n) ...	... 한 대 빌리고 싶습니다. *... han de peellee-gaw seep-sumneeda*
2-/4-door car	투도어식 차/포도어식 차 *too daw-o-seek cha/paw daw-o-seek cha*
automatic car	오토메틱 차 *aw-taw-me-teek cha*
car with 4-wheel drive	사륜 구동식차 *sa-ryoon koo-dawng-seek cha*
car with air conditioning	냉방장치가 된 차 *neng-bang jang-chee-ga dwen cha*
I'd like it for a day/a week.	하루/일주일 빌리고 싶습니다. *haroo/eel-jooeel peellee-gaw seep-sumneeda*
How much does it cost per day/week?	하루에/일주일에 얼마입니까? *haroo-e/eel-jooee-re olma-eemneekka*
Is mileage/insurance included?	마일리지/보험 포함돼 있습니까? *maeel-leejee/pawhom pawham dwe-ee-ssumneekka*
Are there weekend rates?	주말 요금이 있습니까? *choomal yogumee ee-ssumneekka*
Can I return the car at ... ?	... 에서 차를 반환할 수 있습니까? *... eso cha-rul panhwan-hal soo eessumneekka*
What sort of fuel does it take?	어떤 기름을 넣어야 합니까? *otdon keeru-mul no-oya hamneekka*
Where is the high [full]/low [dipped] beam?	하이빔/로우빔 어디 있습니까? *haee-beem/law-oobeem odee ee-ssumneekka*
Could I have full insurance?	종합보험으로 할 수 있습니까? *chawng-hap pawhom-uraw hal-soo ee-ssumneekka*

Gas [Petrol] station 주유소

Where's the next gas [petrol] station, please?	다음 주유소가 어디 있습니까? *taum chooyoo-saw-ga odee ee-ssumneekka*
Is it self-service?	셀프서비스입니까? *selpu-sobeesu eemneekka*
Fill it up, please.	가득 채워주십시요. *kaduk chewo jooseep-seeyo*
… liters of gasoline [petrol], please.	… 리터 넣어주십시요. *… leeto no-o jooseep-seeyo*
premium [super]/regular	고급/보통 *kaw-gup/paw-tawng*
lead-free/diesel	무연/디젤 *mooyon/deejel*
Where is the air pump/water?	공기펌프/물 어디 있습니까? *kawng-gee-pompu/mool odee ee-ssumneekka*

⊘	리터당 가격 price per liter	⊖

Parking 주차

In most cities (except Seoul) there is very little legal parking. And while local drivers seem to ignore the posted parking regulations, indicated by signs or white lines on the curb, you should not.

Is there a parking lot [car park] nearby?	근처에 주차장 있습니까? *kuncho-e choocha-jang ee-ssumneekka*
What's the charge per hour/ per day?	시간당/하루에 얼마입니까? *see-gan-dang/haroo-e olma-eemneekka*
Do you have some change for the parking meter?	주차 미터기에 넣을 잔돈 있습니까? *choocha meeto-gee-e noul chandawn ee-ssumneekka*
My car has been impounded by the police. Who do I call?	제 차가 견인됐습니다. 어디로 전화해야 합니까? *che cha-ga kyon-een dwe-ssumneeda. odee-raw chonhwa-heya hamneekka*

NUMBERS ➤ 216; DIRECTIONS ➤ 94

Breakdown 고장

Your car insurance or rental company will provide emergency numbers for help in the event of a breakdown.

Where is the nearest garage?	가장 가까운 정비소가 어디 있습니까? *kajang katgoon chong-bee-saw-ga odee ee-ssumneekka*
My car broke down.	차가 고장 났습니다. *cha-ga kawjang na-ssumneeda*
Can you send a mechanic/ tow [breakdown] truck?	정비공/견인차 보내 주시겠습니까? *chong-bee-gawng/kyon-een-cha pawne chooseege-ssumneekka*
I belong to … recovery service.	저는 … 복구수리 서비스 회원입니다. *cho-nun … pawk-goo sooree-sobeesu hwe-won eemneeda*
My registration number is …	제 차번호는 … 입니다. *che cha-bonhaw-nun … eemneeda*
The car is …	제 차는 … 있습니다. *che cha-nun … ee-ssumneeda*
on the highway [motorway]	고속도로에 *kawsawk-tawraw-e*
2 km from …	…에서 2킬로 떨어져 *… eso ee-keeraw dorojo*
How long will you be?	오는데 얼마나 걸립니까? *awnun-de olmana kolleem-neekka*

What is wrong? 무엇이 잘못됐습니까?

My car won't start.	시동이 걸리지 않습니다. *seedawng-ee kollee-jee an-ssumneeda*
The battery is dead.	바테리가 나갔습니다. *pateree-ga naga-ssumneeda*
I've run out of gas [petrol].	기름이 떨어졌습니다. *keeru-mee dorojo-ssumneeda*
I have a flat [puncture].	타이어가 펑크났습니다. *ta-ee-o-ga pong-ku na-ssumneeda*
I've locked the keys in the car.	열쇠를 차안에 두고 문을 잠갔습니다. *yol-swe-rul cha-ane toogaw moonul chamga-ssumneeda*

Repairs 수리

Do you do repairs?	수리 합니까? *sooree hamneekka*
Can you repair it (temporarily)?	(임시로) 고칠 수 있습니까? *(eemsee-raw) kaw-cheel soo ees-sumneekka*
Please make only essential repairs.	꼭 필요한 수리만 해 주십시오. *gawk peeryo-han sooree-man he chooseep-seeaw*
Can I wait for it?	기다릴까요? *keeda-reelgayo*
Can you repair it today?	오늘 고칠 수 있습니까? *awnul kaw-cheel soo ee-ssumneekka*
When will it be ready?	언제 다 됩니까? *onje ta dwem-neekka*
How much will it cost?	얼마입니까? *olma-eemneekka*
That's outrageous!	말도 안됩니다! *maldaw an-dwem-needa*
Can I have a receipt for the insurance?	보험용 영수증 주십시오. *paw-hom-yong yong-soo-jung chooseep-seeyo*

... 작동하지 않습니다.	The ... isn't working.
필요한 부속이 없습니다.	I don't have the necessary parts.
부속을 주문해야 합니다.	I'll have to order the parts.
임시로만 고칠 수 있습니다.	I can only repair it temporarily.
차가 크게 망가졌습니다.	Your car is beyond repair.
수리할 수 없습니다.	It can't be repaired.
... 다 됩니다.	It will be ready ...
오늘 늦게	later today
내일	tomorrow
... 일 후에	in ... days

DAYS OF THE WEEK ➤ 218; NUMBERS ➤ 216

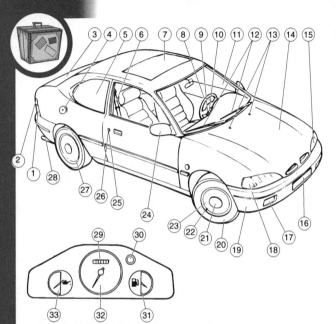

1 taillights [back lights] 후미등 *hoo-mee-dung*
2 brakelights 브레이크등 *pure-ee-ku-dung*
3 trunk [boot] 트렁크 *turongku*
4 gas tank door [petrol cap] 연료탱크 뚜껑 *yollyo-tengku dook-gong*
5 window 창문 *chang-moon*
6 seat belt 안전벨트 *anjon-beltu*
7 sunroof 선루프 *son-roopu*
8 steering wheel 핸들 *hendul*
9 ignition 점화 장치 *chomhwa chang-chee*
10 ignition key 점화키 *chomhwa-kee*
11 windshield [windscreen] 앞유리 *ap-nyooree*
12 windshield [windscreen] wipers 와이퍼 *wa-ee-po*
13 windshield [windscreen] washer 워셔 *wosyo*
14 hood [bonnet] 보넷 *pawnet*
15 headlights 헤드라이트 *hedu-laeetu*
16 license [number] plate 번호판 *ponhaw-pan*

17 fog lamp 안개등 *ange-dung*
18 turn signals [indicators] 방향 지시등 *pang-hyang cheesee-dung*
19 bumper 범퍼 *pompo*
20 tires [tyres] 타이어 *ta-ee-o*
21 hubcap 휠캡 *hweel-kep*
22 valve 밸브 *pelbu*
23 wheels 바퀴 *pa-kwee*
24 outside [wing] mirror 사이드 미러 *sa-ee-du meero*
25 central locking 중앙집중식 잠금장치 *choong-ang cheep-choong-seek cham-gum jangchee*
26 lock 잠금장치 *cham-gum jangchee*
27 wheel rim 외륜 *we-ryoon*
28 exhaust pipe 배기관 *pe-gee-gwan*
29 odometer [milometer] 주행기록계 *chooheng geerawk-ge*
30 warning light 경고등 *kyong-gaw-dung*

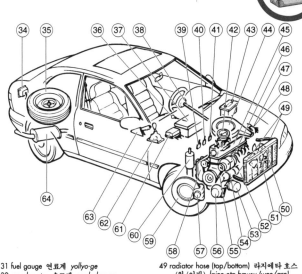

31 fuel gauge 연료계 yollyo-ge
32 speedometer 속도계 sawk-daw-ge
33 oil gauge 오일게이지 aw-eel ge-eejee
34 backup [reversing] lights 후진등
  hoojeen-dung
35 spare tire [tyre] 스페어 타이어
  supe-o taeeo
36 choke 초크 chaw-ku
37 heater 난방장치 nanbang jang-chee
38 steering column 핸들축 hendul-chook
39 accelerator 가속장치 kasawk chang-chee
40 pedal 페달 pedal
41 clutch 클러치 kul-lo-chee
42 carburetor 캬뷰레타 kyabu-reta
43 battery 바테리 pateree
44 alternator 교류기 kyo-ryoo-gee
45 camshaft 캠축 kem-chook
46 air filter 공기필터 kawng-gee peelto
47 distributor 디스트리뷰터 deesu-turee-byooto
48 points 포인트 paw-een-tu

49 radiator hose (top/bottom) 라지에타 호스
  (위/아래) lajee-eta hawsu (wee/are)
50 radiator 라지에타 lajee-eta
51 fan 팬 pen
52 engine 엔진 enjeen
53 oil filter 오일 여과장치
  aw-eel yo-gwa jang-chee
54 starter [motor] 스타터 모터 sutato mawto
55 fan belt 팬벨트 pen-beltu
56 horn 경적 kyong-jok
57 brake pads 브레이크 패드 pure-eeku pedu
58 transmission [gearbox] 변속기
  pyon-sawk-gee
59 brakes 브레이크 pure-eeku
60 shock absorbers 완충장치
  wan-choong jang-chee
61 fuses 퓨즈 pyooju
62 gear shift [gear lever] 기어 keeo
63 handbrake 핸드브레이크 hendu-bure-eeku
64 muffler [silencer] 머플러 mo-pullo

Accidents 사고

Remember to put out the red warning triangle (which you will find in the trunk of your rental car) if you are involved in a breakdown or accident and your car is blocking the flow of traffic.

There has been an accident.	사고가 났습니다. *sagaw-ga na-ssumneeda*
It's ...	... 입니다. *... eemneeda*
on the highway [motorway]	고속도로에서 *kawsawk tawraw-eso*
near ...	... 근처에서 *... kuncho-eso*
Where's the nearest telephone?	가장 가까운 전화 어디 있습니까? *kajang katgaoon chonhwa odee ee-ssumneekka*
Call ...	... 불러주십시오. *... poollo jooseepseeaw*
the police	경찰 *kyong-chal*
an ambulance	구급차 *koo-gup-cha*
a doctor	의사 *ueesa*
the fire department [fire brigade]	소방차 *sawbang-cha*
Can you help me, please?	도와주세요. *taw-wa jooseyo*

Injuries 부상

There are people injured.	부상자가 있습니다. *poosang-ja-ga ee-ssumneeda*
No one is hurt.	아무도 안다쳤습니다. *amoo-daw an-dacho-ssumneeda*
He is seriously injured.	그 남자는 중상입니다. *ku namja-nun choong-sang eemneeda*
She's unconscious.	그 여자는 의식을 잃었습니다. *ku yoja-nun ueesee-gul eero-ssumneeda*
He can't breathe/move.	그 남자는 숨 쉴 수/움직일 수 없습니다. *ku namja-nun soom sweel soo/ oomjeeg-eel soo op-sumneeda*
Don't move him.	그 남자를 움직이지 마십시오. *ku namja-rul oom-jeeg-eejee maseepseeaw*

INJURIES ➤ 162; DIRECTIONS ➤ 94

Legal matters 법률문제

What's your insurance company?

보험회사가 어디입니까?
pawhom-hwesaga odee-eemneekka

What's your name and address?

이름과 주소를 말씀해 주십시오.
eerum-gwa choosaw-rul malssumhe chooseep-seeaw

He ran into me.

그 사람이 제 차를 박았습니다.
ku saram-ee che cha-rul paga-ssumneeda

She was driving too fast/too close.

그 여자가 너무 빠르게/너무 가까이 운전하고 있었습니다. *ku yoja-ga nomoo baruge/nomoo katgaee oonjon-hagaw eesso-ssumneeda*

I had right of way.

제게 우선권이 있었습니다.
che-ge ooson-gwonee eesso-ssumneeda

I'd like an interpreter.

통역을 불러 주십시오.
tawng-yogul poollo chooseep-seeaw

He/She saw it happen.

그 남자가/그 여자가 그것을 보았습니다.
ku namja-ga/ku yoja-ga ku ko-sul pwa-ssumneeda

... 보여주십시오.	Can I see your ..., please?
운전면허증	driver's license
보험증서	insurance card
자동차 등록증	vehicle registration (document)
몇시에 사고가 났습니까?	What time did it happen?
어디서 사고가 났습니까?	Where did it happen?
목격자가 있습니까?	Are there any witnesses?
과속하셨습니다.	You were speeding.
선생님 차의 라이트가 작동하지 않습니다.	Your lights aren't working.
(여기서 바로) 벌금을 내셔야 합니다.	You'll have to pay a fine (on the spot).
경찰서에서 진술서를 작성하셔야 합니다.	We need you to make a statement at the station.

Asking directions 방향 물어보기

Excuse me, please.	실례합니다. *seelle-hamneeda*
How do I get to ?	... 어떻게 갑니까? ... *otdoke kamneekka*
Where is ...?	... 어디 있습니까? ... *odee ee-ssumneekka*
Can you show me on the map where I am?	여기가 어딘지 지도에서 보여주시겠습니까? *yogee-ga odeen-jee cheedaw-eso paw-yo-jooseege-ssumneekka*
I've lost my way.	길을 잃었습니다. *kee-rul eero-ssumneeda*
Can you repeat that, please?	다시 말씀해 주시겠습니까? *tasee malssumhe chooseege-ssumneekka*
More slowly, please.	더 천천히 해 주십시오. *to chon-chonee he-chooseep-seeaw*
Thanks for your help.	도와주셔서 감사합니다. *taw-wa joosyoso kamsa-hamneeda*

Traveling by car 자동차 여행

Is this the right road for ... ?	이 길이 ... 가는 길 맞습니까? *ee kee-ree ... kanun-geel ma-ssumneekka*
How far is it to ... from here?	여기서 ... 까지 얼마나 멉니까? *yogeeso ... gajee olmana mom-neekka*
Where does this road lead?	이건 어디로 가는 길입니까? *ee-gun odeeraw kanun-geel eemneekka*
How do I get onto the highway [motorway]?	고속도로로 어떻게 갑니까? *kawsawk-dawraw-raw otdoke kamneekka*
What's the name of the next town?	다음 도시 이름은 무엇입니까? *taum-tawsee eeru-mun moo-o-seemneekka*
How long does it take by car?	차로 얼마나 걸립니까? *cha-raw olmana kolleemneekka*

– seelle-hamneeda. keecha-yoguraw otdoke kamneekka?
  – sebonze eso oo-hwe-jon haseep-seeaw.
– wen-zawg sebonzeyo. momneekka?
  – koroso seep-boon eemneeda.
– taw-wa-joosyoso kamsa-hamneeda.
  – chon-maneyo.

94

Location 위치

... 있습니다.	It's ...
직진 방향에	straight ahead
왼쪽에	on the left
오른쪽에	on the right
이 길 끝에	at the end of the street
코너에	on the corner
코너를 돌아서	around the corner
... 방향에	in the direction of ...
... 맞은 편에 /... 뒤에	opposite .../behind ...
... 옆에 /... 지나서	next to .../after ...
... 따라 가십시오.	Go down the ...
옆 길 / 큰 길	side street/main street
... 건너십시오.	Cross the ...
광장 / 다리	square/bridge
세번째에서 우회전하십시오	Take the third right.
... 좌회전하십시오	Turn left ...
첫 교통 신호등을 지나서	after the first traffic lights
두번째 교차로에서	at the second intersection [crossroad]

By car 차로

여기의 ...입니다.	It's ... of here.
북쪽 / 남쪽	north/south
동쪽 / 서쪽	east/west
... 가는 길을 타십시오.	Take the road for ...
길을 잘못 들었습니다.	You're on the wrong road.
... 로 되돌아가야 합니다.	You'll have to go back to ...
... 가는 도로표지를 따라가십시오.	Follow the signs for ...

How far? 얼마나 멉니까?

가깝습니다/멉니다.	It's close/a long way.
걸어서 오분입니다.	It's 5 minutes on foot.
차로 십분입니다.	It's 10 minutes by car.
이 길을 따라서 약 백미터입니다.	It's about 100 m down the road.
약 10킬로 떨어져 있습니다.	It's about 10 km away.

TIME ➤ 220; NUMBERS ➤ 216

Road signs 도로표지

우회로	detour [diversion]
차선 변경 금지	stay in lane
양보	yield [give way]
높이 제한	low bridge
일방통행	one-way street
막힌 길	road closed
학교	school
라이트를 켜시오	use headlights

Town plans 시가지 지도

공항	airport
버스노선	bus route
버스정류장	bus stop
교회	church
안내	information office
중심가	main [high] street
영화관	movie theater [cinema]
구시가지	old town
공원	park
주차장	parking lot [car park]
횡단보도	pedestrian crossing
보행자 보호구역	pedestrian zone [precinct]
운동장	playing field [sports ground]
경찰서	police station
우체국	post office
공공건물	public building
경기장	stadium
역	station
지하철	subway [metro] station
택시 승차장	taxi stand [rank]
극장	theater
지하도	underpass
현재 위치	you are here

Sightseeing

Tourist information office 여행정보안내소

The Korean National Tourism Organization (**KNTO**) in Seoul
(☎ 02-757-2000) provides a wealth of information including free maps,
brochures, and advice on travel. There are also tourist information centers
in Pusan (☎ 051-460-3331-7), Chejoo (☎ 064-42-8866), and in Kyongjoo
(☎ 0561-772-3843). For information about long-distance buses, call the
main bus station in Seoul (☎ 02-537-9198).

Where's the tourist office?	여행 안내소가 어디 있습니까? *yoheng annesaw-ga odee ee-ssumneekka*
What are the main points of interest?	주요 볼거리가 무엇입니까? *choo-yaw pawl koree-ga moo-o-seemneekka*
We're here for ...	우리는 여기 ... 동안 있습니다. *ooree-nun yogee ... tawng-an ees-sumneeda*
only a few hours	겨우 두세시간 *kyo-oo too-se seegan*
a day	하루 *haroo*
a week	일주일 *eeljoo-eel*
Can you recommend ...?	... 추천해 주시겠습니까? *... choo-chonhe chooseege-ssumneekka*
a sightseeing tour	관광코스 하나 *kwan-gwang kawsu hana*
an excursion	일일여행 하나 *eereel-yoheng hana*
a boat trip	보트관광 하나 *bawtu kwan-gwang hana*
Do you have any information on ...?	...에 대한 정보를 갖고 계십니까? *... e dehan chong-baw-rul katgaw keseem-neekka*
Are there any trips to ...?	... 가는 여행코스 있습니까? *... kanun yoheng-kawsu ee-ssumneekka*

DAYS OF THE WEEK ➤ 218; DIRECTIONS ➤ 94

97

Excursions 일일여행

How much does the tour cost?	비용이 얼마입니까? *peeyong-ee olma ee-umneekka*
Is lunch included?	점심이 포함돼 있습니까? *chomsee-mee pawham-dwe ee-ssumneekka*
Where do we leave from?	어디서 떠납니까? *odeeso donamneekka*
What time does the tour start?	몇시에 떠납니까? *myossee-e donamneekka*
What time do we get back?	몇시에 돌아옵니까? *myossee-e tawra aw-mneekka*
Do we have free time in …?	… 에서 자유시간이 있습니까? *… eso chayoo-seega-nee ee-ssumneekka*
Is there an English-speaking guide?	영어안내가 있습니까? *yong-o anne-ga ee-ssumneekka*

On tour 여행 도중

Are we going to see …?	… 구경합니까? *… koo-gyong hamneekka*
We'd like to have a look at the …	… 구경하고 싶습니다. *… koo-gyong-hagaw seep-sumneeda*
Can we stop here …?	… 여기 멈출 수 있습니까? *… yogee momchool soo ee-ssumneekka*
to take photographs	사진 찍기 위해 *sajeen zeek-gee weehe*
to buy souvenirs	기념품 사기위해 *kee-nyom-poom sagee weehe*
to use the bathrooms [toilets]	화장실 가기 위해 *hwajang-seel kagee weehe*
Would you take a photo of us, please?	사진 좀 찍어 주시겠습니까? *sajeen chawm zeego chooseege-ssumneekka*
How long do we have here/in …?	여기서/… 에서 얼마나 머뭅니까? *yogeeso/… eso olmana momoom-neekka*
Wait! … isn't back yet.	잠깐! … 아직 안 돌아왔습니다. *cham-gan! … ajeek an-tawra wa-ssumneeda*

Sights 구경

In larger cities you will be able to get maps of the area with useful tourist information in English.

Where is the …	… 어디 있습니까? … odee ee-ssumneekka
art gallery	미술관 mee-sool-gwan
battle site	전적지 chon-jok-zee
botanical garden	식물원 seeng-mul-won
castle	성 song
cathedral	성당 song-dang
cemetery	공동묘지 kawng-dawng myo-jee
church	교회 kyo-hwe
downtown area	중심가 choong-seem-ga
fountain	분수 poon-soo
market	시장 see-jang
(war) memorial	(전쟁)기념물 (chon-jeng) kee-nyom-mool
monastery	수도원 soodaw-won
museum	박물관 pang-mool-gwan
old town	구시가지 koo seegajee
opera house	오페라하우스 awpera ha-oosu
palace	궁전 koong-jon
park	공원 kawng-won
parliament building	국회의사당 kookwe ueesa-dang
ruins	폐허 peho
shopping area	상가 sang-ga
statue	동상 tawng-sang
theater	극장 kuk-zang
tower	탑 tap
town hall	시청 see-chong
viewpoint	전망대 chonmang-de
Can you show me on the map?	지도에서 보여 주시겠습니까? cheedaw-eso pawyo chooseege-ssumneekka

DIRECTIONS ➤ 94

Admission 입장

Museums are usually open daily from 9 a.m. to 6 p.m.
(March–October) or 5 p.m. (November–February), though
some are closed on Mondays.

Is the ... open to the public?	... 일반인도 볼 수있습니까? *... eelban-eendo pawl-soo ee-ssumneekka*
Can we look around?	둘러 볼 수 있습니까? *toollo pawl-soo ee-ssumneekka*
What are the opening hours?	언제 문을 엽니까? *onje moonul yomneekka*
Is ... open on Sundays?	... 일요일에 엽니까? *... eeryoee-re yomneekka*
When's the next guided tour?	다음 안내는 언제입니까? *taum anne-nun onje eemneekka*
Do you have a guidebook (in English)?	(영어) 안내책 있습니까? *(yong-o) anne-chek ee-ssumneekka*
Can I take photos?	사진 찍어도 됩니까? *sajeen zeego-daw dwem-neekka*
Is there access for the disabled?	장애자가 구경할 수 있습니까? *chang-eja-ga koo-kyong-hal soo ee-ssumneekka*
Is there an audioguide in English?	영어 녹음 안내가 있습니까? *yong-o nawg-um anne-ga ee-ssumneekka*

Paying/Tickets 표사기

How much is the entrance fee?	입장료 얼마 입니까? *eep-zang-nyo olma eemneekka*
Are there any discounts for ...?	... 할인 있습니까? *... hareen ee-ssumneekka*
children	어린이 *oreenee*
the disabled	장애 자 *chang-eja*
groups	단체 *tanche*
senior citizens	노인 *naw-een*
students	학생 *hak-sseng*
1 adult and 2 children, please.	어른 한 장, 어린이 두 장 주십시요. *orun han-jang, oreenee too-jang chooseep-seeaw*

- tasot-jang chooseep-seeaw. hareenee
ee-ssumneekka?
- ne. oreenee-wa naw-eenun chon-won
eemneeda.
- orun too-jang, oreenee se-jang
chooseep-seeaw.
- cheel-chon-won eemneeda.

무료입장	free admission
휴관	closed
선물가게	gift shop
마지막 입장 5시	latest entry at 5 p.m.
다음 투어	next tour at …
들어가지 마시오/출입금지	no entry
사진찍지 마시오/사진 촬영 금지	no flash photography
개관	open
관람시간	visiting hours

Impressions 인상

It's amazing.	놀랍습니다. *nawllap-ssumneeda*
It's awful.	엉망입니다. *ong-mang eemneeda*
It's beautiful.	아름답습니다. *arum-dap-ssumneeda*
It's boring.	따분합니다. *daboon-hamneeda*
It's incredible.	훌륭합니다. *hool-lyoong-hamneeda*
It's lots of fun.	아주 재미있습니다. *ajoo chemee-ee-ssumneeda*
It's interesting.	흥미롭습니다. *hung-mee-rawp sumneeda*
It's magnificent.	웅장합니다. *oong-jang hamneeda*
It's romantic.	낭만적입니다. *nang-man-jog eemneeda*
It's strange.	이상합니다. *eesang-hamneeda*
It's stunning.	멋집니다. *mozeem-needa*
It's superb.	최고입니다. *chwe-gaw eemneeda*
It's terrible.	끔찍합니다. *gumzeek-hamneeda*
It's good value.	볼 만 합니다. *pawl-man hamneeda*
It's a rip-off.	바가지 썼습니다. *pagajee sso-ssumneeda.*
I like it.	마음에 듭니다. *maume tum-needa*
I don't like it.	마음에 안 듭니다. *maume antum-needa*

101

사찰, 절	*sachal, chol*	Buddhist temple
묘지	*myo-jee*	burial site
궁	*koong*	palace
사적지	*sajok-jee*	historical site
온천	*awn-chon*	hot spring
박물관	*pang-mool-gwan*	museum
기념물	*kee-nyom-mool*	monument
국립공원	*koong-neep kawng-won*	national park
정원	*chong-won*	garden
사당	*sadang*	shrine

건축	*kon-chook*	architecture
미술	*meesool*	art
서예	*soye*	calligraphy
도예	*taw-ye*	ceramics/pottery
수공예	*soo-gawng-ye*	handicrafts
칠기	*cheel-gee*	lacquerware
회화	*hwe-hwa*	painting
지공예	*chee-gawng-ye*	papercrafts
직물	*cheeng-mool*	textiles
목공예	*mawk-kawng-ye*	woodcrafts

Who/What/When?
누가/무엇/언제?

What's that building?	저 건물은 무엇입니까? *cho konmoo-run moo-o-seemneekka*
When was it built?	언제 지어졌습니까? *onje chee-o-jo-ssumneekka*
Who was the artist/architect?	화가/건축가가 누구입니까? *hwaga/* *konchook-ga-ga noo-goo eemneekka*
What style is that?	무슨 양식입니까? *moosun yangseeg-eemneekka*
What period is that?	어느 시대 것입니까? *onu seede-got eemneekka*

Ko-Choson period   2333 B.C. – 57 B.C.
According to Korean myth, the Korean race was born in 2333 B.C. The traditional calendar used this as the "birth year," making the Western year 2000 the Korean year 4333.

Period of the Three Kingdoms   57 B.C. – 668 A.D.
During the period of the Three Kingdoms – Koguryo, Paekche, and Silla – Buddhism became the state religion and Chinese culture was absorbed. There were many wars for supremacy until the Silla Dynasty, with the help of the Chinese Tang Dynasty, was able to defeat the other two kingdoms.

Unified Silla period   676 – 935
This was a golden age for Korean culture when Buddhist art flourished.

Koryo period   918 – 1392
Buddhism reached the height of its development during this period.

Choson dynasty   1392 – 1910
This was the peninsula's final dynasty. During this time, Confucianism became the state religion and in 1443 the unique Hangul phonetic script for the Korean language was invented, which lead to a vast increase in literacy.

Japanese invasion   1910 – 1945
The Japanese annexed Korea in 1910 and remained there until the Second World War. When the war ended, Japan withdrew. Korea was then occupied by the U. S. military in the South and by the Soviet Military in the North. A UN commission attempted to oversee free elections but was denied access to the North. The new government in the South declared independence followed by the North doing likewise. In 1948, both the United States and the Soviet Union withdrew their forces but continued to supply arms.

Korean War 1950 – 1953

The Korean War started with the invasion of the South by the North. Millions of people were killed and the countryside was devastated. In 1953, a truce was negotiated in Panmunjom with the creation of a demilitarized zone.

Post Korean War

North Korea became a Marxist regime under the leadership of Kim Il-Sung, followed by Kim Jong-Il. The North Korean ideology of **juche** (self-reliance) isolated it from the rest of the world and made it hard for the country to accept overseas aid and trade. South Korea recovered from the ravages of war and its post-war reconstruction efforts resulted in relative prosperity and stability.

Dance and theater 춤과 놀이

The two major forms of folk dance and theater are **Nawng-ak** and **Talchoom**, or **Kamyon-kuk**. Nawng-ak (Farmers' Festival Music and Dance) is the oldest of the Korean folk performing arts. The musical instruments, mainly percussion, are played by the dancers themselves, who wear hats with long paper streamers which they twirl around in circular fashion.

Talchoom, or **Kamyon-kuk** (Mask Dance-Drama), represents one of the major forms of traditional folk theater in Korea today. **Pansawree** is a mixture of music, drama, and verse. The stories are acted out by one performer (**sawreet-goon**) who is accompanied by a drum.

Performances of traditional dance and theater can be enjoyed at the Korean Folk Village near Suwon and at the Sejong Cultural Center in Seoul.

Places of worship 교회

South Korea guarantees freedom of religion and has two major religious influences: Buddhism and, since its introduction in the late 18th century, Christianity. Confucianism remains strong as a moral, ethical principle for the people, regardless of their religion.

Catholic/Protestant church	카톨릭/개신교 교회 *ka-tawl-leek/keseen-gyo kyo-hwe*
mosque	회교사원 *hwe-gyo sawon*
synagogue	유대교회 *yoode gyo-hwe*
What time is ...?	... 몇시입니까? *... myossee ee-mneekka*
mass/the service	미사/예배 *mee-sa/yebe*

In the countryside 시골에서

I'd like a map of ...	... 지도 하나 주십시오. *... cheedaw hana chooseep-seeaw*
this region	이 지역 *ee chee-yok*
walking routes	산책로 *sancheng-naw*
cycle routes	자전거 길 *chajon-go geel*
How far is it to ...?	...까지 얼마나 멉니까? *... gajee olmana mom-neekka*
Is there a right of way?	지나갈 수 있는 길이 있습니까? *cheenagal soo eennun keeree eessumneekka*
Is there a trail/scenic route to ...?	... 산책로/경치좋은 길 있습니까? *... sancheng-naw/kyong-chee jaw-un keeree ee-ssumneekka*
Can you show me on the map?	지도에서 보여 주시겠습니까? *cheedaw- eso pawyo chooseege-ssumneekka*
I'm lost.	길을 잃었습니다. *kee-rul eero-ssumneeda*

Organized walks 안내 도보여행

When does the guided walk/ hike start?	안내 도보여행은 언제 시작합니까? *anne tawbaw yoheng-un onje seejak-hamneekka*
When will we return?	언제 돌아옵니까? *onje tawra-awmneekka*
What is the walk/hike like?	도보여행은 어떻습니까? *tawbaw yoheng-un ot-do-ssumneekka*
It's gentle/medium/tough.	쉽습니다/보통입니다/힘듭니다. *sweep-sumneeda/pawtawng-eemneeda/ heem-dumneeda*
I'm exhausted.	지쳤습니다. *cheecho-ssumneeda*
How long are we resting here?	여기서 얼마나 쉽니까? *yogeeso olmana sweem-neekka*
What kind of ... is that?	그것은 어떤 ... 입니까? *kugo-sun ot-don ... ee-mneekka*
animal/bird	동물/새 *tawng-mool/se*
flower/tree	꽃/나무 *gawt/namoo*

 WALKING/HIKING GEAR ➤ 145

Geographic features 지형

bridge	다리 *taree*
cave	동굴 *tawng-gool*
cliff	절벽 *chol-byok*
farm	농장 *nawng-jang*
field	들판 *tulpan*
footpath	오솔길 *awsawl-geel*
forest	삼림 *samneem*
hill	언덕 *ondok*
lake	호수 *hawsoo*
mountain	산 *san*
mountain pass	산길 *san-geel*
mountain range	산맥 *sanmek*
nature reserve	자연 보호지구 *chayon pawhaw jee-goo*
panorama	전경 *chon-gyong*
park	공원 *kawng-won*
peak	정상 *chong-sang*
picnic area	취사지역 *chweesa jeeyok*
pond	연못 *yon-mawt*
rapids	급류 *kum-nyoo*
river	강 *kang*
sea	바다 *pada*
stream	시내 *seene*
valley	계곡 *ke-gawk*
viewpoint	전망대 *chonmang-de*
village	마을 *maul*
waterfall	폭포 *pawk-paw*
winery [vineyard]	포도밭 *pawdaw-bat*
wood	숲 *soop*

Leisure

Events 문화정보

Two English-language newspapers, **The Korea Times** and **The Korea Herald**, are published daily (except Mondays) and are available at most newsstands, especially in large cities.

Do you have a program of events?	행사 프로그램 있습니까? *hengsa puraw-gurem ee-ssumneekka*
Can you recommend a good ...?	볼만한 ... 하나 있습니까? *pawl-manhan ... hana eessumneekka*
ballet/concert	발레공연 / 음악회 *palle gawng-yon/umak-hwe*
movie [film]	영화 *yong-hwa*
opera	오페라공연 *awpera gawng-yon*

Availability 표 구입

When does it start?	언제 시작합니까? *onje seejak-hamneekka*
When does it end?	언제 끝납니까? *onje gun-namneekka*
Are there any seats for tonight?	오늘밤 자리가 남아 있습니까? *awnul-bam charee-ga nama ee-ssumneekka*
Where can I get tickets?	어디서 표를 삽니까? *odeeso pyo-rul samneekka*
There are ... of us.	...명입니다. *... myong ee-mneeda*

Tickets 표

How much are the seats?	그 자리 얼마입니까? *ku charee olma eemneekka*
Do you have anything cheaper?	더 싼 것 있습니까? *to ssan ko ee-ssumneekka*
I'd like to reserve ...	... 예매하고 싶습니다. *... yeme-hagaw seep-sumneeda*
3 for Sunday evening	일요일 저녁 세 장 *eeryo-eel cho-nyok se-jang*
1 for the Friday matinee	금요일 낮공연 한 장 *kumyo-eel nat kawng-yon han-jang*

신용카드 번호가 어떻게 됩니까?	What's your credit card number?
신용카드 종류가 무엇입니까?	What's your credit card type?
신용카드 만기가 언제입니까?	What's your credit card's expiration [expiry] date?
... 표를 찾으십시오.	Please pick up the tickets ...
일곱시까지	by 7 p.m.
예매창구에서	at the reservations desk

May I have a program, please?	프로그램 주십시오. *puraw-gurem chooseep-seeaw*
Where's the coatcheck [cloakroom]?	휴대품 보관소 어디 있습니까? *hyoode-poom paw-gwan-saw odee ee-ssumneekka*

– moo-ol taw-wa dureel-kkayo.
– awnul cho-nyok yonjoo hwe pyo se-jang chooseep-seeaw.
– alge-ssumneeda.
– seen-yong kaduraw kesan halsoo eesumneekka?
– moollawn-eemneeda.
– kadu yogee eessumneeda.
– kamsa-hamneeda. yogee-e so-myong-he chooseep-seeaw.

예매	Advance reservations
오늘표 파는 곳	Tickets for today

NUMBERS ➤ *216*

Movies [Cinema] 영화관

Foreign films are not dubbed but run in their original version, subtitled in Korean. Films usually run continuously from 11 a.m. but downtown theaters can be very busy on weekends so it's worth buying tickets in advance. The U.S. military also runs an English-language TV station AFKN.

Is there a multiplex theater [cinema] near here?	근처에 복합 영화관있습니까? *kuncho-e paw-kap yong-hwa-gwan ee-ssumneekka*
What's playing at the movies [on at the cinema] tonight?	오늘밤 무슨 영화합니까? *awnul-bam moosun yong-hwa hamneekka*
Is the film dubbed/subtitled?	그 영화 더빙/자막 입니까? *ku yong-hwa tobeeng/chamak eemneekka*
Is the film in the original English?	그 영화 영어로 상영됩니까? *ku yong-hwa yong-o-raw sang-yong dwem-neekka*
A ..., please.	... 하나 주십시오. *... hana chooseep-seeaw*
box [carton] of popcorn	팝콘 *pap-kawn*
hot dog	핫도그 *hat-dawgu*
soft drink	청량음료 *chong-nyang um-nyo*
small/regular/large	작은 거/보통/큰 거 *chagun ko/ paw-tawng/kun ko*

Theater 극장

What's playing at the ... Theater?	... 극장에서 무엇을 합니까? *... kukzang-eso moo-o-sul hamneekka*
Who's the playwright?	극작가는 누구입니까? *kuk-jak-ga-nun noo-goo ee-mneekka*
Do you think I'd enjoy it?	재미 있을 것 같습니까? *chemee eessul ko ka-ssumneekka*
I don't know much Korean.	저는 한국어 잘 모릅니다. *cho-nun han-googo chal mawrum-needa*

Opera/Ballet/Dance
오페라/발레/무용

Where's the opera house?
오페라 하우스가 어디
있습니까? *awpera
haoosu-ga odee ee-ssumneekka*

Who is the composer/soloist?
작곡가는/독주자는 누구입니까?
*chak-gawk-ga-nun/tawk-zoo-ja-nun
noo-goo ee-mneekka*

Is formal dress required?
정장해야 합니까?
chong-jang heya ham-neekka

Who's dancing?
누가 춤을 춥니까?
noo-ga choomul choom-neekka

I'm interested in
contemporary dance.
저는 현대무용에 관심있습니다.
*cho-nun hyon-de mooyong-e kwan-seem
ee-ssumneeda*

Music/Concerts 음악/연주회

Where's the concert hall?
연주회장이 어디 있습니까? *yonjoo-
hwe-jang-ee odee ee-ssumneekka*

Which orchestra/band is
playing?
어느 오케스트라가/악단이 연주합니까?
*onu awkesutura-ga/ak-danee
yonjoo ham-neekka*

What are they playing?
무슨 곡을 연주합니까? *moo-sun kawgul
yonjoo ham-neekka*

Who is the conductor/soloist?
지휘자/독주자는 누구입니까?
*chee-hwee-ja-nun/tawk-zoo-ja-nun
noo-goo eemneekka*

I really like …
… 아주 좋아합니다.
… ajoo chaw-a-hamneeda

folk/country music
민속음악 *meen-sawk umak*

jazz
재즈 *cheju*

pop/rock music
팝/록 음악 *pap/rawk umak*

Have you ever heard of
her/him?
그 여자/그 남자 노래를 들어 봤습니까?
*ku yoja/ku namja nawre-rul
turo-baw-ssumneekka*

Are they popular?
그들은 인기 있습니까? *kudunun
een-gee eessumneekka*

Nightlife 야간 유흥

What is there to do in the evenings?	저녁에 할 만한 것 있습니까? *chonyo-ge hal manhan go eessumneekka*
Can you recommend a …?	갈만한 … 있습니까? *kalman-han … eessumneekka*
Is there a … in town?	시내에 … 있습니까? *seene-e … eessumneekka*
bar/restaurant	바/음식점 *pa/umseek-chom*
casino	카지노 *kajee-naw*
discotheque	디스코텍 *deeskaw-tek*
gay club	게이클럽 *ke-ee-kullop*
nightclub	나이트클럽 *naeetu-kullop*
What type of music do they play?	어떤 음악을 연주합니까? *otdon umagul yonjoo ham-neekka*
How do I get there?	거기 어떻게 갑니까? *ko-gee otdoke kam-neekka*

Admission 입장

What time does the show start?	몇시에 시작합니까? *myossee-e seejak-hamneekka*
Is formal [evening] dress required?	정장해야 합니까? *chong-jang heya hamneekka*
Is a reservation necessary?	예약해야 합니까? *yeyakeya hamneekka*
Do we need to be members?	회원이어야 합니까? *hwe-won ee-o-ya hamneekka*
Is it customary to dine there?	거기서 식사하는 것이 관례입니까? *ko-geeso seeksa-hanun kosee gwalle-eemneekka*
How long will we have to stand in line [queue]?	얼마나 줄을 서야 합니까? *olmana chool-ul soya hamneekka*
I'd like a good table.	좋은 테이블로 주십시오. *chaw-un te-ee-bullaw chooseep-seeaw*

무료 음료수 한병 포함	includes one complimentary drink

Children 어린이

Can you recommend something for the children?	어린이가 볼만한 것 있습니까? *oreenee-ga pawl-manhan-go ee-ssumneekka*
Are there changing facilities here for babies?	여기 아기 기저귀 가는 시설 있습니까? *yogee keejo-gee kanun seesol ee-ssumneekka*
Where are the bathrooms [toilets]?	화장실 어디 있습니까? *hwajang-seel odee ee-ssumneekka*
amusement arcade	오락실 *awrak-seel*
fairground	행사장 *heng-sa-jang*
kiddie [paddling] pool	어린이풀 *oreenee-pool*
playground	놀이터 *nawree-to*
zoo	동물원 *tawng-mool-won*

Baby-sitting 아기보기

Can you recommend a reliable baby-sitter?	믿을 만한 애보는 사람 누구 있습니까? *meedul manhan e-bawnun saram noo-goo ee-ssumneekka*
Is there constant supervision?	아이를 쉬지않고 계속 돌봅니까? *aee-rul sweejee ankaw kesawk tawlbawm-neekka*
Is the staff properly trained?	직원이 제대로 훈련 받았습니까? *jeegwo-nee chederaw hool-lyon pada-ssumneekka*
When can I drop them off?	언제 아이를 맡길 수 있습니까? *onje aee-rul matgeel soo ee-ssumneekka*
I'll pick them up at ...	...에 아이를 데려 가겠습니다. *...-e aee-rul teryo-kage-ssumneeda*
We'll be back by ...	...까지 오겠습니다. *... gajee awge-ssumneeda*
She's 3 and he's 18 months.	여자애는 세살이고 남자애는 십팔개월입니다. *yoja-enun se-sareegaw namja-enun seepal-gewol-eemneeda*

Sports 운동

In addition to the traditional martial art of tae kwon do (**tek-kwon-daw**), practically every sport played in the West is also popular in Korea (tennis, soccer, basketball, skiing, swimming, table tennis, etc.). Baseball has gained such popularity that there is now a professional baseball league. Korean traditional-style wrestling (**ssee-rum**) can still be seen at various tournaments held all over the country and is often accompanied by traditional folk music and dance.

Spectating 관람 경기

Is there a soccer [football] game [match] this Saturday?	이번 토요일에 축구시합 있습니까? *eebon tawyo-eere chook-goo seehap ee-ssumneekka*
Which teams are playing?	어느 팀이 경기합니까? *onu teemee kyong-gee ham-neekka*
Can you get me a ticket?	표 한장 구해 주시겠습니까? *pyo han-jang koohe chooseege-ssumneekka*
What's the admission charge?	입장료는 얼마입니까? *eep-jang-nyo-nun olma ee-mneekka*
Where's the race track [course]?	경마장은 어디입니까? *kyong-ma-jang-un odee eemneekka*
Where can I place a bet ?	어디서 내기를 합니까? *odeeso negee-rul ham-neekka*
What are the odds on ...?	... 승산이 어떻습니까? *... sungsa-nee otdo-ssumneekka*
athletics	육상경기 *yook-sang gyong-gee*
basketball	농구 *nawng-goo*
cycling	자전거경주 *chajon-go gyong-joo*
golf	골프 *kawl-poo*
horse racing	경마 *kyong-ma*
soccer [football]	축구 *chookgoo*
swimming	수영 *soo-yong*
tennis	테니스 *teneesu*
volleyball	배구 *pe-goo*
tae kwon do	태권도 *tekkwon-daw*
traditional wrestling	씨름 *ssee-rum*

114

Playing 운동하기

Where's the nearest ...?	가장 가까운 ... 어디 있습니까? kajang katgaoon ... odee ee-ssumneekka 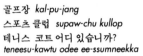
golf course	골프장 kal-pu-jang
sports club	스포츠 클럽 supaw-chu kullop
Where are the tennis courts?	테니스 코트 어디 있습니까? teneesu-kawtu odee ee-ssumneekka
What's the charge per ...?	... 당 얼마입니까? ... tang olma ee-mneekka
day/round/hour	하루/경기/시간 haroo/kyong-gee/seegan
Do I need to be a member?	회원이어야 합니까? hwe-won ee-o-ya hamneekka
Where can I rent ...?	어디서 ... 빌릴 수 있습니까? odeeso ... peelleel soo ee-ssumneekka
boots	신발 seen-bal
clubs/a racket	골프채/라켓 kawl-pu-che/laket
equipment	장비 chang-bee
Can I get lessons?	레슨 받을 수 있습니까? lessun padul-soo ee-ssumneekka
Do you have a fitness room?	체력단련실 che-ryok tal-lyon-seel
Can I join in?	제가 가입할 수 있습니까? che-ga ka-ee-pal soo ee-ssumneekka

죄송합니다. 만원입니다.	I'm sorry, we're booked up.
보증금이 ... 입니다	There is a deposit of ...
어떤 크기 원하십니까?	What size are you?
여권용 사진이 필요합니다.	You need a passport size photo.

탈의실	changing
낚시 금지	no fishing
허용자만 출입	permit holders only

At the beach 해변에서

Most of the lakes in South Korea are reservoirs and swimming is forbidden. In July and August the beaches are open to the public, but are often crowded.

Is the beach pebbly/sandy?	그 해변은 자갈이/모래가 많습니까? *ku he-byon-un chagaree/mawrega man-ssumneekka*
Is there a … here?	여기 … 있습니까? *yogee … ee-ssumneekka*
children's pool	어린이풀 *oreenee-pool*
swimming pool	수영장 *soo-yong-jang*
indoor/open-air	실내/실외 *seel-le/seel-we*
Is it safe to swim/dive here?	여기서 수영해도/다이빙 해도 안전합니까? *yogeeso soo-yong-hedo/ta-ee-beeng-hedaw anjon ham-neekka*
Is it safe for children?	어린이에게 안전합니까? *oreenee-ege anjon ham-neekka*
Is there a lifeguard?	구조원 있습니까? *koojaw-won ee-ssumneekka*
I want to rent a/some …	… 하나/몇개 빌리고 싶습니다. *… hana/myotge peellee-gaw seep-sumneeda*
deck chair	접는 의자 *chom-nun ueeja*
jet-ski	제트스키 *chetu-sukee*
motorboat	모터보트 *mawto-bawtu*
scuba equipment	스쿠버 다이빙 장비 *sukoobo daee-beeng chang-bee*
surfboard	서핑보드 *sopeeng-bawdu*
umbrella [sunshade]	햇빛 가리개 *hetbeet karee-ge*
water skis	수상스키 *soosang-sukee*
For … hours.	… 시간 동안. *… seegan tawng-an*

Skiing 스키타기

The ski season in South Korea lasts from early December to mid-March, and there are several resorts. The Korean Travel Bureau (**KTB**) and other agencies organize package tours to the most popular places, which can get crowded on weekends.

Is there much snow?	눈이 많습니까? *noon-ee man-ssumneekka*
What's the snow like?	눈이 어떻습니까? *noon-ee otdo-ssumneekka*
It's heavy/icy.	많습니다/얼었습니다. *man-ssumneeda/oro-ssumneeda*
It's powdery/wet.	잘 뭉쳐지지 않습니다/잘 뭉쳐집니다. *chal moong-cho-jeejee an-ssumneeda/ chal moong-cho-jeem-needa*
I'd like to rent some ...	... 몇개 빌리고 싶습니다. *... myotge peellee-gaw seep-sumneeda*
poles/skis	스키폴대/스키 *su-kee pawl-de/su-kee*
skates	스케이트 *suke-eetu*
ski boots	스키화 *sukee-hwa*
These are too ...	이건 너무 ... *eegon nomoo ...*
big/small	큽니다/작습니다 *kum-needa/chak-sumneeda*
A lift pass for a day/ 5 days, please.	하루/5일 리프트 사용권 주십시오. *haroo/aw-eel leeputu sayong-gwon chooseep-seeaw*
I'd like to join the ski school.	스키학교에 참가하고 싶습니다. *sukee hakgyo-e chamga-hagaw seep-sumneeda*
I'm a beginner.	저는 초보자입니다. *cho-nun chaw-baw-ja ee-mneeda*
I'm experienced.	저는 경험자입니다. *cho-nun kyong-hom-ja ee-mneeda*

cable car/gondola	케이블카
chair lift	체어 리프트
drag lift	견인 리프트

Making Friends

Introductions 소개

Korean rules of etiquette are based on Confucianism and can be quite complex, but allowances are made for foreigners. Make an effort to be polite as the concept of harmonious relationships is very important to Koreans.

Korean names consist mostly of a family name (mostly one syllable), which comes first, and a given name (usually two syllables). Women do not take their husband's name when they marry, but children have their father's family name. When greeting someone or departing, Koreans usually nod or bow their heads. Pointing or gesturing with one finger is considered impolite. Physical contact between men and women should be avoided in public. When you address Korean people by name, add **ssee** after the full name regardless of their gender. For older people, however, add **sonseng-neem**.

Hello, we haven't met.	안녕하세요, 처음 뵙겠습니다 *an-nyong haseyo. choum pwep-ke-ssumneeda*
My name is …	제 이름은 … 입니다. *che eerumun … eemneeda*
Pleased to meet you.	만나서 반갑습니다. *manaso pan-gap-sumneeda*
What's your name?	이름이 어떻게 되십니까? *eerumee otdoke dwe-seemneekka*
How are you?	어떻게 지내십니까? *otdoke jeene-seemneekka*
Fine, thanks. And you?	네, 좋습니다. 어떠십니까? *ne, chaw-ssumneeda. otdo-seemneekka*

> – *otdoke jeene-seemneekka?*
> – *ne, chaw-ssumneeda. otdo-seemneekka?*
> – *chodaw chal jeenemneeda.*

Where are you from?
어디서 오셨습니까?

Where do you come from?	어디서 오셨습니까? *odeeso awsyo-ssumneekka*
Where were you born?	고향이 어디십니까? *kaw-hyang-ee odee-seemneekka*
I'm from ...	... 에서 왔습니다. *...-eso wassumneeda*
Australia	호주 *haw-joo*
Britain	영국 *yong-gook*
Canada	캐나다 *kenada*
Ireland	아일랜드 *a-eel-lendu*
the United States	미국 *mee-gook*
Where do you live?	어디 사십니까? *odee saseem-neekka*
What part of ... are you from?	... 어느 지방에서 오셨습니까? *... onu chee-bang-eso awsyo-ssumneekka*
Japan	일본 *eel-bawn*
South Korea	한국 *han-gook*
China	중국 *choong-gook*
We come here every year.	우리는 매해 여기 옵니다. *ooree-nun mehe yogee awm-needa*
It's my/our first visit.	처음 왔습니다. *cho-um wassumneeda*
Have you ever been to ...?	... 에 가신 적 있습니까? *...-e kaseen-jok ee-ssumneekka*
Britain/the United States	영국/미국 *yong-gook/mee-gook*
What do you think of the ...?	... 어떻게 생각하십니까? *... otdoke seng-gak ha-seemneekka*
I love the ... here.	저는 여기 ... 좋아합니다. *cho-nun yogee ... chaw-a hamneeda*
I don't really like the ... here.	저는 여기 ... 좋아하지 않습니다. *cho-nun yogee ... chaw-a hajee-an-ssumneeda*
food/people	음식/사람 *umseek/saram*

Who are you with?
누구와 사십니까?

In Korea, members of a family live together until the children get married. Siblings have different names according to their gender relations. Boys call their older sister **noo-na** and their older brother **hyong** while girls use **on-nee** for their older sister and **awtba** for their older brother. Younger siblings are generally called **tawng-seng**.

Who are you with?	누구와 사십니까? *noo-goo-wa saseem-neekka*
I'm on my own.	혼자 삽니다. *hawn-ja samneeda*
I'm with a friend.	친구와 같이 삽니다. *cheen-goo-wa kachee samneeda*
I'm with my ...	... 와 같이 삽니다. *... wa kachee samneeda*
husband/wife	남편/아내 *nam-pyon/ane*
family	가족 *ka-jawk*
boyfriend/girlfriend	애인/애인 *e-een/e-een*
father/son	아버지/아들 *abo-jee/adul*
mother/daughter	어머니/딸 *omonee/dal*
uncle/aunt	삼촌/고모 *sam-chawn/kaw-maw*
What's your son's/wife's name?	아들/부인 이름이 무엇입니까? *adul/poo-een eerumee moo-o-seemneekka*
I'm ...	저는 ... *cho-nun ...*
married/single	기혼/미혼입니다. *kee-hawn/mee-hawn eemneeda*
divorced/separated	이혼했습니다/별거중입니다. *ee-hawn he-ssumneeda/pyol-go hagaw-ee-ssumneeda*
Do you have any children?	아이가 있으십니까? *a-ee-ga eessu-seemneekka*
2 boys and a girl.	남자애 둘, 여자애 하나 있습니다. *namja-e tool yoja-e hana ee-ssumneeda*
How old are they?	아이들이 몇살입니까? *a-eeduree myo-ssal ee-mneekka*
They're 10 and 12.	열살, 열두살 입니다. *yol-sal yoldoo-sal eemneeda*

What do you do?
직업이 무엇입니까?

What do you do?	직업이 무엇입니까? *cheeg-obee moo-o-seemneekka*
What line are you in?	무슨 일을 하십니까? *moo-sun eerul ha-seemneekka*
What are you studying?	무엇을 공부하십니까? *moo-o-sul* *kawng-boo ha-seemneekka*
I'm studying ...	... 공부합니다. *... kawng-boo hamneeda*
I'm in ...	... 합니다. *... hamneeda*
business	사업 *sa-op*
engineering	엔지니어일 *enjee-nee-o-eel*
retail/sales	가게/영업직 *kage/yong-op cheek*
Who do you work for?	어디서 일하십니까? *odee-eso eel-ha-seemneekka*
I work for ...	저는 ...에서 일합니다. *cho-nun ...-eso eel-ham-needa*
I'm (a/an) ...	저는 ... 입니다. *cho-nun ... eemneeda*
accountant	회계사 *hwe-ge-sa*
housewife	가정주부 *kajong jooboo*
student	학생 *hak-seng*
self-employed	자영업자 *cha-yong-op ja*
between jobs/unemployed	실업자 *seerop-ja*
I'm retired.	저는 은퇴했습니다. *cho-nun untwe-he-ssumneeda*
What are your interests/ hobbies?	취미가 무엇입니까? *chwee-mee-ga moo-o-seemneekka*
I like ...	저는 ... 좋아합니다. *cho-nun ... chaw-a hamneeda*
music/reading/sports	음악/독서/운동 *umak/tawk-so/oon-dawng*
Would you like to play ...?	... 좋아하십니까? *... chaw-a ha-seemneekka*
cards	카드놀이 *kadu-nawree/*
chess/Korean chess	체스/바둑 *chesu/pa-dook*

What weather! 날씨

What a lovely day!	날씨 참 좋지요. nalssee cham chaw-cheeyo
What awful weather!	날씨 정말 나쁘군요. nalssee chong-mal natbu-goon-yo
It's cold/hot today!	오늘 춥지요/덥지요! awnul choop-jeeyo/top-jeeyo
Do you think it's going to ... tomorrow?	내일 ... 것 같습니까? ne-eel ... hal-go kasumneekka
be a nice day	날이 좋을 naree chaw-ul
rain	비가 올 pee-ga awl
snow	눈이 올 noo-nee awl
What is the weather forecast?	일기예보는 어떻습니까? eel-gee yebaw-nun otdo-ssumneekka
It's ...	날씨가 ... nalssee-ga ...
cloudy	흐립니다. hu-reem-needa
icy	매우 춥습니다. me-oo choop-sumneeda
It's stormy.	폭풍이 붑니다. pawkpoong-ee boom-needa
It's windy.	바람이 붑니다. param-ee poom-needa
It's raining.	비가 내립니다. pee-ga nereem-needa
It's snowing.	눈이 내립니다. noo-nee nereemneeda
It's sunny.	맑습니다. mal-ssumneeda
Has the weather been like this for long?	날씨가 한참동안 이랬습니까? nalssee-ga hancham tawng-an eere-ssumneekk
What's the pollen count?	꽃가루 지수는 어떻습니까? gawt-karoo cheesoo-nun otdo-ssumneekka
It's high/medium/low.	높습니다/보통입니다/낮습니다. nawp-sumneeda/paw-tawng-eemneeda/ na-sumneeda

일기예보	weather forecast

122

Enjoying your trip?
여행이 재미있으십니까?

휴가로 오셨습니까?	Are you on vacation?
무얼 타고 오셨습니까?	How did you travel here?
어디 묵고 계십니까?	Where are you staying?
얼마나 계셨습니까?	How long have you been here?
얼마나 계실겁니까?.	How long are you staying?
지금까지 무얼 하셨습니까?	What have you done so far?
다음은 어디로 가실 겁니까?	Where are you going next?
휴가 즐거우십니까?	Are you enjoying your vacation?

I'm here ...	여기 ... 왔습니다. yogee ... wa-ssumneeda
on a business trip	일때문에 eel-demoon-e
on vacation [holiday]	휴가로 hyoo-ga-raw
We came by ...	... 로 왔습니다. ...-raw wa-ssumneeda
train/bus/plane	기차/버스/비행기 keecha/posu/peeheng-gee
car/ferry	차/배 cha/pe
I have a rental car.	차를 빌렸습니다. cha-rul peellyo-ssumneeda
We're staying ...?	... 묵고 있습니다. ... mookgaw ee-ssumneeda
in an apartment	아파트에 apatu-e
at a hotel/campsite	호텔에/야영장에 hawtere/yayong-jang-e
with friends	친구와 cheen-goowa
Can you suggest ...?	... 있습니까? ... ee-ssumneekka
things to do	할만한 것 hal manhan-go
places to eat	먹을만한 곳 mogul manhan-gawt
places to visit	가 볼만한 곳 kapawl manhan-gawt
We're having a great/ terrible time.	즐겁게/지루하게 보내고 있습니다. chul-gopge/cheeroo-hage pawnegaw ee-ssumneeda

123

Invitations 초대

Would you like to have dinner with us on ...?	...에 저녁 함께 하시겠습니까? ...-e cho-nyok hamge haseege-ssumneekka
May I invite you to lunch?	점심 초대해도 될까요?. chom-seem chaw-de-hedaw dwelkkayo
Can you come for a drink this evening?	오늘 저녁 한잔 하러 오시겠습니까? awnul cho-nyok hanjan haro awseege-ssumneekka
We are having a party. Can you come?	파티가 있습니다. 오시겠습니까? patee-ga ee-ssumneeda. awseege-ssumneekka
May we join you?	우리가 가도 되겠습니까? ooree-ga kadaw dwege-ssumneekka
Would you like to join us?	함께 가시겠습니까? hamge kaseege-ssumneekka

Going out 외출

What are your plans for ...?	... 무엇을 할 계획입니까? ... moo-o-sul hal kehweg eemneekka
today/tonight	오늘/오늘밤 awnul/awnul-bam
tomorrow	내일 ne-eel
Are you free this evening?	오늘 저녁 시간 있으십니까? awnul cho-nyok seegan eessu-seemneekka
Would you like to ...?	... 가시겠습니까? ... kaseege-ssumneekka
go dancing	춤추러 choom-choo-ro
go for a drink	한잔 하러 hajan haro
go out for a meal	외식하러 weseek haro
go for a walk	산책 하러 sanchek haro
go shopping	쇼핑 하러 syopeeng haro
I'd like to go to ...	... 가고 싶습니다. ... kagaw seep-sumneeda
I'd like to see ...	... 보고 싶습니다. ... paw-gaw seep-sumneeda
Do you enjoy ...?	... 재미있습니까? ... che mee ee-ssumneekka

Accepting/Declining 수락/거절

Thank you. I'd love to.	감사합니다. 좋습니다. *kamsa-hamneeda.* *chaw-ssumneeda*
Thank you, but I'm busy.	감사합니다만, 바쁩니다. *kamsa-hamneeda-man pat-bum-needa*
May I bring a friend?	친구를 데려가도 되겠습니까? *cheen-goo-rul teryo-gadaw dwege-ssumneekka*
Where shall we meet?	어디서 만날까요? *odeeso mannal-gayo*
I'll meet you ...	... 만납시다. *... mannap-seeda*
in front of your hotel	호텔 앞에서 *hawtel a-peso*
I'll call for you at 8.	여덟시에 부르러 가겠습니다. *yodol-see-e pooruro kage-ssumneeda*
Could we make it a bit later/earlier?	약간 늦게/일찍 만날까요? *yak-gan nut-ge/eelzeek mannal-gayo*
How about another day?	다른 날은 어떻습니까? *tarun na-run otdo-ssumneekka*
That will be fine.	좋습니다. *chaw-ssumneeda*

Dining out/in 외식/집에서 식사

Koreans are very hospitable, so when going out with Koreans you may find it very hard to pay for the bill, which is always paid by one person only. If you want to pay it is best to arrange this beforehand to avoid causing embarrassment. When invited to a Korean family's home for a meal, it is common to take a gifts, e.g., flowers for the hostess, drinks for the men, and candy or small toys for the children.

Let me buy you a drink.	제가 한잔 사겠습니다. *che-ga hanjan sage-ssumneeda*
Do you like ...?	... 좋아하십니까? *... chaw-a ha-seemneekka*
What are you going to have?	무엇을 드시겠습니까? *moo-o-sul duseege-ssumneekka*
That was a lovely meal.	잘 먹었습니다. *chal mogo-ssumneeda*

TIME ➤ 220

Encounters 만남

Do you mind if ...?	... 되겠습니까? ... dwege-ssumneekka
I sit here/I smoke	여기 앉아도/담배 피워도 yogee an-jadaw/tambe peewo-daw
Can I get you a drink?	음료수 갖다 드릴까요? um-nyosoo kat-da dureel-kkayo
I'd love to have some company.	누군가 동행이 있으면 좋겠습니다. noo-goon-ga tawng-heng-ee eessu-myon chaw-ke-ssumneeda
Why are you laughing?	왜 웃으십니까? we oosu-seemneekka
Is my Korean that bad?	제 한국어 그렇게 형편없습니까? che han-googo kuroke hyong-pyon op-sumneekka
Shall we go somewhere quieter?	더 조용한 곳으로 갈까요? to chaw-yong- han kaw-suraw kalgayo
Leave me alone, please!	혼자 있게 해주세요! hawn-ja eetge he-jooseep-seeaw
You look great!	멋집니다. motjeem-needa
Would you like to come back with me?	저와 다시 오시겠습니까? cho-wa tasee awseege-ssumneekka
I'm not ready for that.	저는 아직 준비가 안됐습니다. cho-nun ajeek choon-bee-ga andwe-ssumneeda
I'm afraid we've got to leave now.	죄송합니다만 지금 떠나야 합니다. chwe-sawng ham-needa-man chee-gum donaya ha-mneeda
Thanks for the evening.	오늘 저녁 감사합니다. awnul cho-nyok kamsa-hamneeda
It was great.	참 좋았습니다. cham chaw-a-ssumneeda
Can I see you again tomorrow?	내일 다시 뵐 수 있습니까? ne-eel tasee pwel-soo ee-ssumneekka
See you soon.	안녕히 가십시오. an-nyong-ee kaseep-seeaw
Can I have your address?	주소를 주시겠습니까? choo-saw-rul chooseege-ssumneekka

Telephoning 전화걸기

There are three different types of public phones in South
Korea: coin-operated, telephone card, and credit card. Phone
cards can be bought in banks and shops close to telephones
and come in denominations of W 2,000, 3,000, 5,000, and 10,000.
Coin-operated phones take denominations of W 10, 50, and 100. Calls
made between 11 p.m. and 8 a.m. can be 30% – 50% cheaper. To call home
from South Korea, dial 001 or 002 (cheaper) followed by the country code
and the area code. To make a collect call, dial 00799. If you need directory
assistance, call 080-211-0114, which is toll-free and where you can find
English-speaking operators.

Can I have your telephone number?	전화번호 주시겠습니까? *chonhwa–bonhaw chooseege-ssumneekka*
Here's my number.	제 전화번호입니다. *che chonhwa-bon-haw eemneeda*
Please call me.	전화 주십시오. *chonhwa chooseep-seeaw*
I'll give you a call.	전화 드리겠습니다. *chonhwa dureege-ssumneeda*
Where's the nearest telephone booth?	가장 가까운 공중전화 어디 있습니까? *kajang kat-gaoon kawng-joong jonhwa odee ee-ssumneekka*
May I use your phone?	전화를 사용해도 되겠습니까? *chonhwa-rul sayong-hedaw dwege-ssumneekka*
It's an emergency.	급한 일입니다. *kuphan eel-eemneeda*
I'd like to call someone in England.	영국으로 전화걸고 싶습니다. *yong-goog-uraw chonhwa-golgaw seep-sumneeda*
What's the area [dialling] code for …?	… 지역번호는 무엇입니까? … *cheeyok -ponhaw-nun moo-o-seemneekka*
I'd like a phone card, please.	전화카드 한 장 주십시오. *chonhwa-kadu han-jang chooseep-seeaw*
What's the number for information [directory enquiries]?	전화번호 안내가 몇번입니까? *chonhwa-bonhaw anne-ga myotbon eemneekka*
I'd like the number for …	… 전화번호 부탁합니다. … *chonhwa-bonhaw pootak-hamneeda*
I'd like to call collect [reverse the charges].	콜렉트콜로 걸겠습니다. *kawllekt kawl-law kolge-ssumneeda*

Speaking 전화통화

Hello. This is …	여보세요. 저는 … 입니다. *yobaw-seyo. cho-nun … eemneeda*
I'd like to speak to …	… 통화하고 싶습니다. *… tawng-hwa-hagaw seep-sumneeda*
Extension …	교환 … *kyo-hwan …*
Speak louder/more slowly, please.	더 크게/더 천천히 말씀해주십시오. *to kuge/to chon-chonee malssume* *chooseep-seeaw*
Could you repeat that, please?	다시 말씀해 주시겠습니까? *tasee* *malssume chooseege-ssumneekka*
I'm afraid he's/she's not in.	지금 자리에 없습니다. *chee-gum charee-e op-sumneeda*
You have the wrong number.	잘못 거셨습니다. *chal-mawt kosyo-ssumneeda*
Just a moment.	잠깐 기다려 주십시오. *chamgan keeda-ryo chooseep-seeaw*
Hold on, please.	잠깐 기다려 주십시오. *chamgan keeda-ryo chooseep-seeaw*
When will he/she be back?	언제 돌아옵니까? *onje tawra-awm-neekka*
Will you tell him/her that I called?	제가 전화했다고 전해 주시겠습니까? *che-ga chonhwa hetdagaw chonhe* *chooseege-ssumneekka*
My name is …	제 이름은 … 입니다. *che eerumun … eemneeda*
Would you ask him/her to phone me?	제게 전화해 달라고 전해 주시겠습니까? *che-ge chonhwa-he tal-lagaw chonhe* *chooseege-ssumneekka*
I must go now.	이만 끊어야 겠습니다. *eeman gunoyo ke-ssumneeda*
Nice to speak to you.	즐거웠습니다. *chugowo-ssumneeda*
I'll be in touch.	다시 연락 드리겠습니다. *tasee yollak tureege-ssumneeda*
Bye.	안녕히 계십시오. *an-nyong-ee keseep-seeaw*

Stores & Services

All major cities in South Korea have department stores and shopping districts with arcades, and souvenir and duty-free stores. **Lotte World** just outside Seoul is one of the largest shopping malls in the world. Open-air markets such as **Nam-demoon-seejang** offer very good deals on sporting equipment, electronic goods, camping equipment, leather goods, ginseng products, and more. There are also some 24-hour convenience stores.

ESSENTIAL

I'd like a(n) ...	... 주십시오. ... *chooseep-seeaw*
Do you have ...?	... 있습니까? ... *ee-ssumneekka?*
How much is that?	얼마입니까? *olma ee-mneekka?*
Thank you.	감사합니다. *kamsa-hamneeda.*

영업합니다.	open
금일 휴업	closed today
세일	sale

Stores and services
상점과 서비스
Where is ...? ... 어디 있습니까?

Where's the nearest ...?	가장 가까운 ... 어디 있습니까?
	kajang katgaoon ... odee ee-ssumneekka
Where's there a good ...?	좋은 ... 어디 있습니까?
	chaw-un ... odee ee-ssumneekka
Where's the main shopping mall [centre]?	큰 상가 어디 있습니까?
	kun sang-ga odee ee-ssumneekka
Is it far from here?	여기서 멉니까? *yogee-so mom-neekka*
How do I get there?	거기 어떻게 갑니까?
	kogee otdoke kam-neekka

Stores 상점

antique store	골동품 가게 *kawl-tawng-poom kage*
bakery	빵집 *bang-jeep*
bank	은행 *unheng*
bookstore	서점 *sojom*
butcher	정육점 *chong-yook-jom*
camera store	사진기 가게 *sajeen-gee kage*
clothing store [clothes shop]	옷가게 *awtgage*
delicatessen	식료품 가게 *seeng-nyo-poom kage*
department store	백화점 *pekwa-jom*
drugstore	약국 *yakook*
fish store [fishmonger]	생선 가게 *seng-son kage*
florist	꽃가게 *gawtgage*
gift store	선물 가게 *sonmool kage*
greengrocer	채소 가게 *chesaw kage*
health food store	건강 식품점 *kon-gang seek-poom-jom*
jeweler	보석상 *pawsok-sang*

liquor store [off-licence]	주류판매점 *choo-ryoo panme-jom*
market	시장 *see-jang*
newsstand [newsagent]	신문가판대 *seen-moon gapande*
pastry store	제과점 *chegwa-jom*
pharmacy [chemist]	약국 *yak-gook*
produce store	식료품 가게 *seeng-nyo-poom kage*
record [music] store	레코드 가게 *rekawdu kage*
shoe store	신발 가게 *seenbal kage*
shopping mall [centre]	상가 *sang-ga*
souvenir store	기념품 가게 *kee-nyom-poom kage*
sporting goods store	운동구점 *oon-dawng-goo jom*
supermarket	슈퍼마켓 *soopo-maket*
tobacconist	담배 가게 *tambe kage*
toy store	장난감 가게 *chang-nan-gam kage*

Services 서비스

clinic	병원 *pyong-won*
dentist	치과의사 *cheetgwa uee-sa*
doctor	의사 *uee-sa*
dry cleaner	세탁소 *setaksaw*
hairdresser (ladies/men)	미장원/이발소 *meejang-won/eebal-saw*
hospital	종합병원 *chawng-hap pyong-won*
laundromat	빨래방 *balle-bang*
optician	안경점 *an-gyong-jom*
police station	경찰서 *kyong-chal-so*
post office	우체국 *oo-che-gook*
travel agency	여행사 *yoheng-sa*

Opening hours 영업 시간

	Opening	Closing	Days closed
Stores	early a.m.	late p.m.	none
Department stores	10:30 a.m.	7:30 p.m.	varies (▶ 158)
Post office	9:00 a.m.	6:00 p.m. (5:00 p.m. in winter)	Saturday p.m., Sunday, and holidays

When does the ... open/close?	... 언제 문 엽니까/닫습니까?
	... onje moon yom-neekka/tassum-neekka
Are you open in the evening?	저녁에 문 엽니까?
	cho-nyoge moon yom-neekka
Do you close for lunch?	점심시간에 문 닫습니까?
	chomseem seegane moon tassum-neekka
Where is the ...	... 어디 있습니까?
	... odee ee-ssumneekka
cashier [cash desk]	계산대 kesande
escalator	에스컬레이터 esukol-le-eeto
elevator [lift]	엘리베이터 ellee-be-eeto
store guide	상점 안내판 sang-jom anne-pan
first [Brit. ground] floor	일층 eel-chung
second [Brit. first] floor	이층 ee-chung
Where's the ... department?	... 백화점 어디 있습니까?
	... pek-hwa-jom odee ee-ssumneekka

영업시간	business hours
점심시간	closed for lunch
연중무휴	open all day
입구	entrance
에스컬레이터	escalator
출구	exit
비상구	emergency/fire exit
엘리베이터	elevator [lift]
계단	stairs

Service 서비스

Can you help me?	도와주시겠습니까? *taw-wa chooseege-ssumneekka*
I'm looking for …	… 찾고 있습니다. *… chatgaw ee-ssumneeda*
I'm just browsing.	그냥 둘러보고 있습니다. *ku-nyang toollo-bawgaw ee-ssumneeda*
It's my turn.	제 차례입니다. *che chare ee-mneeda*
Do you have any …?	… 있습니까? *… ee-ssumneekka*
I'd like to buy …	… 사고 싶습니다. *… sagaw seep-sumneeda*
Could you show me …?	… 보여주시겠습니까? *… paw-yo chooseege-ssumneekka*
How much is this/that?	이건/그건 얼마입니까? *eegon/kugon olma-eemneekka*
That's all, thanks.	됐습니다. 감사합니다. *dwe-ssumneeda. kamsa-hamneeda*

안녕하십니까?	Good morning/afternoon.
점원이 도와드리고 있습니까?	Are you being served?
무엇을 원하십니까?	What would you like?
그게 다입니까?	Is that everything?
더 필요한 것 없으십니까?	Anything else?

– *taw-wa dureel-gayo?*

– *ku-nyang toollo-bawgaw ee-ssumneeda.*

– *kuro-seep-seeaw …*

– *yobaw-seyo.*

– *moo-ol taw-wa dureel-gayo?*

– *ku-gon olma-eemneekka?*

– *chamgan pawl-gayo … ee-man-won eemneeda.*

고객 서비스	customer service
셀프서비스	self-service
특별 가격	clearance

Preference 선호

I want something ...	저는 ...것을 원합니다. cho-nun ... kosul won-hamneeda
big/small	큰/작은 kun/chagun
cheap/expensive	싼/비싼 ssan/pee-ssan
dark/light (color)	어두운/밝은 odoo-oon/palgun
light/heavy	가벼운/무거운 kabyo-oon/moogo-oon
genuine/imitation	진품인/모조품인 cheen-poom-een/mawjaw-poom-een
It must be ...	틀림없이 ...것입니다. tulleem-opsee ... ko-seemneeda
big/small	클/작을 kul/chagul
cheap/expensive	쌀/비쌀 ssal/pee-ssal
I don't want anything too expensive.	저는 너무 비싼 건 원치 않습니다. cho-nun nomoo pee-ssan gon wonchee an-ssumneeda
In the region of ... Won.	...원대에서 ... won-de-eso

어떤 ... 원하십니까?	What ... would you like?
색/모양	color/shape
질	quality
얼마나 원하십니까?	How much/many would you like?
어떤 종류를 원하십니까?	What sort would you like?
어느 정도 가격대를 생각 하고 계십니까?	What price range are you thinking of?

Do you have anything ...?	...것 있습니까? ... ko ee-ssumneekka
larger/smaller	더 큰/더 작은 to kun/to chagun
better quality/cheaper	더 질좋은/더 싼 to jeel-chaw-un/to ssan
Can you show me ...?	...보여주시겠습니까? ... paw-yo chooseege-ssumneekka
that/this one	그것/이것 kugot/eegot
these/those ones	이것들/그것들 eegodul/kugodul
some others	다른 것들 tarun kodul

COLORS ➤ 143

Conditions of purchase 구매 조건

Is there a guarantee?
보증됩니까?
paw-jung dwem-neekka

Are there any instructions
with it?
설명서가 있습니까?
sol-myong-soga ee-ssumneekka

Out of stock 품절

죄송합니다만, 없습니다.	I'm sorry, we don't have any.
품절되었습니다.	We're out of stock.
다른 걸/종류를 보여드릴까요?	Can I show you something else / a different sort?
주문해 드릴까요?	Shall we order it for you?

Can you order it for me?
주문해 주시겠습니까?
choo-moon-he chooseege-ssumneekka

How long will it take?
얼마나 걸립니까?
olmana kolleem-neekka

Where else can I get ...?
어디 다른데서 ... 구할 수 있습니까?
*odee tarun-deso ... koohal soo
ee-ssumneekka*

Decision 결정

That's not quite what I want.
그건 제가 원하는 게 아닙니다. *kugon
chega wonha-nun-ge aneem-needa*

That's too expensive.
너무 비쌉니다.
nomoo pee-ssam-needa

I'd like to think about it.
생각해 보겠습니다.
seng-gake pawge-sumneeda

I'll take it.
이걸로 하겠습니다.
eegol-law hage-ssumneeda

– *an-nyong ha-seemneekka. tootgo-oon*
suweto-rul sagaw seep-sumneeda.
– *otdon segul won-ha-seemeekka?*
– *aw-renjee se-guraw chooseep-seeaw. chonun*
kun-gosul won-hamneeda.
– *yogee ee-ssumneeda. sa-man-won eemneeda.*
– *kugon chega wonha-nun-ge aneem-needa. meean-hamneeda.*

135

Paying 계산

Sales tax of 10% is added to almost all good and services, except in duty-free shops.

Where do I pay?	어디서 계산합니까? *odee-so kesan ham-neekka*
How much is that?	그건 얼마입니까? *kugon olma eem-neekka*
Could you write it down, please?	써주시겠습니까? *sso chooseege-ssumneekka*
Do you accept traveler's checks [cheques]?	여행자 수표 받습니까? *yoheng-ja soopyo pa-ssumneekka*
I'll pay …	… 계산하겠습니다. *… kesan hage-ssumneeda*
by cash	현금으로 *hyon-gumuro*
by credit card	신용 카드로 *seen-yong kadu-raw*
I don't have any smaller change.	잔돈이 없습니다. *chan-daw-nee op-sumneeda*
Sorry, I don't have enough money.	미안합니다, 돈이 모자랍니다. *mee-an* *ham-needa, taw-nee mawja-ram-needa*

어떻게 계산하시겠습니까?	How are you paying?
이 거래는 승인되지 않았습니다.	This transaction has not been approved/accepted.
이 카드는 유효하지 않습니다.	This card is not valid.
다른 신분증을 보여주시겠습니까?	May I have further identification?
잔돈 있으십니까?	Do you have any smaller change?

Could I have a receipt, please?	영수증 주십시오. *yong-soo-jung chooseep-seeaw*
I think you've given me the wrong change.	잔돈을 잘못 주신 것 같습니다. *chan-daw-nul chal-mawt chooseen-go ka-ssumneeda*

계산	please pay here

Complaints 불만사항

This doesn't work.	이것이 작동하지 않습니다. *eego-see chaktawng-hajee an-ssumneeda*
Can I exchange this?	이것을 바꿔 주시겠습니까? *eegosul pakgwo chooseege-ssumneekka*
I'd like a refund.	환불을 원합니다. *hwan-boorul won-hamneeda*
Here's the receipt.	영수증 여기 있습니다. *yong-soo-jung yogee ee-ssumneeda*
I don't have the receipt.	영수증이 없습니다. *yong-soo-jung-ee op-ssumneeda*
I'd like to see the manager.	지배인을 만나고 싶습니다. *cheebe-een-ul man-agaw seep-sumneeda*

Repairs/Cleaning 수리/세탁

This is broken. Can you repair it?	이것이 고장났습니다. 수리할 수 있습니까? *eegosee kawjang na-ssumneeda. sooree hal soo ee-ssumneekka*
Do you have … for this?	여기 맞는 … 있습니까? *yogee man-nun … ee-ssumneekka*
a battery	전전지 *kon-jon-jee*
replacement parts	교체 부품 *kyo-che poo-poom*
There's something wrong with …	…에 문제가 있습니다. *…e moon-jega ee-ssumneeda*
Can you … this?	이것을 … 주시겠습니까? *eego-sul … chooseege-ssumneekka*
clean	세탁해 *setake*
press	다림질해 *tareem-jeel-he*
patch	기워 *kee-wo*
Could you alter this?	이것을 수선해 주시겠습니까? *eego-sul sooson-he chooseege-ssumneekka*
When will it be ready?	언제 다 됩니까? *onje ta dwem-neekka*
This isn't mine.	이것은 제 것이 아닙니다. *eegosun che ko-see ameem-needa*
There's … missing.	… 없습니다. *… op-sumneeda*

Bank/Currency Exchange
은행 / 환전소

Banks are open from 9:30 – 5:00 on weekdays and from 9:30 – 2:00 on Saturdays. All banks are closed on Sundays and holidays, but Kimpo airport's bank is open from 6:30 a.m. – 9.30 p.m. all year round. Foreign bank notes and traveler's checks [cheques] can be exchanged into Won at currency exchange offices and other authorized money changers. It may, however, be more difficult to find places to change money in rural areas.

Where's the nearest …?	가장 가까운 … 어디 있습니까? *kajang katgaoon … odee ee-ssumneekka*
bank	은행 *unheng*
currency exchange office [bureau de change]	환전소 *hwan-jon-saw*
Can I exchange foreign currency here?	여기서 외국돈 바꿀 수 있습니까? *yogee-so wegook tawn pakgool soo ee-sumneekka*

현금자동 인출기	ATMs [cash machines]
모든 거래	all transactions
영업중/영업끝	open/closed
현금출납원	cashiers

I'd like to change some dollars/ pounds into Won.	달라를/파운드를 원화로 바꾸고 싶습니다. *dalla-rul/pa-oon-durul won- hwa-raw pakgoo-gaw seep-sumneeda*
I want to cash some traveler's checks [cheques].	여행자수표를 현금으로 바꾸고 싶습니다. *yoheng-ja soopyo-rul hyon-gum-uraw pakgoo-gaw seep-sumneeda*
What's the exchange rate?	환율은 얼마입니까? *hwan-nyoo-run olma ee-mneekka*
Could I have some small change, please?	잔돈으로 주시겠습니까? *chan-dawn-uraw chooseege-ssumneekka*
I've lost my traveler's checks [cheques]. These are the numbers.	여행자수표를 잃어버렸습니다. 여기 수표 번호가 있습니다. *yoheng-ja soopyo-rul eero-boryo-ssumneeda. yogee soopyo ponhaw-ga ee-ssumneeda*

Security 신분확인

... 보여주시겠습니까?	Could I see ...?
여권	your passport
신분증	some identification
은행 카드	your bank card
주소가 어떻게 되십니까?	What's your address?
어디 묵고 계십니까?	Where are you staying?
이 용지를 작성해주십시오.	Fill out this form, please.
여기 서명해주십시오.	Please sign here.

ATMs [Cash machines] 현금 자동 인출기

Can I withdraw money on my credit card here?

여기서 신용 카드로 돈 찾을 수 있습니까? *yogeeso seen-yong kaduraw tawn chajul soo ee-ssumneekka*

Where are the ATMs [cash machines]?

현금 자동 인출기 어디 있습니까? *hyon-gum chadawng een-chool-gee odee ee-ssumneekka*

Can I use my ... card in the cash machine?

그 현금 자동 인출기에 제 ... 카드를 사용할 수 있습니까? *ku hyon-gum chadawng een-chool-gee-e che kadurul sayong hal-soo ee-ssumneekka*

The cash machine has eaten my card.

현금 자동 인출기가 제 카드를 먹어버렸습니다. *hyon-gum chadawng een-chool-gee-ga che kadurul mogo-boryo-ssumneeda*

ATM [cash machine]	현금 자동 인출기

Currency	The monatery system is the Won, abbreviated to W.
Won (W)	*Coins:* 1; 5; 10; 50; 100; 500
	1 Won and 5 Won coins are virtually unused
	Notes: 1,000; 5,000; 10,000

Pharmacy 약국

There are plenty of pharmacies, and most Western-type drugs are available. As not all pharmacists speak English it is best to write down what you want as they may recognize the names of the products.

Where's the nearest (all-night) pharmacy?	가장 가까운 (24시간 하는) 약국 어디 있습니까? *kajang katga-oon (ee-seep sa-seegan hanun) yakgoog odee ee-ssumneekka*
What time does the pharmacy open/close?	약국 몇시에 문엽니까/문닫습니까? *yakgoog myo-ssee-e moon yom-neekka/ moon dassu-mneekka*
Can you make up this prescription for me?	이 처방대로 약지어 주시겠습니까? *ee chobang-deraw yag-jee-o choosee-ge-ssumneekka*
Should I wait?	기다려야 합니까? *keeda-ryoya ham-neekka*
I'll come back for it.	찾으러 다시 오겠습니다. *chajuro tasee awge-ssumneeda*

Dosage instructions 복용법

How much should I take?	얼만큼 먹습니까? *olman-kum mok-ssumneekka*
How often should I take it?	얼마 간격으로 먹습니까? *olma kan-gyoguraw mok-ssumneekka*

두알/두스푼 ... 드십시오.	Take two tablets/teaspoons ...
식사 전에/후에	before/after meals
물과 함께	with water
전부	whole
아침에/밤에	in the morning/at night
... 일간	for ... days

외용제	for external use only
내복 절대 불가	not to be taken internally

Asking advice 질문 사항

What would you recommend for ...?	...에 좋은 약 있습니까? ...-e chaw-un yak ee-ssumneekka
a cold/cough	감기/기침 kam-gee/gee-cheem
diarrhea	설사 sol-ssa
a hangover	숙취 sook-chwee
hay fever	꽃가루 알레르기 gawtgaroo alle-rugee
insect bites	벌레 물린데 polle mool-leen-de
a sore throat	목 아픈데 mawk apunde
sunburn	일광 화상 eel-gwang hwa-sang
motion [travel] sickness	차멀미 chamolmee
an upset stomach	배탈 petal
Can I get it without a prescription?	그것을 처방전 없이 살 수 있습니까? kugosul chobang-jon opsee sal-soo ee-ssumneekka

Over-the-counter treatment 처방전 없이 살 수 있는 약

Can I have ...?	... 주십시오. ... chooseep-seeaw
antiseptic cream	소독용 크림 sawdawk-yong kureem
(soluble) aspirin	(물에 녹는) 아스피린 (moore nawng-nun) asu-peereen
condoms	콘돔 kawn-dawm
cotton [cotton wool]	솜 sawm
gauze [bandages]	붕대 poong-de
insect repellent	구충제 koo-choong-je
pain killers	진통제 cheen-tawng-je
vitamins	비타민 정제 pee-tameen chong-je

Toiletries 욕실용품

I'd like a(n) …	… 주십시오. … *chooseep-seeaw*
after shave	아프터 세이브로션 *aputo sye-eebu law-syon*
after-sun lotion	아프터선 로션 *aputo-son law-syon*
deodorant	탈취제 *tal-chwee-je*
razor blades	면도날 *myon-daw-nal*
sanitary napkins [towels]	생리대 *seng-nee-de*
soap	비누 *peenoo*
sun block	자외선 차단 크림 *chaweson chadan kureem*
suntan lotion	선탠 크림 *sonten kureem*
factor …	자외선 차단지수 … *chaweson chadan-jeesoo …*
tampons	탐폰 *tampawn*
tissues	화장지 *hwajang-jee*
toilet paper	화장실 휴지 *hwajang-seel hyoo-jee*
toothpaste	치약 *cheeyak*

Haircare 머리손질

comb	빗 *peet*
conditioner	린스/컨디셔너 *leensu/kondee-syono*
hair mousse/gel	헤어 무스/젤 *he-o moosu/jel*
hair spray	헤어 스프레이 *he-o supu-re-ee*
shampoo	샴푸 *syam-poo*

For the baby 아기용

baby food	이유식 *ee-yoo-seek*
baby wipes	아기용 물휴지 *agee-yong mool-hyoo-jee*
diapers [nappies]	기저귀 *keejo-gee*
sterilizing solution	젖병 소독액 *jotbyong sawdawg-ek*

Clothing 의복

Large department stores are good places to buy clothing. They display all kinds of brands and types. They often have sales, especially at the end of each season. **Namdemoon See-jang** market near downtown Seoul is a good place to buy clothing at reasonable prices. Itaewon (**eetewon**) is a Seoul shopping street for foreigners. Prices are given in dollars and you can find good bargains there.

숙녀복	ladieswear
신사복	menswear
아동복	childrenswear

General 일반 사항

I'd like …	… 사고 싶습니다.
	… *sagaw seep-sumneeda*
Do you have any …?	… 있습니까? … *ee-ssumneekka*

Color 색상

I'm looking for something in …	… 색을 찾고 있습니다.
	… *segul chatgaw ee-ssumneeda*
beige	베이지 *pe-ee-jee*
black/white	검은/흰 *komun/heen*
blue/green	파란/초록 *paran/chaw-rawk*
brown	갈색 *kalseg*
gray	회 *hwe*
orange	오렌지 *aw-renjee*
purple	자주 *chajoo*
red/pink	빨간/분홍 *balgan/poon-hawng*
yellow	노란 *nawran*
light …	밝은 … *palgun …*
dark …	어두운 … *odoo-oon …*
I want a darker/lighter shade.	더 어두운/더 밝은 색조를 원합니다.
	to odoo-oon/to palgun sekchaw-rul won-hamneeda

Clothes and accessories
의복과 액세서리

belt	벨트	*peltu*
blouse	블라우스	*pulla-oosu*
bra	브래지어	*pure-jee-o*
coat	코트	*kawtu*
dress	드레스	*duresu*
handbag	핸드백	*hendu-bek*
hat	모자	*mawja*
jacket	자켓	*chaket*
jeans	청바지	*chong-bajee*
leggings	레깅스바지	*le-geeng-su bajee*
pants (U.S.)	바지	*pajee*
pantyhose [tights]	팬티스타킹	*pentee-suta-keeng*
raincoat	레인코트	*le-een-kawtu*
scarf	스카프	*sukapu*
shirt	와이셔츠	*wa-ee-syochu*
shorts	반바지	*pan-bajee*
skirt	치마	*cheema*
socks	양말	*yang-mal*
stockings	스타킹	*sutakeeng*
suit	양복	*yang-bawk*
sweater	스웨터	*suweto*
sweatshirt	보온용 스웨터	*paw-awn-nyong suweto*
swimming trunks	수영팬츠	*sooyong-penchu*
swimsuit	수영복	*sooyong-bawk*
T-shirt	티셔츠	*tee-syochu*
tie	넥타이	*nek-ta-ee*
trousers	바지	*pajee*
underpants	속바지	*sawk-pajee*
with long/short sleeves	긴/짧은 소매	*keen/zalbun sawme*
with a V-/round neck	브이 넥/라운드 넥	*pu-ee nek/la-oonde nek*

Shoes 신발

boots	부츠 *poo-chu*
flip-flops	고무 슬리퍼 *kawmoo sullee-po*
running [training] shoes	운동화 *oon-dawng-hwa*
sandals	샌들 *sendul*
shoes	신발 *seenbal*
slippers	슬리퍼 *sullee-po*

Walking/Hiking gear 등산용품

knapsack	배낭 *penang*
hiking boots	등산화 *tungsan-hwa*
waterproof jacket [anorak]	방수자켓 *pang-soo-jaket*
windbreaker [cagoule]	방풍자켓 *pang-poong-jaket*

Fabric 천

I want something in ...	...으로 된 걸 원합니다. *...-uraw dwen-gol won-hamneeda*
cotton	면 *myon*
denim	데님 *te-neem*
lace	레이스 *le-eesu*
leather	가죽 *kajook*
linen	마 *ma*
wool	모 *maw*
Is this ...?	이것 ... 입니까? *eegot ... eemneekka*
pure cotton	순면 *soon-myon*
synthetic	합성섬유 *hapsong somyoo*
Is it hand/machine washable?	손빨래/기계세탁 합니까? *sawn-balle/keege-setak hamneekka*

드라이크리닝	dry clean only
손빨래	handwash only
다림질하지 마시오	do not iron
물 빠지지 않음	colorfast

Does it fit? 맞습니까?

Can I try this on? (clothing)	입어 볼 수 있습니까?	*eebo pawl-soo ee-ssumneekka*
Can I try these on? (shoes)	신어 볼 수 있습니까?	*seeno pawl-soo ee-ssumneekka*

Where's the fitting room?
탈의실이 어딥니까?
taluee-see-ree odeem-neekka

It fits well. I'll take it.
잘 맞습니다. 이걸로 사겠습니다. *chal massumneeda. eegol-law sage-ssumneeda*

It doesn't fit.
맞지 않습니다. *mazee an-ssumneeda*

It's too ...
너무 ... *nomoo ...*

short/long
짧습니다/깁니다
zal-ssumneeda/keem-needa

tight/loose
낍니다/헐렁합니다 *geem-needa/hollong-hamneeda*

What size is this?
이건 사이즈가 어떻게 됩니까?
eegun sa:ee-zu-ga otdoke dwem-neekka

Size 사이즈

	Women's dresses/suits						Women's shoes			
American	8	10	12	14	16	18	6	7	8	9
British	10	12	14	16	18	20	$4^{1/2}$	$5^{1/2}$	$6^{1/2}$	$7^{1/2}$
Continental	36	38	40	42	44	46	37	38	40	41
Korean	43	44	45	46	47	48	$22^{1/2}$	23	$23^{1/2}$	24

	Men's shirts				Men's shoes									
American } British	15	16	17	18	5	6	7	8	$8^{1/2}$	9	$9^{1/2}$	10	11
Continental	38	41	43	45	38	39	41	42	43	43	44	44	45
Korean	$14^{1/2}$	15	$15^{1/2}$	16	$24^{1/2}$	25	$25^{1/2}$	26	$26^{1/2}$	27	$27^{1/2}$	28	$28^{1/2}$

대	large (L)
중	medium (M)
소	small (S)

1 centimeter (cm.) = 0.39 in.	1 inch = 2.54 cm.
1 meter (m.) = 39.37 in.	1 foot = 30.5 cm.
10 meters = 32.81 ft.	1 yard = 0.91 m.

Health and beauty 건강과 미용

I'd like a …	… 해 주십시오.
	… he chooseep-seeaw
facial	얼굴마사지 *olgool-massajee*
manicure	손톱 손질 *sawn-tawp sawnjeel*
massage	마사지 *massajee*
waxing	피부팩 *peeboo-pek*

Hairdresser/Hairstylist 미용실

Normally you don't need an appointment at beauty salons and barber's shops. Shampoo, haircut, and blow-dry are usually provided as a package rather than as separate services.

I'd like to make an appointment for …	… 예약하고 싶습니다.
	… yeyak-hagaw seep-sumneeda
Can you make it a bit earlier/later?	좀 더 일찍/좀 더 늦게 할 수 있습니까?
	chawm to eelzeek/chawm to nutge hal soo ee-ssumneekka
I'd like a …	… 해 주십시오. *… he chooseep-seeaw*
cut and blow-dry	커트와 드라이 *kotu-wa tura-ee*
shampoo and set	샴푸와 세트 *syampoo-wa setu*
trim	다듬기 *tadum-gee*
I'd like my hair …	머리를 … 하고 싶습니다.
	moree-rul … hagaw seep-sumneeda
colored/tinted	염색 *yomsek*
highlighted	부분염색 *pooboon yomsek*
permed	퍼머 *pomo*
Don't cut it too short.	너무 짧게 자르지 마세요.
	nomoo zalge charu-jee maseyo
A little more off the …	… 좀 더 잘라 주세요.
	… chawm to challa chooseyo
back/front/top	뒤/앞/위 *dwee/ap/wee*
neck/sides	목부분/옆 *mawk-pooboon/yop*
That's fine, thanks.	좋습니다, 감사합니다.
	chaw-ssumneeda. kamsa-hamneeda

Household articles 가정용품

I'd like (a/an) ...	... 주십시오.	... chooseep-seeaw
adapter	어댑터	odepto
alumin(i)um foil	알루미늄 호일	alloo-mee-nyoom haw-eel
bottle opener	병따개	pyong-dage
can [tin] opener	통조림따개	tawng-jawreem-dage
clothes pins [pegs]	빨래 집게	balle cheepke
corkscrew	마개뽑기	mage-bawp-gee
light bulb	전구	chon-goo
matches	성냥	song-nyang
paper napkins	종이 냅킨	chawng-ee nepkeen
plastic wrap [cling film]	랩	lep
plug	플러그	pulogu
scissors	가위	kawee
screwdriver	드라이버	tura-eebo

Cleaning items 세척용품

bleach	표백제	pyo-bek-che
detergent [washing powder]	세제	seje
dish cloth	행주	heng-joo
dishwashing [washing-up] liquid	식기용 세제	seekgee-yong seje
garbage [refuse] bags	쓰레기봉투	ssuregee-bawng-too
sponge	수세미	soosemee

Crockery/Cutlery 그릇/수저

cups/glasses	컵/유리잔	kop/yooree-jan
knives/forks	나이프/포크	na-ee-pu/pawku
spoons	숟가락	sootgarak
mugs	머그잔	mogu-jan
plates	접시	chopsee
bowls	공기	kawng-gee
chopsticks	젓가락	chotgarak

Jeweler 보석상

Could I see …?	… 볼 수 있습니까? … *pawl soo ee-ssumneekka*
this/that	이것/그것 *eegot/kugot*
It's in the window/display cabinet.	진열대에 있습니다. *cheen-yol-de-e ee-ssumneeda*
alarm clock	자명종 *cha-myong-jawng*
bracelet	팔찌 *palzee*
brooch	브로치 *puraw-chee*
chain	줄 *chool*
clock	시계 *seege*
earrings	귀걸이 *kwee-goree*
necklace	목걸이 *mawkgoree*
ring	반지 *panjee*
watch	손목시계 *sawn-mawk seege*

Materials 재료

Is this real silver/gold?	이것은 진짜 은/금 입니까? *eego-sun cheenza un/kum eemneekka*
Is there a certificate for it?	보증서가 있습니까? *pawjung-soga ee-ssumneekka*
Do you have anything in …?	…으로 된 것 있습니까? *…-uraw dwen-go eessumneekka*
copper	구리 *kooree*
crystal	수정 *soojong*
cut glass	세공 유리 *segawng yooree*
diamond	다이아몬드 *ta-ee-a-mawndu*
enamel	에나멜 *enamel*
gold/gold-plate	금/금도금 *kum/kum-dawgum*
pearl	진주 *cheenjoo*
pewter	백랍 *peng-nap*
platinum	백금 *pekkum*
silver/silver-plate	은/은도금 *un/un-dawgum*
stainless steel	스테인레스 *sute-een-lesu*

Newsstand [Newsagent]/ Tobacconist 신문가게/담배가게

Newspapers and magazines are usually sold at kiosks rather than in bookstores. Large hotels and bookstores in Seoul may also sell some foreign publications. Cigarettes and candy can be bought at most groceries and convenience stores.

Do you sell English-language books/newspapers?	영어 책/신문 팝니까? *yong-o chek/seenmoon pamneekka*
I'd like (a/an) …	… 주십시오. … *chooseep-seeaw*
book	책 *chek*
candy [sweets]	사탕 *satang*
chewing gum	껌 *gom*
chocolate bar	초콜렛 *chaw-kawl-let*
cigarettes (pack of)	담배 한갑 *tambe han-gap*
cigars	시가 *seega*
dictionary	사전 *sajon*
English-Korean	영한 *yong-han*
envelopes	편지 봉투 *pyon-jee pawng-too*
guidebook of …	… 안내서 … *anneso*
lighter	라이타 *la-ee-ta*
magazine	잡지 *chap-chee*
map	지도 *cheedaw*
map of the town	시내 지도 *seene cheedaw*
road map of …	… 도로 지도 … *tawraw cheedaw*
matches	성냥 *song-nyang*
newspaper	신문 *seenmoon*
American/English	미국/영국 *mee-gook/yong-gook*
paper	종이 *chawng-ee*
pen	펜 *pen*
stamps	우표 *oo-pyo*
tobacco	담배 *tambe*
writing pad	편지지 *pyon-jee-jee*

Photography 사진촬영

I'm looking for a(n) ... camera.	... 사진기를 찾고 있습니다. ... sajeen-geerul chatgaw ee-ssumneeda
automatic	자동 chadawng
compact	소형 saw-hyong
disposable	일회용 eel-hwe-yong
SLR	싱글 렌즈 리플렉스 seeng-gul lenju leepul-leksu
I'd like a(n) ...	... 주십시오. ... chooseep-seeaw
battery	건전지 kon-jon-jee
camera case	사진기 케이스 sajeen-gee ke-ee-su
(electronic) flash	(전자) 플래시 (chonja) pullesee
filter	필터 peelto
lens	렌즈 lenju
lens cap	렌즈 덮개 lenju topke

Film/Processing 필름/현상

I'd like a ... film for this camera.	이 사진기에 넣을 ... 필름 주십시오. ee sajeen-gee-e no-ul ... peelleem chooseep-seeaw
black and white	흑백 hukpek
color	칼라 kalla
24/36 exposures	이십사 방/삼십육 방 eeseep-sa pang/ samseep-yook pang
I'd like this film developed, please.	이 필름 현상하고 싶습니다. ee peelleem hyon-sang-hagaw seep-sumneeda
How much do ... exposures cost?	... 방은 얼마입니까? ... pang-un olma ee-mneekka
When will the photos be ready?	언제 다 됩니까? onje ta dwem-neekka
I'd like to collect my photos.	사진을 찾고 싶습니다. sajee-nul chatgaw seep-sumneeda
Here's the receipt.	영수증 여기 있습니다. yong-soo-jung yogee ee-ssumneeda

Police 경찰

The emergency telephone number in South Korea for the police is 112; the number for the fire department is 119.

Where's the nearest police station?	가장 가까운 경찰서 어디 있습니까? *kajang katgaoon kyong-chal-so odee ee-ssumneekka*
Does anyone here speak English?	여기 영어하는 분 계십니까? *yogee yong-o-hanun poon ke-seemneekka*
I want to report a(n) ...	...을 신고하고 싶습니다. *...-ul seen-gaw-hagaw seep-sumneeda*
accident/attack	사고/폭행 *sagaw/pawkeng*
mugging/rape	노상 강도/강간 *nawsang kang-daw/kang-gan*
My child is missing.	제 아이가 실종됐습니다. *che a-ee-ga seel-zawng dwe-ssumneeda*
Here's a photo of him/her.	여기 그애 사진이 있습니다. *yogee ku-e sajeen-ee ee-ssumneeda*
I need an English-speaking lawyer.	저는 영어하는 변호사가 필요합니다. *cho-nun yong-o-hanun pyon-haw-sa-ga peeryo-hamneeda*
I need to make a phone call.	전화를 해야겠습니다. *chon-hwa-rul heya-ge-ssumneeda*
I need to contact the ... Consulate.	... 영사관에 연락해야겠습니다. *... yong-sa-gwane yollak-heya-ge-ssumneeda*
American/British	미국/영국 *mee-gook/yong-gook*

그 남자/그 여자 인상착의를 묘사해 주십시오.	Can you describe him/her?
남자/여자	male/female
금발/갈색/적갈색/백발	blonde/brunette/red-haired/gray-headed
진/짧은 머리/대머리	long/short hair/balding
대략 키가 ...	approximate height ...
(대략) ... 살	aged (approximately) ...
그 남자는/그 여자는 ... 입고 있었습니다.	He/She was wearing ...

CLOTHES ➤ 144; COLORS ➤ 143

Lost property/Theft 분실물/도난

I want to report a theft/break-in.	도난/주거침입 신고하고 싶습니다. *tawnan/choogo-cheemeep seen-gaw-hagaw seep-sumneeda*
I've been robbed/mugged.	강도를 당했습니다. *kang-dawrul tang-he-ssumneeda*
I've lost my ...	... 잃어버렸습니다. *... eero-boryo-ssumneeda*
My ... has been stolen.	제 ... 도난당했습니다. *che ... tawnan dang-he-ssumneeda*
bicycle	자전거 *cha-jon-go*
camera	사진기 *sajeen-gee*
(rental) car	(빌린) 차 *peelleen-cha*
credit cards	신용 카드 *seen-yong kadu*
handbag	핸드백 *hendu-bek*
money	돈 *tawn*
passport	여권 *yokgwon*
purse/wallet	지갑 *chee-gap*
watch	손목시계 *sawn-mawk seege*
I need a police report for my insurance claim.	보험 청구용 경찰 증명서가 필요합니다. *paw-hom chong-gooyong kyong-chal chung-myong-so-ga peeryo-hamneeda*

무엇이 없어졌습니까?	What's missing?
무엇을 도둑맞았습니까?	What's been taken?
언제 도둑맞았습니까?	When was it stolen?
언제 일어났습니까?	When did it happen?
어디 묵고 계십니까?	Where are you staying?
어디에서 훔쳐갔습니까?	Where was it taken from?
그때 어디 계셨습니까?	Where were you at the time?
통역을 불러드리겠습니다.	We're getting an interpreter for you.
그 사건을 우리가 조사하겠습니다.	We'll look into the matter.
이 용지를 작성해 주십시오.	Please fill out this form.

Post office 우체국

Post offices are open from 9:00 a.m. to 5:00 p.m. Monday to Friday and from 9:00 a.m. to 2:00 p.m. on Saturdays. You can recognize them by their red and white (**oochegook**) sign. Mailboxes are red. Large post offices also offer a cheap packing service.

General queries 일반 문의사항

Where is the nearest/main post office?	가장 가까운 우체국/큰 우체국 어디 있습니까? *kajang katgaoon ooche-gook/ kun ooche-gook odee ee-ssumneekka*
What time does the post office open/close?	우체국 몇시에 문엽니까/문닫습니까? *ooche-goog myossee-e moon yom-neekka/tassum-neekka*
Does it close for lunch?	점심시간에 문닫습니까? *chomseem-seega-ne moon tassumneekka*
Where's the mailbox [postbox]?	우체통 어디 있습니까? *ooche-tawng odee ee-ssumneekka*
Is there any mail for me?	제 편지 있습니까? *che pyon-jee ee-ssumneekka*

Buying stamps 우표 사기

A stamp for this postcard, please.	이 엽서용 우표 한 장 주십시오. *ee yopso-yong oopyo han-jang chooseep-seeaw*
A … Won stamp, please.	… 짜리 우표 한 장 주십시오. *… zaree oopyo han-jang chooseep-seeaw*
What's the postage for a letter to …?	… 가는 편지 우편요금이 얼마입니까? *… kanun pyon-jee oopyon yogumee olma ee-mneekka*
Is there a stamp machine here?	여기 우표 자동판매기 있습니까? *yogee oopyo chadawng-panmegee eessumneekka*

– annyong-haseemneekka, ee yopso-rul mee-gook-uraw pawne-gaw seep-sumneeda.
– *mawdoo myotzang-eemneekka?*
– *ahawp-zang eemneeda.*
– *aw-beg-won zaree ahawp-chang eemneekka?*
sa-chon aw-beg-won chooseep-seeaw.

154

Sending parcels 소포 보내기

I want to send this parcel/package ...	이 소포/짐 ... 보내고 싶습니다. *ee sawpaw/cheem ... pawne-gaw seep-sumneeda*
by air mail	항공우편으로 *hang-gawng oopyon-uraw*
by special delivery [express]	속달로 *sawktal-law*
It contains ...	안에 ... 들어 있습니다. *ane ... turo ee-ssumneeda*

통관 신고서를 작성해 주십시오.	Please fill in the customs declaration.
가격은 어느 정도입니까?	What's the value?
안에 무엇이 들어 있습니까?	What's inside?

Other services 기타 서비스

I'd like a phonecard, please.	전화 카드 한 장 주십시오. *chon-hwa kadu hanjang chooseep-seeaw*
3,000/5,000/10,000 Won	삼천원/오천원/만원 짜리 *samchon-won/awchon-won/man-won zaree*
Do you have a photocopier ?	복사기 있습니까? *pawk-sa-gee ee-ssumneekka*
I'd like to send a message ...	서신 한 장을 ... 보내고 싶습니다. *soseen hanjang-ul ... pawne-gaw seep-sumneeda*
by e-mail/fax	이메일로/팩스로 *ee-me-eellaw/peksuraw*
What's your e-mail address?	이메일 주소가 어떻게 되십니까? *ee-me-eel choosaw-ga otdoke dweseem-neekka*
Can I access the Internet here?	여기서 인터넷 접속할 수 있습니까? *yogeeso een-tonet chopsawk-hal soo ee-ssumneekka*
What are the charges per hour?	시간당 얼마입니까? *seegan-dang olma ee-mneekka*
How do I log on?	어떻게 접속합니까? *otdoke chopsawk-hamneekka*

소포	packages
유치 우편	general delivery [poste restante]
우표	stamps

Souvenirs 기념품

You will find no difficulty in finding any number of souvenirs and presents to take home. There is something for everybody and in every price range.

The following are just a few suggestions: brass, bamboo and lacquerware, wooden masks, fans, kites, leather goods, furs, jewelry, jade and other semiprecious stones, dolls dressed in traditional costume, embroidery, and macrame.

Other bargains are Ginseng (not more than three kilos per person should be taken out of the country), custom-made silk and cotton shirts and blouses, sports equipment (rackets, skis, baseball gloves), and sportswear.

ginseng liquor	인삼주	*eensam-joo*
ginseng tea	인삼차	*eensam-cha*
pottery/percelain	도자기	*taw-ja-gee*
handicrafts	수공예품	*soo gawng-ye-poom*
woodcrafts	목공예품	*mawk kawng-ye-poom*
fans	부채	*pooche*

Gifts 선물

bottle of wine	포도주 한병	*pawdaw-joo han-byong*
box of chocolates	초콜렛 한 상자	*chaw-kawllet han-sangja*
calendar	달력	*tal-lyok*
key ring	열쇠고리	*yolswe-gawree*
postcard	엽서	*yopso*
souvenir guidebook	기념품 안내	*kee-nyom-poom anne*
tea towel	티 타월	*tee tawol*
T-shirt	티셔츠	*tee-syochu*

Music 음악

I'd like a(n) ...
... 사고 싶습니다.
... sagaw seep-sumneeda

cassette
카세트 테이프
kasetu te-ee-pu

compact disc
시디 *see-dee*

record
레코드판 *rekawdu-pan*

videocassette
비디오 테이프 *pee-dee-aw te-eepu*

Who are the popular native singers/bands?
국내 인기가수가/인기그룹이 누구입니까?
koong-ne een-gee-kasoo-ga/een-gee-guroop-ee noo-goo ee-mneeka

Toys and games 장난감과 오락기구

I'd like a toy/game ...
... 장난감/게임기 사고 싶습니다.
... chang-nan-gam/ge-eem-gee sagaw seep-sumneeda

for a boy
남자애용 *namja-e-yong*

for a 5-year-old girl
다섯살 여자애용
tasot-sal yoja-e-yong

ball
공 *kawng*

chess set
체스 세트 *chesu-setu*

doll
인형 *een-hyong*

electronic game
컴퓨터 게임 *kompyoo-to ge-eem*

teddy bear
곰인형 *kawm een-hyong*

Antiques 골동품

How old is this?
이것은 얼마나 됐습니까?
eego-sun olmana dwe-ssumneekka

Do you have anything from the ... era?
... 시대 것 있습니까?
... seede go ee-ssumneekka

Can you send it to me?
보내 줄 수 있습니까?
pawne chool-soo ee-ssumneekka

Will I have problems with customs?
세관에서 문제가 될까요?
segwan-eso moon-jega dwel-gayo

Is there a certificate of authenticity?
감정서 있습니까?
kamjong-so ee-ssumneekka

HISTORICAL PERIODS ➤ 104

Supermarket/Minimart
슈퍼마켓/가게

Department stores in major cities in South Korea, such as **Lotte** (closed Monday) and **Midopa** (closed Wednesday), often have supermarkets in the basement or lower level. In Seoul **Crown Bakery** offers a variety of Western foods, such as breads, jams, and cheeses. You will find supermarkets on the basement floor of department stores.

At the supermarket 슈퍼마켓에서

Excuse me. Where can I find (a) …?	여보세요. … 어디 있습니까? *yobaw-seyo. … odee ee-ssumneekka*
Do I pay for this here or at the checkout?	여기서 계산합니까, 아니면 계산대에서 합니까? *yogeeso kesan-ham-neekka, anee-myon kesande-eso ham-neekka*
Where are the shopping carts [trolleys]/baskets?	손수레/바구니 어디 있습니까? *sawnsoore/pagoonee odee eessumneekka*
Is there a … here?	여기 … 있습니까? *yogee … eessumneekka*
delicatessen	델리카테슨 *dellee-katesun*
pharmacy	약국 *yakgook*

현금만 받습니다	cash only
세척용품	cleaning products
유제품	dairy products
생선	fresh fish
정육	fresh meat
농산물	fresh produce
냉동식품	frozen foods
가정용품	household goods
닭고기	poultry
과일/야채 통조림	canned fruit/vegetables
주류	wines and spirits
빵과 케이크	bread and cakes

Weights and measures

- **1 kilogram** or **kilo (kg.)** = **1000 grams (g.)**; **100 g.** = 3.5 oz.; **1 kg.** = 2.2 lb; 1 oz. = **28.35 g.**; 1 lb. = **453.60 g.**
- **1 liter (l.)** = 0.88 imp. quart or 1.06 U.S. quart; 1 imp. quart = **1.14 l.**; 1 U.S. quart = **0.951 l.**; 1 imp. gallon = **4.55 l.**; 1 U.S. gallon = **3.8 l.**

Food hygiene 식품 위생

개봉후 ... 안에 드십시오	eat within ... days of opening
냉장 요	keep refrigerated
전자렌지 사용 가능	microwaveable
데워서 드십시오	reheat before eating
유효 기간 ...	use by ...

At the minimart 가게에서

I'd like some of that/those.	그것/그것들 약간 주십시오. *kugo/kugotdul yakgan chooseep-seeaw*
This one/these.	이것/이것들. *eego/eegotdul*
To the left/right.	왼쪽으로/오른쪽으로. *wen-zawguraw/awrun-zawguraw*
Over there/here.	저쪽에/여기. *cho-zawge/yogee*
Which one(s)?	어느 것? *onu got*
That's all, thanks.	됐습니다. 감사합니다. *dwe-ssumneeda. kamsa-hamneeda*
I'd like ...	... 주십시오. *... chooseep-seeaw*
... kilo of apples	사과 ... 킬로 *sagwa ... keellaw*
half-kilo of tomatoes	토마토 반 킬로 *tawmataw pan-keellaw*
100 grams of cheese	치즈 백 그램 *cheeju pek-gurem*
... liter of milk	우유 ... 리터 *oo-yoo ... leeto*
half-dozen eggs	계란 여섯개 *keran yosotge*
... slices of ham	햄 ... 장 *hem ... jang*
... pieces of cake	케이크 ... 조각 *ka-ee-ku ... chawgak*
... bottles of wine	포도주 ... 병 *pawdaw-joo ... pyong*
... cartons of milk	우유 ... 팩 *oo-yoo ... pek*
... jars of jam	잼 ... 병 *chem ... pyong*
... bags of potato chips [crisps]	감자 칩 ... 봉지 *kamja-cheep ... pawng-jee*
... cans of cola	캔콜라 ... 개 *ken-kawlla ... ge*

– ku cheeju pan-keellaw chooseep-seeaw.
– *eego-yo?*
– ne, gugo chooseep-seeaw.
– ne... *dwe-ssumneekka?*
– kureegaw tak han maree
chooseep-seeaw.
– *yogee ee-ssumneeda.*

Provisions/Picnic 식품/소풍

butter	버터 *poto*
cheese	치즈 *cheeju*
cookies [biscuits]	쿠키 *kookee*
eggs	계란 *keran*
French fries [chips]	감자 튀김 *kamja-tweegeem*
grapes	포도 *pawdaw*
ice cream	아이스크림 *a-eesu-kureem*
instant coffee	인스탄트 커피 *een-su-tantu kopee*
loaf of bread	식빵 *seekbang*
margarine	마가린 *ma-gareen*
milk	우유 *oo-yoo*
potato chips [crisps]	감자칩 *kamja-cheep*
rolls	롤빵 *lolbang*
sausages	소세지 *saw-sejee*
six-pack of beer	맥주 여섯병짜리 포장 *mek-joo yosot-pyong-zaree pawjang*
soft drink	청량음료 *chong-ryang umnyo*
tea bags	봉지차 *pawng-jee-cha*

You can get bread in bakeries (**pe-eeko-ree** or **che-gwajom**). You can also get croissants in bakery chains such as **Paris Baguette** in large cities. However, it might be difficult to find bakeries in rural areas.

Health

Before you leave, make sure your health insurance policy covers any illness or accident while abroad. You do not need any vaccinations in order to enter the either South or North Korea, but it is advisable not to drink tap water (ice included) and check that the milk is pasteurized. For minor ailments your hotel or embassy can contact or give you the name of an English-speaking doctor. Asia Emergency Assistance (☎ 02-790–7561) provides a 24-hour service for foreigners for a fee. In a medical emergency, dial 129 or 119 for an ambulance.

Doctor (general) 의사 (일반 사항)

Where can I find a doctor/ dentist?	의사/치과의사 어디서 찾을 수 있습니까? *ueesa/cheetgwa-ueesa odeeso chajul-soo ee-ssumneekka*
Where's there a doctor/dentist who speaks English?	영어 하는 의사/치과의사 어디 있습니까? *yong-o hanun ueesa/cheetgwa-ueesa odee ee-ssumneekka*
What are the office [surgery] hours?	진료시간이 언제입니까? *cheel-lyo seegan-ee onje eem-neekka*
Could the doctor come to see me here?	의사가 여기로 왕진을 수 있습니까? *ueesa-ga yogee-raw wang-jeen-awl soo ee-ssumneekka*
Can I make an appointment for …?	… 예약할 수 있습니까? *… yeyakal soo ee-ssumneekka*
today/tomorrow	오늘/내일 *awnul/ne-eel*
as soon as possible	가능한 한 빨리 *kanung-han han ballee*
It's urgent.	응급입니다. *ung-gup eem-needa*
I've got an appointment with Doctor …	… 의사와 약속돼 있습니다. *… ueesa-wa yaksawk dwe-eessumneeda*

Accident and injury 사고와 부상

My ... is hurt/injured.	제 ... 아픕니다/다쳤습니다. *che ... apum-needa/tacho-ssumneeda*
husband/wife	남편/아내 *nam-pyon/ane*
son/daughter	아들/딸 *adul/dal*
friend	친구 *cheen-goo*
baby	아기 *agee*
He/She is ...	... 상태 입니다. *... sang-te eemneeda*
unconscious	의식불명 *ueeseek pool-myong*
(seriously) injured	(심 하게) 다친 *(seemhage) tacheen*
He/She is bleeding (heavily).	(심 하게) 출혈하고 있습니다. *(seemhage) chool-hyol-hagaw ee-ssumneeda*
I have a blister.	물집이 생겼습니다. *mool-jeebee seng-gyo-ssumneeda*
I have a boil.	종기가 났습니다. *chawng-geega na-ssumneeda*
I have a bruise.	멍이 들었습니다. *mong-ee turo-ssumneeda*
I have a burn.	화상을 입었습니다. *hwa-sangul eebo-ssumneeda*
I have a cut.	베었습니다. *pe-o-ssumneeda*
I have a graze.	찰과상을 입었습니다. *chal-gwa-sangul eebo-ssumneeda*
I have an insect bite.	벌레에 물렸습니다. *polle-e moollyo-ssumneeda*
I have a lump.	혹이 생겼습니다. *hawgee seng-gyo-ssumneeda*

Short-term symptoms 단기 증세

I've been feeling ill for … days.	… 일 동안 계속 아픕니다. *… eel tawng-an kesawk* *apum-needa*
I feel feverish.	열이 납니다. *yoree nam-needa*
I've been vomiting.	계속 토하고 있습니다. *kesawk tawha-gaw ee-ssumneeda*
I have diarrhea.	설사를 합니다. *solsarul ham-needa*
It hurts here.	여기가 아픕니다. *yogee-ga apum-needa*
I have (a/an) …	저는 … 있습니다. *cho-nun … ee-ssumneeda*
backache	요통 *yo-tawng*
earache	귀 통증 *kwee tawng-zung*
headache	두통 *too-tawng*
stomachache	위통 *wee-tawng*
sunstroke	일사병 *eelssa-byong*
sore throat	목이 아픕니다. *maw-gee apum-needa*
cold	감기 걸렸습니다. *kamgee kollyo-ssumneeda*

Health conditions 건강 상태

I have arthritis.	저는 관절염이 있습니다. *cho-nun kwan-jol-lyomee ee-ssumneeda*
I have asthma.	저는 천식이 있습니다. *cho-nun chonseeg-ee ee-ssumneeda*
I am …	저는 … 입니다. *cho-nun … eemneeda*
diabetic	당뇨병 *tang-nyo-byong*
epileptic	간질병 *kanjeel-byong*
(… months) pregnant	임신 (… 개월) *eemseen (… kewol)*
I am deaf.	저는 귀가 멀었습니다. *cho-nun kwee-ga moro-ssumneeda*
I have a heart condition.	저는 심장병이 있습니다. *cho-nun* *seemjang-byong-ee ee-ssumneeda*
I have high blood pressure.	저는 고혈압입니다. *cho-nun kaw-hyo-rap eemneeda*

Doctor's inquiries 진찰

얼마나 이렇게 아팠습니까?	How long have you been feeling like this?
이번이 처음이십니까?	Is this the first time you've had this?
복용중인 다른 약이 있습니까?	Are you taking any other medication?
알레르기 있으십니까?	Are you allergic to anything?
파상풍 예방 주사를 맞으셨습니까?	Have you been vaccinated against tetanus?
식욕을 잃으셨습니까?	Have you lost your appetite?

Examination 검사

체온/혈압을 재겠습니다.	I'll take your temperature/blood pressure.
소매를 걷으십시오.	Roll up your sleeve, please.
상의를 벗으십시오.	Please undress to the waist.
누으십시오.	Please lie down.
입을 벌리십시오.	Open your mouth.
호흡을 크게 하십시오.	Breathe deeply.
기침을 하십시오.	Cough, please.
어디가 아픕니까?	Where does it hurt?
여기가 아픕니까?	Does it hurt here?

Diagnosis 진단

엑스레이를 찍겠습니다.	I want you to have an X-ray.
혈액/대변/소변 검사를 하겠습니다.	I want a specimen of your blood/stools/urine.
전문의를 만나 보십시오.	I want you to see a specialist.
종합병원으로 가보십시오.	I want you to go to a hospital.
부러졌습니다/삐었습니다.	It's broken/sprained.
탈구되었습니다/ 찢어졌습니다.	It's dislocated/torn.

... 입니다.	You have (a/an) ...
맹장염	appendicitis
방광염	cystitis
독감	flu
식중독	food poisoning
골절상	fracture
위염	gastritis
치질	hemorrhoids
탈장	hernia
... 염	inflammation of ...
홍역	measles
폐염	pneumonia
좌골 신경통	sciatica
편도선염	tonsilitis
종양	tumor
성병	venereal disease
감염되었습니다.	It's infected.
전염됩니다.	It's contagious.

Treatment 치료

... 드리겠습니다.	I'll give you ...
소독약	an antiseptic
진통제	a painkiller
... 처방하겠습니다.	I'm going to prescribe ...
일련의 항생제	a course of antibiotics
좌약 약간	some suppositories
약 알레르기가 있으십니까?	Are you allergic to any medication?
... 한 알씩 드십시오.	Take one pill ...
... 시간마다	every ... hours
하루에 ... 번	... times a day
식사 전에/후에	before/after each meal
통증이 있을 때	in case of pain
... 일간	for ... days
본국에 돌아가시면 의사에게 진찰 받으십시오.	Consult a doctor when you get home.

Parts of the body 신체 부위

appendix	맹장 meng-jang
arm	팔 pal
back	등 tung
bladder	방광 pang-gwang
bone	뼈 byo
breast	유방 yoo-bang
chest	가슴 kasum
ear	귀 gwee
eye	눈 noon
face	얼굴 ol-gool
finger	손가락 sawn-garak
foot	발 pal
gland	선 son
hand	손 sawn
head	머리 moree
heart	심장 seem-jang
jaw	턱 tok
joint	관절 kwan-jol
kidney	신장 seen-jang
knee	무릎 moorup
leg	다리 taree
lip	입술 eep-sool
liver	간 kan
mouth	입 eep
muscle	근육 kun-yook
neck	목 mawk
nose	코 kaw
rib	늑골 nukgawl
shoulder	어깨 okke
skin	피부 peeboo
stomach	위 wee
thigh	넓적다리 nobzok-daree
throat	목구멍 mawk-goo-mong
thumb	엄지 손가락 omjee sawn-garak
toe	발가락 pal-garak
tongue	혀 hyo
tonsils	편도 pyon-daw
vein	정맥 chong-mek

Gynecologist 부인과

I have ...
저는 ... 있습니다.
cho-nun ... ee-ssumneeda

abdominal pains
복통 *pawk-tawng*

period pains
생리통 *seng-nee-tawng*

a vaginal infection
질감염 *cheel-gam-yom*

I haven't had my period for ... months.
저는 ... 달간 생리가 없었습니다.
cho-nun ... talgan seng-nee-ga op-sossum-needa

I'm on the Pill.
저는 경구피임약을 먹고 있습니다.
cho-nun kyong-goo pee-eem-yagul mokgaw ee-ssumneeda

Hospital 종합병원

Please notify my family.
제 가족에게 연락해 주십시오.
che kajawg-ege yollake chooseep-sseeaw

I'm in pain.
아픕니다. *apum-needa*

I can't eat/sleep.
먹을 수가/잘 수가 없습니다. *mogul soo-ga/chal soo-ga op-sumneeda*

When will the doctor come?
의사는 언제 옵니까?
ueesa-nun onje awm-neekka

Which ward is ... in?
... 어느 병동에 있습니까?
... onu pyong-dawng-e ee-ssumneekka

I'm visiting ...
... 문병 왔습니다.
... moon-byong wa-ssumneeda

Optician 안경사

I'm near- [short-] sighted/ far- [long-] sighted.
저는 근시/원시 입니다.
cho-nun kunsee/wonsee eem-needa

I've lost ...
... 잃어버렸습니다.
... eero-boryo-ssumneeda

one of my contact lenses
콘택트 렌즈 한 짝
kawn-tektu lenju han-zak

my glasses/a lens
안경/안경알 *angyong/angyong-al*

Could you give me a replacement?
대체품을 주시겠습니까?
teche-poom-ul chooseege-ssumneekka

Dentist 치과

I have a toothache.	이가 아픕니다. *eega apum-needa*
This tooth hurts.	이 이빨이 아픕니다. *ee eetbaree apum-needa*
I've lost a filling/tooth.	봉이/이빨이 빠졌습니다. *pawng-ee/eetbaree bajo-ssumneeda*
Can you repair this denture?	이 틀니를 수리해 주시겠습니까? *ee tullee-rul sooree-he choosee-ge-ssumneekka*
I don't want it extracted.	저는 그 이빨을 뽑고 싶지 않습니다. *cho-nun ku eetbarul bawp-gaw seep-chee an-ssumneeda*

주사/국소마취주사 놓겠습니다.	I'm going to give you an injection/ a local anesthetic.
봉을 박겠습니다/이를 씌우겠습니다/크라운을 하겠습니다.	You need a filling/cap/crown.
그것을 뽑아야겠습니다.	I'll have to take it out.
그것을 임시로만 고칠 수 있습니다.	I can only fix it temporarily.
... 시간동안 아무 것도 먹지 마십시오.	Don't eat anything for ... hours.

Payment and insurance 계산과 보험

How much do I owe you?	얼마 내야 합니까? *olma neya ham-neekka*
I have insurance.	저는 보험이 있습니다. *cho-nun pawhom-ee ee-ssumneeda*
Can I have a receipt for my health insurance?	의료보험용 영수증을 주시겠습니까? *ueeryo pawhom-yong yong-soo-jung-ul choosege-ssumneekka*
Would you fill out this health insurance form, please?	이 의료보험 용지를 작성해 주시겠습니까? *ee ueeryo pawhom yong-jeerul chaksong-he choosege-ssumneekka*

MAKING APPOINTMENTS ➤ 161

To enable correct usage, most terms in this dictionary are either followed by an expression or cross-referenced to pages where the word appears in a phrase. The notes below provide some basic grammar guidelines.

Nouns

Korean nouns have no articles (a, an, the) and no plural forms. Whether the noun is singular or plural is judged from the context, or by a number modifying the noun:

pyo	ticket
pyo se-jang	three tickets

Adjectives

Adjectives are usually placed in front of the noun (➤ 15).

Verbs/Levels of politeness

Korean has various levels of politeness depending on who you are talking to. For example, when having a drink with a close friend you use a very different style to that you would use when addressing a meeting or talking to somebody for the first time. The level of politeness is shown principally by the verb ending. Although English has formal and informal styles of speech, it does not have the same all-inclusive Korean system of verb endings indicating degrees of politeness.

For example, the verb stem **ka-** ("to go") with the addition of the polite sentence ending **-m-nee-da** – **kam-nee-da** – has the meaning "I go, he/she goes, we go, they go," depending on the context. There is no need to specify *who* is going. If, however, you are talking about a friend then a different familiar form is used.

The phrases in this book follow the **-m-nee-da** style of polite speech, as this is the form you are most likely to need.

an ("no/not") is added in front of the verb to indicate negation:

Sine-e kam-nee-da.	[I] am going to town.
Sine-e an kam-nee-da.	[I] am not going to town.

(Question formation ➤ 12.)

Word order

In Korean the main verb always comes at the *end* of the sentence. So the sentence above reads literally: "to town am going" (➤ 16 for additional information).

a few of 조금 *chaw-gum* 15

a little 조금 *chaw-gum* 15

a lot of 많이 *manee* 15

a.m. 오전 *awjon*

about *(approximately)* 약 *yak* 15

abroad 외국에 *wegoo-ge*

accept, to 받다 *patda* 136

access 접근 *chobgun*

accident *(road)* 사고 *sa-gaw* 92, 152; **accidentally** 실수로 *seelssoo-raw* 28

accompany, to 같이 가다 *kachee kada* 65

accountant 회계사 *hwegesa* 121

acne 여드름 *yodurum*

acrylic 아크릴 *akureel*

actor/actress 남자배우/여배우 *namjabe-oo/yobe-oo*

adaptor 어댑터 *odepto* 26, 148

address 주소 *choosaw* 84, 93, 126

adjoining room 붙어있는 방 *pooto-eennun pang* 22

admission charge 입장료 *eep-jang-nyo* 114

adult 어른 *orun* 81, 100

after *(place)* 지나서 *cheena-so* 95
(time) 후 *hoo* 13

after shave 아프터셰이브 로션 *aputo sye-eebu law-syon* 142

after-sun lotion 아프터선 로션 *aputo-son law-syon* 142

afternoon, in the 오후에 *awhoo-e* 221

aged, to be 살이다 *sal-eeda* 152

ago 전에 *jone* 221

agree: I don't agree 동의 안합니다 *tawng-vee anhamneeda*

air conditioning 에어컨 *eokon* 22, 25

air mail 항공우편 *hang-gawng-oopyon* 155

air pump 공기펌프 *kawng-gee-pompu* 87

airport 공항 *kawng-hang* 96

aisle seat 복도쪽 자리 *pawk-daw-zawk charee* 69, 74

alarm clock 자명종 *cha-myong-jawng* 149

alcoholic *(drink)* 주류 *chooryoo*

all-night pharmacy 24시간 하는 약국 *ee-seep sa-seegan hanun yakgook* 140

all 모두 *mawdoo*

allergic, to be 알레르기가 있다 *alle-rugee-ga eetda* 164, 165

allergy 알레르기 *allerugee*

allowance 허용한도 *hoyong-handaw* 67

almost 거의 *ko-uee*

alone 혼자 *hawnja*

already 이미 *eemee* 28

also 또한 *daw-han*

alter, to 수선하다 *sooson-hada* 137

alumin(i)um foil 알루미늄 호일 *alloo-mee-nyoom haw-eel* 148

always 항상 *hang-sang* 13

am: I am ... 저는 ... 입니다 *cho-nun ... eemneeda*

amazing 놀라운 *nawlla-oon* 101

ambassador 대사 *tesa*

ambulance 구급차 *koo-gup-cha* 92

American 미국 *mee-gook* 150, 152

American Plan (A.P.) 하루 세끼 포함 *haroo sekgee paw-ham* 24

amount 금액 *kumek* 42

amusement arcade 오락실 *awrak-seel* 113

anaesthetic 마취제 *machweeje*

and 그리고 *kureegaw*

animal 동물 *tawng-mool* 106

anorak 아노락 *anawrak*

another 다른 *tarun* 21, 125

antacid 제산제 *chesanje*

antibiotics 항생제 *hang-seng-je* 165

antifreeze 부동액 *poodawng-ek*

antique 골동품 *kawl-dawng-poom* 157;
~ **shop** 골동품가게 *kawl-tawng-poom kage* 130

antiseptic 소독약 *sawdawk-yak* 165;
~ **cream** 소독용 크림 *sawdawk-yong kureem* 141

anyone: does anyone speak English?
영어 하시는 분 계십니까?
yong-o haseenun boon keseemneekka

anything else? 더 필요한 것
없으십니까? *to peeryohan kot opsuseemneekka*

apartment 아파트 *apatu* 28, 123

apologize: I apologize 사과합니다
sagwahamneeda

appendicitis 맹장염 *meng-jang-nyom* 165

appendix 맹장 *meng-jang* 166

appetite 식욕 *seegyok* 164

apple 사과 *sagwa*

appointment 약속/예약
yaksawk/yeyak

approximately 대략 *te-ryak* 152

April 사월 *sa-wol* 218

architect 건축가 *konchook-ga* 104

are there ...? ... 있습니까?
... *ee-ssumneekka/*

arm 팔 *pal* 166

around (time) 쯤 *zum* 13

arrive, to 도착하다 *tawchak-hada*
68, 70, 71, 76

art gallery 미술관 *mee-sool-gwan* 99

arthritis, to have 관절염이 있다
kwan-jol-lyomee eetda 163

artificial sweetener 감미료 *kam-meeryo* 38

artist 화가 *hwga* 104

ashtray 재떨이 *chetdoree* 39

ask: I asked for ... 저는 ... 시켰습니다
cho-nun ... seekyo-ssumneeda 41

aspirin (물에 녹는) 아스피린
asu-peereen 141

asthma, to have 천식이
있다
chonseegee eetda 163

at (place) 에 *e* 12; (time)
에 *e* 13

at last! 드디어! *tu-dee-o* 19

at least 적어도 *cho-godaw* 23

athletics 육상경기 *yook-sang gyong-gee* 114

ATM 현금 자동 인출기 *hyon-gum chadawng een-chool-gee* 139

attack 폭행 *pawkeng* 152

attractive 매력적인 *meryok-chogeen*

audioguide 녹음안내 *nawgum anne* 100

August 팔월 *pal-wol* 218

aunt 고모 *kaw-maw* 120

Australian (person) 호주(사람)
haw-joo (saram) 119

Australia 호주 *haw-joo* 119

authentic: is it authentic? 이것 진짜입
니까? *eegot cheenza-eemneekka*

authenticity 감정 *kamjong* 157

automatic (car) 오토매틱 차 *aw-taw-me-teek cha* 86; (camera) 자동
(사진기) *chadawng (sajeen-gee)* 151

automobile 자동차 *chadawngcha*

autumn 가을 *ka-ul* 219

avalanche 눈사태 *noonsate*

awful 엉망인 *ong-mang-een* 101;
나쁜 *natbun* 122

B **baby** 아기 *agee* 39, 113, 162;
~ **food** 이유식 *ee-yoo-seek* 142;
~ **wipes** 아기용 물휴지 *agee-yong mool-hyoo-jee* 142; ~**sitter** 애보는
사람 *e-bawnun saram* 113

back (part of body) 등 *tung* 166;
~**ache** 요통 *yo-tawng* 163

backpacking 배낭여행 *penang-yoheng*

bad 나쁜 *napbun* 14

bag 가방 *gabang* 67

baggage 짐 *cheem* 32, 69, 71; ~ **check** 짐보관소 *cheem baw-gwan-saw* 73; ~ **reclaim** 짐 찾는 곳 *cheem channun-kawt* 71

bakery 빵집 *bang-jeep* 130

balcony 발코니 *pal-kawnee* 29

ball 공 *kawng* 157

ballet 발레공연 *palle gawng-yon* 108

band (*musical*) 악단 *akdan* 111; 그룹 *guroop* 157

bank 은행 *unheng* 130, 138 ~ **card** 은행 카드 *unheng kadu* 139

bar 바 *pa* 26, 112

barber 이발소 173 *eebalsaw*

basement 지하실 *cheehaseel*

basket 바구니 *pagoonee* 158

basketball 농구 *nawng-goo* 114

bath 욕조 *yokzaw* 21 ~ **towel** 욕실 수건 *yoksel soogon* 27

bathroom (*toilet*) 화장실 *hwajang-seel* 26; (*with tub*) 욕실 *yoksel* 29

battery 전지 *kon-jon-jee* 137, 151; 바테리 *pateree* 88

battle site 전적지 *chon-jok-zee* 99

be, to 있다 *eetda* 17

beach 해변 *he-byon* 116

beard 턱수염 *toksooyom*

beautiful 아름다운 *arum-daoon* 101; 예쁜 *yepbun* 14

because 때문이다 *demoon-eeda* 15 ~ **of** 때문에 *demoone* 15

bed 침대 *cheemde* 21; ~ **and breakfast** 아침식사 포함 *acheem-seeksa paw-ham* 24

bedding 침구 *cheem-goo* 29

bedroom 침실 *cheemseel* 29

beer 맥주 *mekjoo* 40

before (*time*) 전에 *jone* 13, 221

begin, to 시작하다 *seejakada*

beginner 초보자 *chaw-baw-ja* 117

beige 베이지 *pe-ee-jee* 143

belong: this belongs to me 이것은 제 것입니다 *eego-sun che koseemneeda*

belt 벨트 *peltu* 144

berth 침대 *cheemde* 74, 77

best 가장 좋은 *kajang chaw-un*

better 더 좋은 *to chaw-un* 134

between (*time*) 사이에 *saee-e* 221

bib 턱받이 *tokpajee*

bicycle 자전거 *chajon-go* 75, 83, 153

bidet 비데 *beede*

big 큰 *kun* 14, 117, 134; **bigger** 더 큰 *to kun* 24

bill 계산서 *kesanso* 32, 42

bin liner 쓰레기 봉지 *ssuregee pawngjee*

binoculars 쌍안경 *ssang-an-gyong*

bird 새 *se* 106

birthday 생일 *seng-eel* 219

biscuits 쿠키 *kookee* 160

bite (*insect*) 벌레 물린데 *polle moolleen-de*

bitter 쓴 *ssun* 41

black 검은 *komun* 143; ~ **and white film** (*camera*) 흑백 필림 *hukpek peelleem* 151; ~ **coffee** 블랙 커피 *pullek kopee* 40

bladder 방광 *pang-gwang* 166

blanket 담요 *tam-nyo* 27

bleach 표백제 *pyo-bek-che* 148

bleeding 출혈 *chool-hyol* 162

blind (*n*) 차양 *chayang* 25

blister 물집 *mool-jeep* 162

blocked, to be 막혀 있다 *makyo eetda* 25

blood 혈액 *hyorek* 164; ~ **group** 혈액형 *hyorekhyong*; ~ **pressure** 혈압 *hyorap* 164

blouse 블라우스 *pulla-oosu* 144

blow-dry 드라이 *tura-ee* 147

blue 파란 *paran* 143

boarding card 보딩 카드 *pawdeeng kadu* 70

boat 보트 *bawtu* 81; **~ trip** 보트관광 *bawtu kwan-gwang* 81, 97

boil 종기 *chawng-gee* 162

boiled 삶은 *salmun*

boiler 보일러 *paw-eel-lo* 29

bone 뼈 *byo* 166

book 책 *chek* 150; **~ store** 서점 *sojom* 150

booked up, to be 만원이다 *manwon-eeda* 115

booked: fully booked 예약이 꽉 차 있는 *yeyagee gwak cha eennun* 161

boots 부츠 *poo-chu* 145

boring 따분한 *daboon-han* 101

born: I was born in 저는 ... 에서 태어났습니다 *cho-nun ... eso te-onassumneeda*

botanical garden 식물원 *seeng-mool-won* 99

bottle 병 *pyong* 37, 159; **~ of wine** 포도주 한병 *pawdaw-joo han-pyong* 156; **~ opener** 병따개 *pyong-dage* 148

bottled (*beer*) 병맥주 *pyong-mekjoo* 40

bowel 내장 *nejang*

box of chocolates 초콜렛 한 상자 *chaw-kawllet han-sangja* 156

boy 남자애 *namja-e* 120, 157

boyfriend 애인 *e-een* 120

bra 브래지어 *pure-jee-o* 144

bracelet 팔찌 *palzee* 149

bread 빵 *bang* 38

break, to 고장나다 *kawjang-nada* 28

break-in 주거침입 *choogo-cheemeep* 153

breakdown truck 견인차 *kyon-een-cha* 88

breakfast 아침식사 *acheem-seeksa* 26, 27

breast 유방 *yoo-bang* 166

breathe, to 숨쉬다 *soom sweeda* 92

bridge 다리 *taree* 107

bring, to (*a friend*) 데려오다 *teryo-awda* 125

Britain 영국 *yong-gook* 119

British 영국 *yong-gook* 152

brochure 브로셔 *purawsyo*

broken, to be 고장난 *kawjang-nan* 25, 137; (*bone*) 뼈가 부러지다 *(byo-ga) pooro-jeeda* 164

bronchitis 기관지염 *keegwanjeeyom*

brooch 브로치 *puraw-chee* 149

brown 갈색 *kalsek* 143

browse, to 둘러보다 *toollo-bawda* 133

bruise 멍 *mong* 162

building 건물 *konmool* 104

built, to be 세워지다 *sewo-jeeda*

bulletin board 안내판 *anne-pan* 26

bureau de change 환전소 *hwan-jon-saw* 138

burger 햄버거 *hembogo* 40; **~ stand** 햄버거집 *hembogo-jeep* 35

burn 화상 *hwa-sang* 162

bus (시내)버스 *(seene)posu* 70, 78; **~ route** 버스노선 *posu nawson* 96; **~ stop** 버스 정거장 *posu chong-gojang* 65, 96

business 사업 *sa-op* 121; **~ class** 비지니스석 *peejee-neesu-sok* 68; **~ trip** 출장 *chool-jang* 123; **on ~** 사업상 *saop-sang* 66

busy 만원 *manwon* 36

butane gas 부탄가스 *pootan-gasu* 30

butcher shop 정육점 *chong-yook-jom* 130

butter 버터 *poto* 38, 160

button 단추 *tanchoo*

buy, to 사다 *sada* 67, 98, 125

by (*near*) 옆에 *yope* 36; (*time*) 에 *e* 221; **~ bus** 버스로 *posu-raw* 123; **~ car** 차로 *cha-raw* 17, 94, 123;

~ cash 현금으로 hyon-gum-uraw 17; **~ credit card** 신용 카드로 seen-yong kadu-raw 17; **~ ferry** 배로 peraw 123; **~ plane** 비행기로 peeheng-gee-raw 123; **~ train** 기차로 keecha-raw 123

bye! 안녕히 계세요(when you're leaving) annyonghee keseyo; 가세요 (to s.o. leaving) annyonghee kaseyo

C **cabin** 선실 sonseel 81

cable TV 유선방송 yooson pang-sawng 22

café 카페 kape 35

cake 케이크 ke-eeku 40

calendar 달력 tal-lyok 156

call, to 부르다 pooruda 92; 전화하다 chonhwa-hada 128; **~ collect** 콜렉트콜로 걸다 kawllekt-kawl-law kolda 127; **call the police!** 경찰을 부르다 koyng-charul pooruda 92

camera 사진기 sajeen-gee 151, 153; **~ case** 사진기 케이스 sajeen-gee ke-ee-su 151; **~ store** 사진기 가게 sajeen-gee kage 130

camp, to 야영하다 kempeenghada

campbed 캠핑용 침대 kempeeng-yong cheemde 31

camping 캠핑 kempeeng 30

campsite 캠핑장 kempeeng-jang 30

can I 할 수 있습니까? hal-soo ee-ssumneekka 18; **can I/we have ...?** ... 주시겠습니까? ... chooseege-ssumneekka 18; **can you help me?** 도와주시겠습니까? taw-wa chooseege-ssumneekka 18

can opener 통조림따개 tawng-jawreem-dage 148

Canadian (person) 캐나다(사람) kenada (saram) 119

Canada 캐나다 kenada 119

cancel, to 취소하다 chweesaw-hada 68

cancer (disease) 암 am

candles 양초 yang-chaw 148

candy 사탕 satang 150

cap (dental) 이를 씌움 ee-rul ssee-oom 168

car 자동차 cha-dawng-cha 86, 88, 89, 90–91; **~ ferry** 카페리 ka-peree 81; **~ hire** 차렌트 cha-rentu 70; **~ park** 주차장 choocha-jang 26, 87, 96 **~ rental** 차렌트 cha-rentu 70; **by ~** 차로 cha-raw 95

caravan 카라반 karaban 30

card (credit) (신용) 카드 (seen-yong) kadu 139

cards 카드놀이 kadu-nawree 121

careful: be careful! 조심 하세요! chawseemhaseyo

carpet (rug) 카페트 kapetu

carrier bag 봉지 pawngjee

carry-cot 여행용 아기침대 yoheng-yong ageecheemde

cart 손수레 sawnsoore 158

carton 팩 pek 159

cases 가방 gabang 69

cash 현금 hyon-gum 136; **~ desk** 계산대 kesande 132, 136; **~ machine** 현금 자동 인출기 hyon-gum chadawng een-chool-gee 139

cash, to 현금으로 바꾸다 hyon-gum-uraw pakgooda 138

cashier 계산대 kesande 132

casino 카지노 kasee-naw 112

cassette 카세트 테이프 casetu te-ee-pu 157

castle 성 song 99

catch, to (bus) 타다 tada

cathedral 성당 song-dang 99

Catholic 카톨릭 ka-tawl-leek 105

cave 동굴 tawng-gool 107

CD 시디 seedee; **~-player** 시디 플레이어 seedee pulle-eeo

cemetery 공동묘지 *kawng-dawng myo-jee* 99

center (of town) 시내 *seene* 21

central heating 중앙난방 *choong-ang nanbang*

ceramics 도자기 *tawjagee*

certificate 보증서 *pawjung-so* 149; 증명서 *chung-myong-so* 157

chain 줄 *chool* 149

change (coins) 잔돈 *chandawn* 87, 136; **keep the change** 거스름돈 가지세요 *kosurum-dawn kajeeseyo* 84

change, to (bus) 갈아타다 *kara-tada* 78, 79; (money) 바꾸다 *pakgooda* 138; (reservation) 변경하다 *pyon-gyong-hada* 68; (train) 갈아타다 *kara-tada* 75, 76, 80

changing facilities 기저귀 가는 시설 *keejo-gee kanun seesol* 113

charcoal 숯 *soot* 31

charge 요금 *yogum* 30, 115, 155

charter flight 전세 비행기 *chonse peehenggee*

cheap 싼 *ssan* 14, 74, 134; **cheaper** 더 싼 *do ssan* 21, 24, 109, 134

check in, to 탑승수속하다 *tapsung-soosawk-hada* 68

check out, to 체크아웃하다 *cheku-aootada*

check-in desk 탑승수속대 *tapsung-soosawk-de* 69

check [cheque] book 수표책 *soopyochek*

checkout 계산대 *kesande* 158

cheers! 건배 *konbe*

cheese 치즈 *cheeju* 160

chemist 약국 *yakgook* 131

chess 체스 *chesu* 121; (Korean) 바둑 *padook* 121

chest 가슴 *kasum* 166

chewing gum 껌 *gom* 150

child(ren) 어린이 *oreenee* 22, 24, 39, *41*, 74, 100, 113; 아이 *a-ee* 81, 152; **children's meals** 어린이 용 식사 *oreenee-yong seeksa* 39; **child seat** 어린이용 의자 *oreenee-yong ueeja* 39

childminder 애보는 사람 *ebawnun saram*

China 중국 *choong-gook* 119

Chinese 중국(음식) *choong-gook (umseek)* 35, 119

chips 감자튀김 *kamja-tweegeem* 160

chocolate bar 초콜렛 *chaw-kawl-let* 150

chopsticks 젓가락 *chotgarak* 148

Christmas 크리스마스/성탄절 *kurees-umasu/song-tan-jol* 219

church 교회 *kyo-hwe* 96, 99, 105

cigarettes, packet of 담배 *tambe* 150; **cigarette kiosk** 담배 가게 *tambe kage* 130

cigars 시가 *seega* 150

cinema 영화관 *yong-hwa-gwan* 96, 110

claim check 짐표 *cheem-pyo* 71

clean (adj) 깨끗한 *getgutan* 14, 39, 41

clean, to 세탁하다 *setak-hada* 137

clearance 특별 가격 *tukpyol kagyok* 133

cliff 절벽 *chol-byok* 107

cling film 랩 *lep* 148

clinic 병원 *pyong-won* 131

cloakroom 휴대품 보관소 *hyoode-poom paw-gwan-saw* 109

clock 시계 *seege* 149

close (near) 가까운 *katga-oon* 95

close, to 닫다 *tatda* 132, 140

clothes pins [pegs] 빨래집게 *balle-cheepke* 148

clothing store [clothes shop] 옷 가게 *awtgage* 130

cloudy, to be 흐리다 *huree-da* 122

clubs (golf) 골프채 kawl-pu-che 115

coach (bus) 장거리버스 chang-goree posu 78; ~ station 고속버스 터미날 kawsawk-posu tomeenal 78

coach [car] (train compartment) 차 cha 75

coast 해안 he-an

coat 코트 kawtu 144; ~check 휴대품 보관소 hyoode-poom paw-gwan-saw 109; ~hanger 양복걸이 yangbawk-koree

cockroach 바퀴벌레 pakweebolle

code (area, dialling) 지역번호 cheeyokponhaw

coffee 커피 kopee 40

coin 동전 tawng-jon

cold (adj) 식은/찬 seegun/chan 14, 41; 추운 choo-oon 122

cold (n) 감기 kam-gee 141, 163

collapse: he's collapsed 그 사람 실신 했습니다 ku saram seelseen-hessumneeda

collect, to 찾다 chatda 151

color 색 sek 134, 143; ~ film (camera) 칼라 필림 kalla peelleem 151

colored 염색 yomsek 147

comb 빗 peet 142

come back 다시 오다 tasee awda 36

compact (camera) 소형(사진기) saw-hyung (sajeen-gee) 151

compact disc 시디 see-dee 157

company (business) 회사 hwesa; (companionship) 동행 tawng-heng 126

compartment (train) 차량 charyang

composer 작곡가 chak-gawk-ga 111

computer 컴퓨터 kompyooto

concert 음악회 umak-hwe 108; ~ hall 연주회장 yonjoo-hwe-jang 111

concession 할인 hareen

conditioner 린스/컨디셔너 leensu/kondee-syono 142

condoms 콘돔 kawn-dawm 141

conductor 지휘자 chee-hwee-ja 111

confirm, to (reservation) 확인하다 hwag-een-hada 22, 68

confirmation 확인 hwag-een 22

congratulations! 축하합니다! chooka ham-needa 219

connection 갈아타는 기차 kara-tanun keecha 76

conscious: he's conscious 그 사람 의식이 있습니다 ku saram ueesee-gee eessumneeda

constipation 변비 pyonbee

consulate 영사관 yong-sa-gwan 152

consult, to 진찰받다 cheen-chal-batda 165

contact, to 연락하다 yollak-hada 28

contact lens 콘택트 렌즈 kawn-tektu lenju 167

contagious, to be 전염되다 chon-yom-dweda 165

contain, to 들어 있다 turo eetda 155; 있다 eetda 39, 69

contemporary dance 현대 무용 hyon-de mooyong 111

contraceptive 피임약 pee-eemyak

cook, to 요리하다 yoreehada

cook (n) 요리사 yoreesa

cookies 쿠키 kookee 160

cooking (cuisine) 요리 yoree

coolbox 아이스 박스 aeesu pax

copper 구리 kooree 149

corkscrew 마개뽑기 mage-bawpgee 148

corner 코너 kawno 95

correct 맞는 mannun

cosmetics 화장품 hwajangpoom

cost, to 비용이 들다 peeyong-ee dulda 98

cot 아기용 침대 agee-yong cheemde 22

cotton 면 *myon* 145; **cotton [wool]** 솜 *sawm* 141

cough (n) 기침 *gee-cheem* 141

cough, to 기침하다 *keecheem-hada* 164

could I have ...? ... 주시겠습니까? ... *chooseege-ssumneekka* 18

country (nation) 나라 *nara*

country music 민속 음악 *meen-sawk umak* 111

courier (guide) 가이드 *kaeedu*

course (meal) 코스 *kawsu*

cousin 사촌 *sachawn*

craft shop 공예품점 *kawng-yepoomjom*

crèche 탁아소 *tagasaw*

credit card 신용카드 *seen-yong kadu* 42, 136, 153; **~ number** 신용카드 번호 *seen-yong-kadu ponhaw* 109

crib (n) 아기용 침대 *agee-yong cheemde* 22

crisps 감자칩 *kamja-cheep* 160

crockery 그릇 *kurut* 29

cross (crucifix) 십자가 *seepjaga*

cross, to (road) 건너다 *konnoda* 95

crossroad 교차로 *kyo-cha-raw* 95

crowded 혼잡한 *hawnjap-han* 31

crown (dental) 크라운 *kura-oon* 168

cruise (n) 선상유람 *sonsangyooram*

crutches 목발 *mawkpal*

crystal 수정 *soojong* 149

cup 컵 *kop* 39, 148

cupboard 찬장 *chanzang*

currency 돈 *tawn* 67, 138; **~ exchange** 환전소 *hwan-jon-saw* 70, 73, 138

curtains 커튼 *kotun*

customer service 고객 서비스 *kawgek sobeesu* 133

customs 세관 *segwan* 157; **~ declaration** 통관 신고서 *tawng-gwan seen-gaw-so* 155

cut 벰 *pem* 162; **cut and blow-dry** 커트와 드라이 *kotu-wa tura-ee* 147

cut glass 세공유리 *segawng yooree* 149

cutlery 나이프와 포크 *naeepu-wa pawku* 29

cycle route 자전거길 *chajon-go geel* 106

cycling 자전거경주 *chajon-go gyong-joo* 114

cystitis 방광염 *pang-gwang-nyom* 165

D **daily** 매일 *me-eel*

damaged, to be 망가지다 *mang-gajeeda* 28; 손상되다 *sawn-sang-dweda* 71

damp (n/adj) 습기/습한 *supkee/suphan*

dance, to 춤추다 *choomchooda* 111

dancing, to go 춤추러 가다 *choom chooro kada* 124

dangerous 위험한 *weehomhan*

dark 어두운 *odoo-oon* 14, 24, 134, 143; **darker** 더 어두운 *to odoo-oon* 143

daughter 딸 *dal* 120, 162

dawn 새벽 *sebyok* 221

day (unit) 하루 *haroo* 97

day trip 당일치기 여행 *tang-eelcheegee yoheng*

dead (battery) 나가다 *nagada* 88

deaf, to be 귀가 멀다 *gwee-ga molda* 163

December 십이월 *seep-ee-wol* 218

deck chair 접는 의자 *chom-nun ueeja* 116

declare, to 신고하다 *seen-gaw-hada* 67

deduct, to (money) 빼다 *beda*

deep 깊은 *keepun*; **~ freeze** 냉동 저장 *nengdawng chojang*

defrost, to 녹이다 *nawgeeda*

degrees (temperature) 도 *taw*

delay 지연 *chee-yon* 70

delicatessen 델리카테슨 *dellee-katesun* 158

deliver, to 배달하다 *pedalhada*

dental floss 치실 *cheeseel*

dentist 치과의사 *cheetgwa vee-sa* 131, 161

dentures 틀니 *tullee* 168

deodorant 탈취제 *tal-chwee-je* 142

depart, to (train, bus) 출발하다 *choolbalhada*

department store 백화점 *pek-wa-jom* 130

departure lounge 출발 라운지 *choolbal laoon-jee* 69

deposit 보증금 *pawjung-gum* 24, 83; (security) 보증금 *pawjung-gum* 115

describe, to 묘사하다 *myosa-hada* 152

destination 목적지 *mawkzokzee*

details 세부사항 *seboosahang*

detergent 세제 *seje* 148

detour 우회로 *oo-hwe-raw* 96

develop, to (photos) 현상하다 *hyon-sang-hada* 151

diabetes 당뇨병 *tangnyoppyong*

diabetic, to be 당뇨병이다 *tang-nyo-byong-eeda* 39, 163

diagnosis 진단 *cheendan* 164

dialling [area] code 지역번호 *cheeyok-ponhaw* 127

diamond 다이아몬드 *ta-ee-a-mawndu* 149

diapers 기저귀 *keejo-gee* 142

diarrhea 설사 *sol-ssa* 141

dice 주사위 *choosawee*

dictionary 사전 *sajon* 150

diesel 디젤 *deejel* 87

diet: I'm on a diet 식이요법 중입니다 *seegeeyoppop choong-eemneeda*

difficult 어려운 *oryo-oon* 14

dining car 식당차 *seektang-cha* 75, 77

dining room 식당 *seek-dang* 26, 29

dinner jacket 정장 *chongjang*

dinner, to have 저녁식사를 하다 *cho-nyok seeksarul hada* 124

direct (train) 직행 *cheekeng* 75

direct, to 길을 가리키다 *kee-rul karee-keeda*

direction: in the ~ of 방향에 *pang-hyang-e* 95

director (of company) 이사 *eesa*

directory (telephone) 전화번호부 *chonhwaponhawboo*; ~ enquiries 전화번화 안내 *chonhwa-bonhaw anne* 127

dirty 더러운 *toro-oon* 14, 28

disabled (n) 장애자 *chang-eja* 22, 100

discotheque 디스코텍 *deesukaw-tek* 112

discount (reduction) 할인 *hareen* 24, 74, 100

dish (meal) 음식 *umseek* 37

dish cloth 행주 *heng-joo* 148

dishwashing detergent 식기용 세제 *seekgee-yong seje* 148

dislocated, to be 탈구되다 *talgoo-dweda* 164

display cabinet 진열대 *cheen-yol-de* 149

disposable (camera) 일회용(사진기) *eelhwe-yong (sajeen-gee)* 151

distilled water 증류수 *chungryoosoo*

disturb: don't disturb 방해 하지 마십시오 *panghehajee maseepseeaw*

dive, to 다이빙하다 *taee-beeng-hada* 116

diversion 우회로 *oo-hwe-raw* 96

divorced, to be 이혼하다 *eehawn hada* 120

dizzy: I feel dizzy 어지럽습니다 *ojeeropsumneeda*

do: things to do 할만한 거 *hal manhan-go* 123

do you accept ...? ... 받습니까? *... pa-ssumneekka* 136

emerald 에메랄드 *emeraldu*

emergency 급한 일 *kuphan eel* 127; **~ exit** 비상구 *peesang-goo* 132

enamel 에나멜 *enamel* 149

end: at the end 끝에 *gute* 95

engine 엔진 *enjeen*

engineering 엔지니어링 *enjeen-eeo-eel* 121

English (adj.) 영국 *yong-gook* 150

English (language) 영어 *yong-o* 11, 67, 110, 150, 152, 161; **~-speaking** 영어하는 *yong-o-hanun* 152; **~-speaking guide** 영어안내 *yong-o anne* 98

enjoy, to 재미있다 *chemee-eetda* 110, 123

enough 충분히 *choong-boon-ee* 15

ensuite bathroom 욕실달린 방 *yokseel-dalleen pang*

entertainment guide 여흥 안내 *yohung anne*

entrance fee 입장료 *eep-zang-nyo* 100

entry visa 입국비자 *eepkkookpeeja*

envelope 편지 봉투 *pyon-jee pawng-too* 150

epileptic, to be 간질병이다 *kanjeel-byong eeda* 163

equipment (sports) 장비 *chang-bee* 115

error 실수 *seelsoo*

escalator 에스컬레이터 *esukol-le-eeto* 132

essential 꼭 필요한 *gawk peeryo-han* 89

EU 유럽연합 *yoorop yonhap*

Eurocheque 유로체크 *yoorawcheku*

evening, in the 저녁에 *cho-nyog-e* 221

evening dress 정장 *chong-jang* 112

events 행사 *hengsa* 108

every: ~ day 매일 *me-eel;* **~ hour** 매시간마다 *me-seegan-mada* 76; **~ week** 매 주 *me choo* 13

examination (medical) 검사 *komsa*

example, for 보기 *pawgee*

except 외에 *we-e*

excess baggage 짐 초과 *cheem chaw-gwa* 69

exchange, to 바꾸다 *pakgooda* 137, 138

exchange rate 환율 *hwan-nyool* 138

excluding meals 식사 제외 *seeksa chewe* 24

excursion 일일 여행 *eereel yoheng* 97

excuse me (apology) 미안합니다! *meean-hamneeda* 10; (attention) 여보세요! *yobaw-seyo* 10; (pardon?) 뭐라 하셨습니까? *moo-o-ra hasyo-ssumeekka* 11

exit 출구 *chool-goo* 132

expected, to be 기대되다 *keede-dweda*

expensive 비싼 *pee-ssan* 14, 134

expiration [expiry] date 만기 *man-gee* 109

exposure (photos) 방 *pang* 151

express 속달 *sawktal* 155

extension 교환 *kyo-hwan* 128

extra (adj) 하나 *hana* to 27; **~ night** 하룻밤 더 *haroop-bam to* 23

extract, to (tooth) 뽑다 *bawpda* 168

eye 눈 *noon* 166

F **fabric** 천 *chon* 145
face 얼굴 *ol-gool* 166
facial 얼굴마사지 *olgool-massajee* 147

facilities 시설 *seesol* 22, 30

fairground 행사장 *heng-sa-jang* 113

fall 가을 *ka-ul* 219

family 가족 *kajawk* 66, 74, 120, 167

famous 유명한 *yoomenghan*

fan (air) 선풍기 *sonpoong-gee* 25

far- [long-] sighted 원시 *wonsee* 167

far: how far is it? 얼마나 멉니까? *olmana momneekka* 73

farm 농장 *nawng-jang* 107

fast 빨리 *ballee* 93; (clock) 빠르다 *baruda* 221; ~ **food restaurant** 패스트푸드 음식점 *pest-poodu umseek-zom* 35

fat 지방 *cheebang* 39

father 아버지 *abo-jee* 120

faucet 수도꼭지 *soodaw gawk-zee* 25

faulty: this is faulty 이것 결함이 있습니다 *eegot kyolha-mee eessumneeda*

favorite 매우 좋아하는 *meoo chaw-ahanun*

fax 팩스 *peksu* 155

February 이월 *ee-wol* 218

feed, to 먹이다 *mogeeda* 39

feeding bottle 젖병 *choppyong*

feel ill, to 아프다 *apuda* 163

female 여자 *yoja* 152

feverish, to feel 열이 나다 *yoree nada* 163

few 조금 *chaw-gum* 15

fiancé/e 약혼자/약혼녀 *yakhawnja/yakhawnnyo*

field 들판 *tulpan* 107

fifteen 십오(열다섯) *seep-aw(yol-tasot)* 216

fifth 다섯째 *tasot-ze* 217

fifty 오십(쉰) *aw-seep(sween)* 216

fight (brawl) 싸움 *ssaoom*

fill in, to (a form) 작성하다 *chaksong-hada* 155, 168

filling (dental) 봉 *pawng* 168

film (camera) 필름 *peelleem* 151; (movie) 영화 *yong-hwa* 108, 110

filter 필터 *peelto* 151

find, to 찾다 *chatda* 18

fine (excellent) 좋은 *chaw-un* 19, 125; **fine, thank you** 잘 지냅니다 *chal cheenem-needa* 19

fine (penalty) 벌금 *polgum* 93

finger 손가락 *sawn-garak* 166

fire: there's a fire! 불이야! *pooreeya!*; ~ **alarm** 화재 경보 *hwaje kyongbaw*; ~ **department [brigade]** 소방소 *sawbang-saw* 92; ~ **escape** 화재 비상구 *hwaje peesanggoo*; ~ **extinguisher** 소화기 *saw-hwagee*; ~**wood** 장작 *changjak*

first 첫 *chot* 68, 76; 첫째 *chot-ze* 217; ~ **[ground] floor** 일층 *eel-chung* 132; ~ **class** 일등석 *eeldung-sok* 68; (train) 특실 *tukseel* 74

fish 생선 *seng-son; ~ **restaurant** 생선 요리 음식점 *sengson-yoree umseekzom* 35; ~ **store [fishmonger]** 생선 가게 *seng-son kage* 130

fit, to (clothes) (옷이) 맞다 *(aw-see) matda* 146

fitting room 탈의실 *taluee-seel* 146

five 오(다섯) *aw(tasot)* 216

fix, to 고치다 *kaw-cheeda* 168

flashlight 후레시 *hooresee* 31

flat [puncture] 펑크 *pong-ku* 83, 88

flea 벼룩 *pyorook*

flight 비행기 *peeheng-gee* 68, 70; ~ **number** 호기 *haw-gee* 68

flip-flops 고무 슬리퍼 *kawmoo sullee-po* 145

floor (level) 층 *chung* 132

florist 꽃가게 *gawtgage* 130

flour 밀가루 *meel-garoo* 39

flu 독감 *tawkkam* 165

flush: the toilet won't flush 화장실 물이 나오지 않습니다 *hwajangseel moo-ree na-awjee anssumneeda*

fly (insect) 파리 *paree*

folk art 민속 예술 *meensawk yesool*

folk music 민속 음악 *meen-sawk umak* 111

follow, to 따라가다 *dara-gada* 95

A-Z

food 음식 *umseek* 39, 41, 119; ~ **poisoning** 식중독 *seek-choong-dawk* 165

foot 발 *pal* 166; ~ **path** 보행길 *paw-heng-geel*

football (*soccer*) 축구 *chook-goo* 114

for (*time*) 동안 *tawng-an* 13; ~ **a day** 하루동안 *haroo tawng-an* 86; ~ **a week** 일주일동안 *eeljooeel tawng-an* 6

foreign currency 외국돈 *wegook tawn* 138

forest 삼림 *samneem* 107

forget, to 잊다 *eetda* 42

fork 포크 *pawku* 39, 41, 148

form 용지 *yong-jee* 23, 153, 168

formal dress 정장 *chong-jang* 111

fortnight 2주일 *eejoo-eel*

fortunately 다행히도 *taheng-eedaw* 19

forty 사십(마흔) *sa-seep (mahun)* 216

fountain 분수 *poon-soo* 99

four 사(넷) *sa(net)* 216; ~-**door car** 포도어식 차 *paw-daw-o-seek cha* 86; ~-**wheel drive** 사륜 구동식 *sa-ryoon koodawng-seek* 86

fourteen 십사(열넷) *seep-sa(yol-let)* 216

fourth 넷째 *net-ze* 217

foyer (*hotel/theater*) 로비 *lawbee*

fracture 골절상 *kawl-zol-sang* 165

frame (*glasses*) 창틀 *changtul*

free (*available*) 빈 *been* 36; **free of charge** 공짜 *kawng-za*

freezer 냉동고 *neng-dawng-gaw* 29

French dressing 프렌치 드레싱 *puren-chee dureseeng* 38

French fries 감자튀김 *kamja-tweegeem* 160

frequent: how frequent? 얼마나 자주 *olmana chajoo* 76; **frequently** 자주 *chajoo*

fresh 신선한 *seenson-han* 41

Friday 금요일 *kum-yo-eel* 218

fried 튀긴 *tweegeen*

friend 친구 *cheen-goo* 125, 162; **friendly** 친절한 *cheenjolhan*

fries 감자튀김 *kamja-tweegeem* 38, 40

frightened, to be 무서워하는 *moosowohanun*

from 에서 *eso* 12, 119; **from ... to** (*time*) 부터 ... 까지 *booto ... gajee* 13, 221

front 앞 *ap* 147; ~ **door** 정문 *chong-moon* 26

frying pan 후라이팬 *hoora-eepen* 29

fuel (*petrol/gasoline*) 기름 *keerum* 86

full: ~ **up** 만원 *manwon* 36; ~ **board** 하루 세끼 포함 *haroo sekgee paw-ham* 24; ~ **insurance** 종합보험 *chawng-hap pawhom* 86

fun, to have 재미 *chemee*

furniture 가구 *kagoo*

further (*extra*) 다른 *tarun* 136

fuse 휴즈 *hooju* 28; ~ **box** 휴즈함 *hooju-ham* 28

G **gallon** (*U.S. = 3.78 liters; U.K. = 4.55 liters*) 갤런 *kellon*

game (*football*) 시합 *seehap* 114; (*toy*) 게임기 *ge-eem-gee* 157

garage 정비소 *chong-bee-saw* 88

garbage bags 쓰레기봉투 *ssuregee-bawng-too* 148

garden 정원 *chongwon*

gas 기름 *keerum* 88; ~ **bottle** 가스통 *kasu-tawng* 23; ~ **station** 주유소 *chooyoo-saw* 87

gasoline 기름 *keerum* 86, 88

gastritis 위염 *wee-yom* 165

gate (*airport*) 탑승구 *tapsung-goo* 70

gauze [*bandage*] 붕대 *poong-de* 141

gay club 게이클럽 *ke-ee-kullop* 112

gel 젤 *jel* 142

gentle 쉬운 *swee-oon* 106

genuine 진품인 *cheen-poom-een* 134, 157

get off, to 내리다 *nereeda* 79

get, to (find) 잡다 *chapda* 84; **how do I get to ...?** ... 에 어떻게 갑니까? *...e otdoke kamneekka* 73

gift 선물 *sonmool* 67; **gift store** 선물 가게 *sonmool kage* 130

girl 여자애 *yoja-e* 120, 157

girlfriend 애인 *e-een* 120

give, to 주다 *chooda*

give way 양보 *yang-paw* 96

gland 선 *son* 166

glass 유리잔 *yooree-jan* 37, 39, 148

glasses (optical) 안경 *angyong* 167

glossy finish (photos) 광택 처리 *kwangtek choree*

glove 장갑 *changgap*

go: let's go! 갑시다! *kapseeda;* **where does this bus go?** 이 버스 어디 갑니까? *ee posu odee kamneekka;* **go away!** 가주세요 *kajooseyo;* **go back** (turn around) 되돌아가다 *twedawra-gada* 95; **go for a walk** 산책 하러 가다 *sanchek haro kada* 124; **go out** (in evening) 외출하다 *wechoolhada;* **go shopping** 쇼핑하러 가다 *syopeeng haro kada* 124

goggles 물안경 *mooran-gyong*

gold 금 *kum* 149; **~-plate** 금도금 *kum-dawgum* 149

golf 골프 *kawl-poo* 114; **~ course** 골프장 *kawl-pu-jang* 115

good (adj) 좋은 *chaw-un* 14, 35, 42; **~ morning/afternoon/evening** 안녕하세요 *an-nyong haseyo* 10; **~ night** 안녕히 주무세요 *an-nyong-ee choomoo-seyo* 10; **~ value** 할 만하다 *halman-hada;* **Good God!** 맙소사! *map-sawsa* 19;

good-bye (you're leaving) 안녕히 계세요 *an-nyong-ee keseyo ;* (to s.o. leaving) 안녕히 가세요 *an-nyong-ee kesayo*

gram 그램 *gurem* 159

grandparents 조부모 *chawboomaw*

grapes 포도 *pawdaw* 160

grass 잔디 *chandee*

gray 회색 *hwesek* 143

graze 찰과상 *chal-gwa-sang* 162

great 근사한 *kunsa-han* 19

green 초록 *chaw-rawk* 143; **~ grocer** 채소 가게 *chesaw kage* 130

grilled 구운 *koo-oon*

grocer (grocery store) 식료품점 *seeng-nyopoomjom*

ground (earth) 바닥 *padak* 31; **~ floor** (= U.S. first floor) 일층 *eelchung;* **~cloth** [groundsheet] 방수깔개 *pangsoo-galge* 31

group 일행 *eelheng* 66

guarantee 보증 *paw-jung* 135

guide (tour) 안내 *anne* 98 ; **~book** 안내책 *anne-chek* 100, 150; **guided tour** 안내 여행 *anne yoheng;* **guided hike** 안내 도보여행 *anne tawbaw yoheng* 106

guitar 기타 *keeta*

gum 검 *gom*

guy rope 밧줄 *pazool* 31

H **hair** 머리 *moree* 147; **~ mousse** 헤어 무스 *he-o moosu* 142; **~ spray** 헤어 스프레이 *he-o supu-re-ee* 142; **~-cut** 이발 *eebal*

hairdresser's (ladies/men) 미장원/이발소 *meejang-won/eebal-saw* 131

half 반 *pan* 217; **~ board** 아침 저녁 포함 *acheem cho-nyok paw-ham* 24; **~ past** 시반 *see pan* 220

hammer 망치 *mang-chee* 31

hand 손 sawn 166; ~
baggage 손가방 sawn-
gabang 69; ~ **washable**
손빨래 sawn-balle 145
handbag 핸드백 hendu-bek
144, 153
handicap (golf) 핸디캡 hendeekep
handicrafts 수공예 sookawng-ye
handkerchief 손수건 sawnsoogon
hanger 옷걸이 awtgoree 27
hangover (n) 숙취 sook-chwee 141
happen: what happened? 무슨
일입니까? moosun ee-reemeekka 93
happy: I'm not happy with the service
서비스가 마음에 안듭니다 sobeesu-
ga mau-me andumneeda
harbor 항구 hanggoo
hat 모자 mawja 144
have, to 갖다 katda 18; (hold stock of)
(가게에)있다 (kage-e) eet-da 133;
(consume) 들다 dulda 125; **I'll have ...**
... 하겠습니다 ... hage-ssumneeda 37;
~ **an appointment** 예약하다 yeyak-
hada 161; ~ **to** (must) 해야 하다
heya hada 79;
hay fever 꽃가루 알레르기
gawtgaroo alle-rugee 141
head 머리 moree 166; ~**ache** 두통
too-tawng 163
heading, to be (in a direction) 로 가다
raw kada 83
health: ~ **food store** 건강식품점 kon-
gang seek-poom-jom 130; ~ **insurance**
의료보험 ueeryo pawhom 168
hear, to 듣다 tutta
hearing aid 보청기 pawchonggee
heart 심장 seem-jang 166; ~ **condition**
심장병 seemjang-byong 163
hearts (cards) 하트 hatu
heat 난방 nanbang 25
heater 난방장치 nanbang-jangchee
heating 난방 nanbang 25
heavy 무거운 moogo-oon 14, 69, 134

height 키 kee 152
hello! 안녕하세요 an-nyong haseyo
10, 118
help, to 돕다 tawpda 18; **can you help
me?** 도와주세요 taw-wa-jooseyo 92:
thanks for your help 도와주셔서 감
사합니다. taw-wa-joosyoso kamsa-
hamneeda 94
hemorrhoids 치질 cheejeel 165
her 그 여자의 ku yoja-e 16
here 여기 yogee 12, 17
hernia 탈장 tal-zang 165
hers 그 여자 것 ku yoja got 16; **it's
hers** 그 여자 것입니다 ku yoja
koseemneeda
hi! 안녕하세요 an-nyong haseyo 10
high 높다 nawp-da 106, 122; ~ **street**
중심가 choong-seem-ga 96
highlight, to 부분염색하다 pooboon
yomsek-hada 147
highway 고속도로 kawsawk-dawraw
94
hike (walk) 도보여행 tawbaw yoheng
106; **hiking boots** 등산화 tungsan-
hwa 145
hill 언덕 ondok 107
hire, to 빌리다 peelleeda
his 그 남자 것 ku namja got 16;
ku namja-e 16; **it's his** 그 남자
것입니다 ku namja koseemneeda
HIV-positive 에이즈 항체보균자 e-
eeju hangche-bawgyoonja
hobby (pastime) 취미 chwee-mee 121
hold on, to 잠깐 기다리다 chamgan
keeda-reeda 128
hole (in clothes) 구멍 koomong
holiday: on ~ 휴가로 hyooga-raw 66;
~ **resort** 휴양지 hyooyangjee
home: we're going ~ 우리는 집에
갑니다 ooree-nun chee-be kamneeda
homosexual (adj) 동성연애의
tawngsong-yone-uee

honeymoon: we're on ~ 신혼여행
중입니다 seenhawn-yoheng choong-
eemneeda

hopefully 바라건대 para-gonde 19

horse 말 mal; **~ racing** 경마 kyong-
ma 114

hospital 종합병원 chawng-hap pyong-
won 131, 164, 167

hot 뜨거운 dugo-oon 14; (weather)
더운 to-oon 122; **~ dog** 핫 도그 hat
dawgu 110; **~ spring** 온천 awnchon;
~ water 더운 물 do-oon mool 25

hotel 호텔 hawtel 21, 123

hour 시간 seegan 97; **in an ~** 한 시간
후에 han-seegan hoo-e 84

house 집 cheep; **~wife** 가정주부
kajong jooboo 121

hovercraft 쾌속정 kwe-sawk-chong 81

how? 어떻게? otdoke 17; **how are
things?** 요즘 어떻습니까? yojum
otdo-ssumneekka 19; **how are you?**
어떻게 지내십니까? otdoke jene-
seemneekka 118

how far 얼마나 먼 olmana mon
94, 106

how long? 얼마나 olmana 23, 76, 78,
88, 94, 98, 135

how many? 몇 정거장 myot chong-
gojang 80; 몇개 myotge 15

how much (money) 얼마 olma 15, 21,
65, 84, 100, 109; (quantity)
얼만큼 olman-kum 140

how often? 얼마 간격으로 olma kan-
gyoguraw 140

how old? 몇살 myo-ssal 120

hundred 백 pek 216

hungry: I'm hungry 배가 고픕니다
pe-ga kawpumneeda

hurry: I'm in a hurry 급합니다
kuphamneeda

hurt: to hurt
아프다 apuda 162, 164;
to be hurt 다치다
tacheeda 92; **my ...
hurts ...** 아픕니다 ...
apum-needa 163

husband 남편 nam-pyon 120, 162

I ice 얼음 orum 38
ice cream 아이스크림 aeesu-
kureem 40, 160; **~ parlor** 아이스크림
가게 aeesu-kureem kage 35

icy, to be 매우 춥다 me-oo choop-ta
122

identification 신분증 seenboon-zung
136

ill: I'm ill 아픕니다 apumneeda

illegal: is it illegal? 그것 불법입니까?
kugot poolppobeemneekka?

imitation 모조품인 mawjaw-poom-een
134

immediately 즉시 chuk-see 13

impounded by the police 견인되다
kyoneen-dweda 87

in (place) (안)에 (an)e 12; **in** (time)
지나서 cheenaso 13

in front of 앞에 ape

included: is ... included? ... 포함돼
있습니까? ... pawham dwe-ee-
ssumneekka 88

incredible 훌륭한 hool-lyoong-han 101

indicate, to 가리키다 kareekeeda

indigestion 소화불량 saw-
hwaboolryang

indoor pool 실내 수영장 seel-le soo-
yong-jang 116

inexpensive 싼 ssan 35

infected, to be 감염되다 kam-yom-
dweda 165

infection 감염 gam-yom 167

inflammation (of ...) 염 yom 165

informal (dress) 평상복의 pyong-sang-
baw-guee

A-Z

information 정보/안내 chong-baw/anne 97; ~
desk 안내 anne 73; ~
office 안내 anne 96
injection 주사 choosa 168
injured, to be 부상당하다
poosang dang-hada 92, 162
innocent 결백한 kyolbekan
insect bite 벌레 물린데 polle moolleen-de 141, 162
insect repellent 구충제 koo-choong-je
141
inside 안에 ane 12
insist: I insist 저는 주장합니다 cho-
nun choojanghamneeda
insomnia 불면증 poolmyonzung
instant coffee 인스턴트 커피 een-su-
tantu kopee 160
instead of 대신에 tesee-ne
instructions 설명서 sol-myong-so 135
instructor 교사 kyosa
insulin 인슐린 eensyoolleen
insurance 보험 pawhom 86, 89, 93,
168; ~ **card** 보험증서 pawhom-jungso
93; ~ **claim** 보험 청구 paw-hom
chong-goo 153; ~ **company** 보험회사
pawhom-hwesa 93
interest (hobby) 취미 chwee-mee 121
interested, to be 관심이 있다
kwansee-mee eetda 111
interesting 흥미로운 hung-mee-raw-
oon 101
International Student Card 국제학생증
kookze hakseng-zung 29
Internet 인터넷 een-tonet 155
interpreter 통역 tawng-yok 93, 153
intersection 교차로 kyo-cha-raw 95
invite, to 초대하다 chaw-de-hada 124
iodine 요오드 yo-awdu
Irish (person) 아일랜드(사람) a-eel-
lendu (saram) 119
Ireland 아일랜드 a-eel-lendu 119

is it ...? ...입니까? ...eemneekka
is there ...? ...있습니까?
... ee-ssumneekka
is this ...? 이것 ... 입니까? eegot ...
eem-neekka 145; **is this seat taken?**
이 자리 임자 있습니까? ee charee
eemja
it is ... ... 입니다 ... eemneeda 17
Italian (cusine) 이태리(음식)
eeteree(umseek) 35
itch: it itches 가렵습니다
karyopsumneeda
itemized bill 계산서 kesanso 32
items 제품 chepoom 69

J
jacket 자켓 chaket 144
jam 잼 chem
jammed, to be 열리지 않다 yolleejee
anta 25
January 일월 eel-wol 218
Japan 일본 eel-bawn 119
Japanese 일본 eelbawn 35, 119
jar 병 pyong 159
jaw 턱 tok 166
jazz 재즈 cheju 111
jeans 청바지 chong-bajee 144
jellyfish 해파리 heparee
jet lag: I'm jet lagged 저는 시차
때문에 피곤합니다 cho-nun seecha
demoo-ne peegawn hamneeda
jet-ski 제트스키 chetu-sukee 116
jeweler 보석상 pawsok-sang 130
job: what's your job? 직업이 무엇입니
까? cheego-bee moo-oseemneekka
join: may we join you? 우리가 가도
되겠습니까? ooree-ga gadaw dwege-
ssumneekka
joint passport 공동여권 kawng-dawng
yokgwon 66
joint 관절 kwan-jol 166
joke 농담 nawngdam
journalist 언론인 ollawneen

journey 여행 *yoheng* 75, 76

jug (of water) 큰잔 *kunjan*

July 칠월 *cheel-wol* 218

jump leads 점프 케이블 *chompu ke-eebul*

jumper 잠바 *chamba*

junction (intersection) 교차로 *kyocharaw*

June 유월 *yoo-wol* 218

K keep: keep the change! 거스름돈 가지세요! *kosurumdawn kajeeseyo!*

kerosene 등유 *tung-yoo*; **~ stove** 휴대용 석유난로 *hyoode-yong sog-yoo nallaw* 31

ketchup 케참 *kechap*

kettle 주전자 *choojon-ja* 29

key 열쇠 *yol-swe* 27, 28, 88; **~ ring** 열쇠고리 *yolswe-gawree* 156

kiddie pool 어린이풀 *oreenee-pool* 113

kidney 신장 *seen-jang* 166

kilo(gram) 킬로(그램) *keellaw(gurem)* 159

kilometer 킬로미터 *keellawmeeto*

kind (pleasant) 친절한 *cheenjolhan*

kind: what kind of ... 어떤 종류의 ... *otton chawng-nyoo-e ...*

kiss, to 키스하다 *keesuhada*

kitchen 부엌 *poo-ok* 29

knapsack 배낭 *penang* 31, 145

knee 무릎 *moorup* 166

knickers 여자 내의 *yoja ne-uee*

knife 나이프 *naeepu* 39, 41

know: I don't know 모르겠습니다 *mawruge-ssumneeda* 23

Korean (language) 한국어 *han-googo* 11, 110, 126

kosher 코셔 *kawsyo*

L label 상표 *sangpyo*
lace 레이스 *le-eesu* 145

ladder 사다리 *sadaree*

lake 호수 *hawsoo* 107

lamp 전등 *chondung* 25, 29

land, to 도착하다 *tawchak-hada* 70

language course 어학 강좌 *ohak kangjwa*

large (adj) 큰 *kun* 40, 69; (size of drink) 큰 거 *kun ko* 110; **larger** 더 큰 *to kun* 134

last, to 지속하다 *cheesawkhada*

last (adj) 마지막 *majee-mak* 68, 76, 80; 지난 *chee-nan* 218

late (delayed) 늦다 *nutda* 70; **later** 늦게 *nut-ge* 125, 147

laugh, to 웃다 *ootda* 126

laundromat 빨래방 *balle-bang* 131

laundry: ~ facilities 세탁 시설 *setak seesol* 30; **~ service** 세탁 서비스 *setak sobeesu* 22

lavatory 화장실 *hwajangseel*

lawyer 변호사 *pyon-haw-sa* 152

laxative 완하제 *wanhaje*

lead, to (road) 가다 *kada* 94

lead-free (petrol/gas) 무연 *mooyon* 87

leader (of group) 지도자 *cheedawja*

leaflet 안내서 *anne-so* 97

leak, to (roof/pipe) 새다 *seda*

learn, to (language/sport) 배우다 *peooda*

leather 가죽 *kajook* 145

leave, to 떠나다 *donada* 32, 68, 70, 76, 81, 98, 126; **I've left my bag** 가방을 두고 왔습니다 *kabang-ul toogaw-wassumneeda*

left: on the ~ 왼쪽 *wen-zawk* 76; 왼쪽에 *wen-zaw-ge* 95; **~ hand side** 왼쪽 *wen-zawk* 95

left-luggage office 짐보관소 *cheem baw-gwan-saw* 71, 73

leg 다리 taree 166

legal: is it legal? 그것 합법입니까? kogot happobeemneekka

leggings 레깅스바지 le-geeng-su bajee 144

lemon 레몬 le-mawn 38

lemonade 레모네이드 lemawne-eedu

lend: could you lend me ...? ... 빌려 주시겠습니까? ... peellyo chooseegessumneekka

length (of) 길이 keeree

lens 렌즈 lenju 151; (in glasses) 안경알 angyong-al 167; ~ **cap** 렌즈 덮개 lenju topke 151

lesbian club 여자 동성연애자 모임 yoja tawngsong-yoneja maw-eem

less (더) 적게 (to) chokge 15

lesson 교훈 kyohoon

let, to: let me know! 알려주세요! allyojooseyo!

letter 편지 pyon-jee 154; ~**box** 우체통 oochetawng

level (ground) 평평한 pyong-pyong-han 31

library 도서관 tawsogwan

lie down, to 눕다 noopta 164

lifebelt 안전벨트 anjonbeltu

lifeboat 구명보트 koomyong-bawtu

lifeguard 구조원 koojaw-won 116

lifejacket 구명조끼 koomyong-jawkkee

lift (elevator) 엘리베이터 ellee-be-eeto 26, 132; (hitchhiking) 태워주기 tewo joo-gee 83; ~ **pass** 리프트 사용권 leeputu sayong-gwon 117

light (bicycle) 등 tung 83; (electric) 전등 chondung 25; ~ **bulb** 전구 chon-goo 148

light (color) 밝은 palgun 134, 143; **lighter** 더 밝은 to palgun 24, 143

light (weight) 가벼운 kabyo-oon 14, 134

lighter (for cigarettes) 라이타 la-ee-ta 150

like this (similar to) 이것 같은 eegot katun

like, to 마음에 들다 maume tulda 101; 좋아하다 chaw-a hada 111, 119, 121; **I like it** 저는 그것을 좋아합니다 cho-nun kugo-sul chaw-ahamneeda; **I don't like it** 저는 그것을 좋아하지 않습니다 cho-nun kugo-sul chaw-ahajee ansumneeda; **I'd like a(n)** ... 주십시요 ... chooseep-seeyo 18; **I'd like to** ... ... 하고 싶습니다 ... hagaw seep-sumneeda 18, 36, 133

limousine 리무진 leemoojeen

line (profession) 일/직업 eel/cheeg-op 121; (subway/metro) 지하철 노선 cheeha-chol nawson 80

linen 마 ma 145

lip 입술 eep-sool 166; ~**stick** 립스틱 leepsuteek

liquor store 주류판매점 choo-ryoo panme-jom 131

liter 리터 leeto 87, 159

little (small) 작은 chagun

live, to 살다 salda 119

liver 간 kan 166

living room 거실 koseel 29

loaf of bread 식빵 seekbang 160

lobby (theater/hotel) 로비 lawbee

local 지방/한국 chee-bang/han-gook 35, 37; ~ **anaesthetic** 국소 마취주사 kooksaw ma-chwee-joosa 168

lock (n) 자물쇠 chamool-swe 25

lock, to 잠그다 cham-guda 88; ~ **oneself out, to** 열쇠를 방안에 둔 채 잠그다 yol-swerul pang-ane toon-che chamguda

locked, to be 잠기다 cham-geeda 26

log on, to 접속하다 chopsawk-hada 155

long 진 keen 144; 먼 mon 95; **how ~?** 얼마나? olmana 164; **how much longer?** 얼마나 더 olmana to 41

long-sighted 원시 wonsee 167

look, to: I'm just looking 그냥 보는 것 입니다 kunyang pawnun koseemneeda; **look around** 둘러 보다 toollo pawda; **look for ...** 찾다 ... chatda 18; **look like** 같이 생기다 kachee seng-geeda 71

loose 헐렁한 hollong-han 146

lorry 대형트럭 tehyong-turok

lose, to 잃어버리다 eero-boreeda 28, 138, 153

lost-and-found office [lost property office] 분실물 신고 poon-seel-mool seen-gaw 73

louder 더 크게 to kuge 128

love: I love you 당신을 사랑합니다 tangsee-nul saranghamneeda

lovely 매우 좋은 me-oo chaw-un 122

low 낮은 najun 122; **~ bridge** 높이 제한 nawpee chehan 96; **~-fat** 저지방 chojeebang

lower (berth) 아래칸 arekan 74

luck: good luck! 행운을 빕니다 heng-oonul peem-needa 219

luggage 짐 cheem

lump 혹 hawk 162

lunch 점심 chomseem 98, 154

lung 폐 pe

Ⓜ machine washable 기계세탁 keege-setak 145

madam 부인 pooeen

magazine 잡지 chap-chee 150

magnificent 웅장한 oong-jang-han 101

maid 청소부 chong-saw-boo 28

mail 편지 pyonjee 27; **by ~** 편지로 pyon-jee-raw 22; **~box** 우체통 ooche-tawng 154

mail, to 우편으로 보내다 oopyo-nuraw pawneda

main 큰 kun 130, 154; **~ course** 주요 리 choo-yoree 38; **~ street** 큰길 kun-geel 95; **~ train station** 중앙 기차 역 choong-ang keecha-yok 73

make an appointment, to 예약하다 yeyak-hada

make-up 화장 hwajang

male 남자 namja 152

mallet 나무 망치 namoo-mang-chee 31

man/male 남자 namja

manager 지배인 cheebe-een 25, 41, 137

manicure 손톱 손질 sawn-tawp sawnjeel 147

manual (car) 수동식 soodawngseek

many 많이 manee 15

map 지도 cheedaw 94, 106, 150

March 삼월 sam-wol 218

margarine 마가린 ma-gareen 160

market 시장 see-jang 99, 131

married, to be 기혼이다 kee-hawn-eeda 120

mascara 마스카라 masukara

mask (diving) 마스크 masuku

mass 미사 mee-sa 105

massage 마사지 massajee 147

match (soccer) 시합 seehap 114

matches 성냥 song-nyang 31, 148, 150

matinee 낮공연 nat kawng-yon 109

matter: it doesn't matter 상관없습니다 sang-gwan-opssumneeda; **what's the matter?** 문제가 무엇입니까? moonje-ga moo-oseemneekka

mattress 매트리스 metureesu

may I 해주시겠습니까? he chooseege-ssumneekka 18

May 오월 aw-wol 218

maybe 아마 ama

me 저 cho

meal 식사 *seeksa* 38, 42, 124, 125, 165

mean, to 뜻하다 *duthada* 11

measles 홍역 *hawng-yok* 165

measurement 치수 *cheesoo*

meat 고기 *kaw-gee* 41

medication 약 *yak* 164, 165

medium (adj) 중간/보통 *choong-gan/bawtawng* 40

meet, to 만나다 *mannada* 125

meeting point [place] 만남의 장소 *manna-me chang-saw* 12

member (of club) 회원 *hwe-won* 112, 115

memorial (war) (전쟁) 기념물 (chon-jeng) *kee-nyom-mool* 99

men (toilets) 신사용 *seensayong*

mention: don't mention it 천만에요 *chon-maneyo* 10

menu 메뉴 *menyoo*

message 연락 *yollak* 27

metal 금속 *kumsawk*

microwave (oven) 전자오븐 *chonja-awbun*

midday 정오 *chong-aw*

midnight 자정 *chajong* 220

migraine 편두통 *pyondootawng*

mileage 마일리지 *maeel-leejee* 86

milk 우유 *oo-yoo* 160; with ~ 우유 넣어서 *ooyoo no-oso* 40

million 백만 *peng-man* 216

mind: do you mind? ... 되겠습니까? ... *dwege-ssumneekka* 77, 126

mine 내 것 *ne got* 16; it's mine! 제 것입니다 *che koseemneeda*

mineral water 광천수 *kwangchonsoo*

mini-bar 미니바 *meenee-ba* 32

minute 분 *poon* 76

mirror 거울 *ko-ool*

missing, to be 없다 *op-da* 137; 실종되다 *seel-zawng-dweda* 152

mistake /잘못 *jalmawt* 41; 실수 *seelssoo* 32, 42

misunderstanding: there's been a misunderstanding 오해가 있었습니다 *awhe-ga eetsso-ssumneeda*

mobile home 이동식 주택 *eedawngseek chootek*

Modified American Plan (M.A.P.) 아침 저녁 포함 *acheem cho-nyok*

moisturizer (cream) 모이스처라이징 크림 *maw-eesuchoraeejeeng kureem*

monastery 수도원 *soodaw-won* 99

Monday 월요일 *wol-yo-eel* 218

money 돈 *tawn* 42, 136, 139, 153; ~ **order** 우편환 *oopyonhwan*

month 달 *dal* 218

moped 소형 오토바이 *saw-hyong awtaw-baee* 83

more (더) 많이 (to) *manee* 15; 더 to 67; I'd like some more 좀 더 주십시오 *chawm to chooseep-seeyo*

morning, in the 아침에 *acheem-e* 221

mosque 회교사원 *hwe-gyo sawon* 105

mosquito bite 모기 물린데 *mawgee moolleende*

mother 어머니 *omonee* 120

motion sickness 차멀미 *chamolmee* 141

motorbike 소형 오토바이 *saw-hyong awtaw-baee* 83

motorboat 모터보트 *mawto-bawtu* 116

motorway 고속도로 *kawsawk-dawraw* 94

mountain 산 *san* 107; ~ **bike** 산악용 자전거 *sanaknyong chajon-go*; ~ **pass** 산길 *san-geel* 107; ~ **range** 산맥 *sanmek* 107

moustache 콧수염 *kawtsooyom*

mouth 입 *eep* 164, 166; ~ **ulcer** 입안 헌데 *eeban honde*

move, to 옮기다 *awm-geeda* 25; **don't move him!** 그 남자를 움직이지 마십시오 *ku namjarul oom-jeeg-eejee maseep-seeyaw*

movie 영화 *yong-hwa* 108, 110; **~ theater** 영화관 *yong-hwa-gwan* 96

Mr. 씨 *ssee*

Mrs. 여사 *yosa*

much (much more) 훨씬 (더 많이) *hwol-sseen (to manee)* 15

mugged, to be 강도를 당하다 *kang-dawrul tang-hada* 153

mugging 노상강도 *nawsang kang-daw* 152

mugs 머그잔 *mogu-jan* 148

multiplex theater [cinema] 복합 영화관 *paw-kap yong-hwa-gwan* 110

mumps 볼거리 *pawlgoree*

muscle 근육 *kun-yook* 166

museum 박물관 *pang-mool-gwan* 13, 99

music 음악 *umak* 111, 121; **~ store** 레코드 가게 *rekawdu kage* 131

musician 음악가 *umakka*

must: I must ... 저는 ... 해야 합니다 *cho-nun ... heya hamneeda*

mustard 겨자 *kyoja* 38

my 제 *che* 16

myself: I'll do it myself 제 스스로 하겠습니다 *che susuraw hagessumneeda*

N **name** 이름 *eerum* 22, 36, 93, 118, 120; **my name is ...** 제 이름은 ... 입니다 *che eerumun ... eemneeda* 118; **what's your name?** 이름이 어떻게 되십니까? *eerumee ot-doke dwe-seemneekka* 118

napkin (serviette) 냅킨 *nepkeen* 39

nappies 기저귀 *keejo-gee* 142

narrow 좁은 *chawbun* 14

national 국가의 *kookkae*

nationality 국적 *kookzok*

nature reserve 자연 보호지구 *chayon pawhaw jee-goo* 107

nausea 메스꺼움 *mesukko-oom*

near 근처에 *kuncho-e* 12; **nearest** 가장 가까운 *kajang kat-gaoon* 80, 88, 92, 130, 140, 154

nearby 근처에 *kuncho-e* 21, 87

necessary 필요한 *peeryo-han* 89

neck 목부분 *mawk-pooboon* 147, 166

necklace 목걸이 *mawkgoree* 149

need: I need to ... 저는 ... 해야 합니다 *cho-nun ... heya hamneeda* 18

nephew 조카 *chawka*

nerve 신경 *seen-gyong*

nervous system 신경계 *seen-gyong-gye*

never 단 한번도 *tan hanbon-daw* 13; **~ mind** 괜찮습니다 *kwen-chan-ssumneeda* 10

new 새것인 *segoseen* 14

New Year 새해 *sehe* 219

newspaper 신문 *seenmoom* 150

newsstand 신문가판대 *seen-moon gapande* 131

next 다음 *taum* 68, 76, 78, 80; **next stop!** 다음 정거장 *taum chong-gojang* 79

next to 옆에 *yope* 95; 바로 옆에 *paraw yope* 12

nice 좋은 *chaw-un*

niece 조카딸 *chawkattal*

night, at 밤에 *pame* 221

nightclub 나이트클럽 *naeetu-kullop* 112

nine 구(아홉) *koo(ahawp)* 216

nineteen 십구(열아홉) *seep-koo (yol-ahawp)* 216

ninety 구십(아흔) *koo-seep (ahun)* 216

no 아니요 *a-neeyo* 10

no-one 아무도 a-moodaw 16, 92
noisy 시끄러운 seekguro-oon 24
non-alcoholic 음료수 umnyosoo
non-smoking (adj) 금연 kumyon 36; (area) 금연석 kumyon-sok 69
none 하나도 없다 hanado-opda 15; 아무 것도 amoo-got-do 16
noon 정오 chong-aw 220
normal 정상 chong-sang 67
north 북쪽 pook-zawk 95
nose 코 kaw 166
not: not bad 나쁘지 않은 napbujee anun 19; not enough 모자란 mawjaran 42, 136; not good 좋지 않은 chaw-chee anun 19; not yet 아직 ajeek 13
nothing else: there is nothing else 더 없습니다 to op-ssumneeda 15
notify, to 연락하다 yollak-hada 167
November 십일월 seep-eel-wol 218
now 지금 jee-gum 13
number 번호 ponhaw 138; ~ plate 번호판 ponhawpan
nurse 간호사 kanhaw-sa
nylon 나일론 naeellawn

O
occasionally 때때로 ttetteraw
October 시월 see-wol 218
odds (betting) 승산 sungsan 114
of course 물론 mool-lawn 19
off-licence 주류판매점 choo-ryoo panme-jom 131
off-peak 한산한 때 hansanhan tte
office 사무실 samooseel
office (surgery) hours 진료시간 cheel-lyo seegan 161
often 종종 chawng-jawng 13
oil 기름 keerum
okay 좋습니다 chaw-ssumneeda 10

old 낡은 nalgun 14; ~ town 구시가지 koo seega-jee 96, 99
olive oil 올리브유 awlleebu-yoo
omelet 오믈렛 awmullet
on (day, date) 에 e 13; ~ foot 걸어서 koroso 95; ~ my own 혼자 hawn-ja 120; ~ the hour 매시 정각에 mesee chong-gage 76; ~ the left 왼쪽에 wen-zawge 12; ~ the right 오른쪽에 awrun-zawge 12; ~ the spot 여기서 바로 yogeeso paraw 93; on/off switch 스위치 켜고/끄고 suweechee kyogaw/gugaw
once 한 번 han-bon 217
one 일(하나) eel(hana) 216; ~ like that 그와 같은 것 kuwa-gatun got 16; ~ way 편도 pyon-daw 65; ~-way street 일방통행 eelbang tawng-heng 96
open, to 열다 yolda 100, 132, 140; (mouth) 벌리다 polleeda 164
open (adj.) 열린 yolleen 14
open-air pool 실외 수영장 seel-we soo-yong-jang 116
opening hours 개관시간 kegwan seegan 100
opera 오페라공연 awpera gawng-yon 108; ~ house 오페라 하우스 awpera haoo-su 99, 111
operation 수술 soosool
opposite 맞은 편 majun-pyon 12
optician 안경점 an-gyong-jom 131, 167
or 또는 ttawnun
orange 오렌지색 aw-renjee-sek 143
orchestra 오케스트라 awke-sutura 111
order, to 주문하다 choomoon-hada 37, 41; 주문 choo-moon 135; (taxi) (택시)를 부르다 (teksee)rul pooruda 32
organized hike/walk 안내 도보여행 anne tawbaw-yoheng
others 다른 것들 tarun kodul 134
our 우리의 ooree-e 16

ours 우리 것 *ooree got* 16

outdoor 실외 *seelwe*

outrageous 말도 안되는 *maldaw andwenun* 89

outside 밖에 *pakge* 12, 36

oven 오븐 *awbun*

over there 저기 *cho-gee* 36; 저쪽 *cho-zawk* 76

overdone (adj) 너무 익은 *nomoo eegun* 41

overheat 과열 *kwayol*

owe, to 내다 *neda* 168; **how much do I owe?** 얼마를 내야 합니까? *olmarul neyahamneekka*

owner 주인 *chooeen*

o'clock: it's ... o'clock ... 시입니다 ... see *eem-needa* 220

P **p.m.** 오후 *aw-hoo*

pacifier 가짜 젖꼭지 *kaza chotkkawkzee*

pack, to 싸다 *ssada* 69

package 소포(짐) *sawpaw (cheem)* 155

packed lunch 도시락 *tawseerak*

packet 봉지 *pawng-jee* 159; **~ of cigarettes** 담배 한갑 *tambe han-gap* 150

paddling pool 어린이풀 *oreenee-pool* 113

padlock 자물쇠 *chamoolswe*

pain, to be in 아프다 *apuda* 167

painkiller 진통제 *cheen-tawng-je* 165

paint, to 그리다 *kureeda*

painter 화가 *hwaga*

painting 그림 *kureem*

pair of ... ... 벌 ... *pol* 217

palace 궁전 *koong-jon* 99

palpitations 심장이 두근두근 *seemjang-ee toogun-toogun*

panorama 전경 *chon-gyong* 107

pants (U.S.) 바지 *pajee* 144

pantyhose 팬티 스타킹 *pentee-suta-keeng* 144

paper 종이 *chawng-ee* 150; **~ napkins** 종이 냅킨 *chawng-ee nep-keen* 148

paracetamol 파라세타몰 *parasetamawl*

paraffin 파라핀 *parapeen* 31

paralysis 마비 *mabee*

parcel 소포(짐) *sawpaw (cheem)* 155

pardon? 뭐라 하셨습니까? *moo-o-ra hasyo-ssumeekka* 11

park 공원 *kawng-won* 96, 99, 107

parking lot 주차장 *choocha-jang* 26, 87, 96

parking meter 주차미터기 *choocha meeto-gee* 87

parliament building 국회의사당 *kookwe ueesa-dang* 99

partner (boyfriend/girlfriend) 애인 *e-een*

parts (components) 부품 *poo-poom* 89

party (social) 파티 *patee* 124

pass through, to 통과하다 *tawng-gwa-hada* 66

pass, to 지나다 *cheenada* 77

passport 여권 *yokgwon* 66, 69, 153

pastry 제과점 *che-gwa-jom* 131

patch, to 깁다 *keep-da* 137

path (foot) 오솔길 *awsawl-geel* 107

patient (n) 환자 *hwanja*

pavement, on the 인도 *eendaw*

pay, to 계산하다 *kesan-hada* 42, 67, 136; **~ a fine** 벌금을 내다 *polgu-mul neda* 93

pay phone 공중전화 *kawngjoong-jonhwa*

payment 계산 *kesan*

peak 정상 *chong-sang* 107

pearl 진주 *cheenjoo* 149

pebbly (beach) 자갈이 많은 *chagaree manun* 116

pedestrian crossing 횡단 보도 hweng-dan pawdaw 96

pedestrian zone [precinct] 보행자 보호구역 paw-heng-ja pawhaw-gooyok 96

pen 펜 pen 150

penicillin 페니실린 pe-nee-seelleen 165

penknife 주머니칼 choo-monee-kal 31

people 사람 saram 92, 119

pepper 후추 hoochoo 38

per: ~ day 하루에 haroo-e 30, 83, 86, 87, 115; **~ hour** 시간당 see-gan-dang 87, 115, 155; **~ night** 하룻밤에 haroop-bame 21; **~ week** 일주일에 eeljooee-re 83, 86

perhaps 아마 ama 19

period (menstrual) 생리 seng-nee 167; **~ pains** 생리통 seng-nee-tawng 167

period (of history) 시대 seede 104

perm, to 퍼머하다 pomo-hada 147

petrol [gasoline] 기름 keerum 86, 87, 88; **~ station** 주유소 chooyoo-saw 87

pewter 백랍 pek-nap 149

pharmacy 약국 yakgook 131, 140, 158

phone, to 전화하다 chonhwahada; **~ call** 전화 chonhwa 152; **~ card** 전화카드 chonhwa-kadu 127, 155

photo 사진 sajeen 98; **passport-size ~** 여권용 사진 yokwon-yong sajeen 115

photocopier 복사기 pawk-sa-gee 155

photographer 사진사 sajeensa

phrase 구절 koojol 11

pick up, to (children) 데려 가다 teryo-kada 113; (ticket) 찾다 chatda 109

picnic 소풍 sawpoong; **~ area** 취사지 역 chweesa jeeyok 107

piece (of baggage) 개 ge 69; **a piece of ... ...** 하나 hana 40

pill 알약 alyak 165; **to be on the Pill** 경구피임약을 먹다 kyong-goo pee-eem-yagul mogda

pillow 베개 pege 27; **~ case** 베갯잇 pegenneet

pink 분홍 poon-hawng 143

pipe (smoking) 파이프 paeepu

pizzeria 피자 가게 peeja kage 35

place (space) 자리/방 charee/pang 29

place a bet, to 내기하다 negee-hada 114

plane 비행기 peeheng-gee 68

plans 계획 kehwek 124

plant (n) 식물 seengmool

plastic bags 비닐 봉지 peeneel pawngjee

plastic wrap 랩 lep 148

plate 접시 chopsee 39, 148

platform 플랫폼 plepawm 73, 76, 77

platinum 백금 pekkum 149

play, to 하다 hada 121; (music) 연주하다 yonjoo-hada 111

playground 놀이터 nawree-to 113

playing field 운동장 oondawng-jang 96

playwright 극작가 kukjak-ga 110

please 부탁합니다 pootak-hamneeda 10

plug 플러그 pulogu 148

pneumonia 폐렴 pye-ryom 165

point to, to 가리키다 karee-keeda 11

poison 독 tawk

poles 스키폴대 sukee pawl-de 117

police 경찰 kyong-chal 92, 152; **~ report** 경찰 증명서 kyong-chal chung-myong-so 153; **~ station** 경찰서 kyong-chalso 96, 131, 152

pollen count 꽃가루 지수 gawtkaroo cheesoo 122

polyester 폴리에스테르 pawllee-esuteru

pond 연못 yon-mawt 107

pop music 팝 음악 pap umak 111

popcorn 팝콘 pap-kawn 110

popular 인기있는 een-gee-eennun 157

port (harbor) 항구 hang-goo

porter 포터 *pawto* 71

portion 분량 *poollyang* 40, 41

possible: as soon as possible 가능한 한 빨리 *kanunghan han ppallee*

post *(mail)* 우편 *oopyon*; ~ **office** 우체국 *ooche-gook* 96, 131, 154

post, to 우편으로 보내다 *oopyonnuraw pawneda*

postage 우편요금 *oopyon-yogum* 154

postbox 우체통 *ooche-tawng* 154

postcard 엽서 *yopso* 154, 156

potato 감자 *kamja* 38; ~ **chips** 감자칩 *kamja-cheep* 160

pottery 도기 *tawgee*

pound *(sterling)* 파운드 *pa-oon-du* 138

power: ~ **cut** 단전 *tanjon*; ~ **points** 전기 콘센트 *chon-gee kawnsentu* 30

pregnant, to be 임신이다 *eemseen eeda* 163

premium *(petrol/gas)* 고급 *kaw-gup* 87

prescribe, to 처방하다 *chobang-hada* 165

prescription 처방 *chobang* 140, 141

present *(gift)* 선물 *sonmool*

press, to 다림질하다 *tareem-jeel-hada* 137

pretty 예쁜 *yeppun*

priest 성직자 *songjeekza*

prison 감옥 *kamawk*

probably 어쩌면 *ozo-myon* 19

produce store 식료품 가게 *seeng-nyopoom kage* 131

program 프로그램 *puraw-gurem* 109; ~ **of events** 행사 프로그램 *hengsa puraw-gurem* 108

pronounce, to 발음하다 *parumhada*

Protestant 개신교 *keseen-gyo* 105

public building 공공건물 *kawnggawng gonmool* 96

puncture *(flat)* 펑크 *pong-ku* 88

puppet show 인형극 *eenhyongguk*

pure cotton 순면 *soon-myon* 145

purple 자주색 *chajoo-sek* 143

purse 지갑 *chee-gap* 153

push-chair 유모차 *yoomawcha*

put 넣다 *notda* 22; **where can I put ...?** ... 어디에 놓을까요 *odee-e naw-ulkkayo*

---

quality 질 *jeel* 134

quarter, a 사분의 일 *saboon-e eel* 217; ~ **past** *(after)* 십오분 *seep-awboon* 220; ~ **to** *(before)* 십오분 전 *seep-awboon jon* 220

queue, to 줄을 서다 *chool-ul soda* 112

quick 빠른 *barun* 14; **quickly** 빨리 *ballee* 17

quieter 더 조용한 *to chaw-yong-han* 24, 126

---

rabbi 랍비 *rappee*

race course [track] 경마장 *kyong-ma-jang* 114

racket *(tennis, squash)* 라켓 *laket* 115

railroad [railway] 철도 *choldaw*

rain, to 비가 내리다 *pee-ga nereeda* 122

raincoat 레인코트 *le-een-kawtu* 144

rape 강간 *kang-gan* 152

rapids 급류 *kum-nyoo* 107

rare *(steak)* 설익힌 *soreekeen*; *(unusual)* 드문 *tumoon*

razor 면도칼 *myondawkal*; ~ **blades** 면도날 *myon-daw-nal* 142

reading 독서 *tawk-so* 121

ready, to be 다 되다 *ta dweda* 89, 137, 151

real *(genuine)* 진짜 *cheenza* 149

really? 정말(입니까)? *chong-mal(eemneekka)* 19

receipt 영수증 *yong-soo-jung* 32, 89, 136, 137, 151, 168

reception (desk) 접수 *chopsoo*

receptionist 접수원 *chopsoowon*

---

reclaim tag 짐표 cheem-pyo 71

recommend, Can you recommend ...? 볼만한 ... 하나 있습니까? pawl-manhan ... hana eessumneekka 108

recommend, to 추천하다 choo-chon-hada

record (music) 레코드판 rekawdu-pan 157; **~ store** 레코드 가게 rekawdu kage 131

red 빨간 balgan 143; **~ wine** 레드 와인 redu waeen 40

refrigerator 냉장고 neng-jang-gaw 29

refund 환불 hwan-bool 137

refuse bags 쓰레기봉투 ssuregee-bawng-too 148

region 지역 chee-yok 106

registered mail 등기우편 tunggee-oopyon

registration: ~ form 등록용지 tung-nawk yong-jee 23; **~ number** 차번호 cha-bonhaw 88

regular (petrol/gas) 보통 paw-tawng 87

regular (size of drink) 보통 paw-tawng 110

religion 종교 chawnggyo

remember: I don't remember 기억이 안납니다 keeo-gee annamneeda

rent, to 빌리다 peelleeda 86, 115, 116, 117

rental car 빌린 차 peelleen-cha 153

repair, to 수리하다 sooree-hada 89, 137, 168

repairs 수리 sooree 89

repeat, to 다시 말하다 tasee mal-hada 94, 128; **please repeat that** 다시 말씀해 주십시요 tasee malssume choosee-seeyo 11

replacement (n) 대체품 teche-poom 167; **~ part** 교체 부품 kyo-che poo-poom 137

report, to 신고하다 seen-gaw-hada 152

required, to be 해야하다 heya-hada

reservation 예약 yeyak 22, 36, 68, 77, 112; **reservations desk** 예매창구 yeme chang-goo 109

reserve, to 예약하다 yeyak-hada 21, 28, 36, 74; (theater) 예매하다 yeme-hada 109

rest, to 쉬다 sweeda 106

restaurant 음식점 umseek-zom 35, 112

retail 가게 kage 121

retired, to be 은퇴하다 untwe-hada 121

return, to (give back) 반환하다 panhwanhada 86; (travel) 돌아오다 tawra-awda 75, 81

return (round-trip) **ticket** 왕복표 wang-bawk pyo 65, 68, 74

reverse the charges, to 콜렉트콜로 걸다 kawllekt-kawl-law kolda 127

rheumatism 류마티즘 ryoomateejum

rib 늑골 nukgawl 166

right (correct) 맞는 mannun 77, 94; **that's right** 맞습니다 massumneeda

right (direction) 맞은 majun 14; **on the ~** 오른쪽 awrun-zawk 76

right of way 우선권 ooson-gwon 93

ring 반지 panjee 149

rip-off (n) 바가지 pagajee 101

river 강 kang 107; **~ cruise** 강유람선 kang yooram-son 81

road 길 keel 95; 도로 tawraw 94; **~ closed** 막힌 길 makeen keel 96; **~ map** 도로지도 tawraw cheedaw 150

robbed, to be 강도를 당하다 kang-dawrul tang-hada 153

robbery 강도 kangdaw

rock music 록 음악 rawk umak 111

rolls 롤빵 lolbang 160

romantic 낭만적인 nang-man-jog-een 101

roof (house/car) 지붕 *cheeboong;*
~-rack 루프랙 *loopurek*
room 방 *pang* 21; **~ service**
룸 서비스 *loom sobeesu* 26
rope 밧줄 *patzool*
round (of golf) 경기당 *kyong-gee-dang* 115
round-trip 왕복 *wang-bawk* 65
route 길 *keel* 106
rubbish 쓰레기 *ssuregee* 28
rucksack 배낭 *penang*
rude, to be 무례한 *moorehan*
ruins 페허 *pejo* 99
run: run into somebody (crash car)
박다 *pakda* 93; **run out** (fuel)
떨어지다 *doro-jeeda* 88
running shoes 운동화 *oon-dong-hwa*
145
rush hour 러시아워 *losee-awo*

S **safe** (lock-up) 금고 *kumgaw* 27
safe (not dangerous)
anjon-han 116; **to feel ~** 안전하다
anjon-hada 65
safety 안전 *anjon;* **~ pins** 안전핀
anjonpeen
salad 샐러드 *sellodu*
sales 영업 *yong-op* 121; **~ tax** 부가가
치세 *pooga gachee-se* 24
salt 소금 *saw-gum* 38, 39; **salty** 짠
zan
same 같은 *katun* 75; **~-day** 당일
tang-eel
sand 모래 *mawre*
sandals 샌들 *sendul* 145
sandwich 샌드위치 *sendu-weechee* 40
sandy (beach) 모래가 많은 *mawre-ga*
manun 145
sanitary napkins [towels] 생리대 *seng-nee-de* 142
satellite TV 위성티비 *weesongteebee*
satin 공단 *kawngdan*

satisfied: I'm not satisfied
with this
이것 마음에 안듭니다
eegot mau-me
andumneeda
Saturday 토요일 *taw-yo-eel*
218
sauce 소스 *sawsu* 38
saucepan 냄비 *nembee* 29
sauna 사우나 *sa-oona* 44
sausages 소세지 *saw-sejee* 160
say: how do you
say ...? ... 뭐라고
합니까? *... mworagaw hamneekka*
scarf 스카프 *sukapu* 144
scenic route 경치 좋은 길 *kyong-chee*
jaw-un keel 106
scheduled flight 정기 비행기
chonggee peehenggee
school 학교 *hakgyo* 96
sciatica 좌골 신경통 *chwa-gawl seen-gyong-tawng* 165
scissors 가위 *kawee* 148
scooter 스쿠터 *sukooto*
screwdriver 드라이버 *tura-eebo* 148
scuba equipment 스쿠버 다이빙 장비
sukoobo daee-beeng chang-bee 116
sea 바다 *pada* 107; **~front** 해안거리
he-an-goree
seasick: I feel ~ 배멀미가 납니다
pemolmee-ga namneeda
season ticket 정기권 *chonggeekkwon*
seasoning 양념 *yang-nyom* 38
seat 자리/좌석 *charee/chwasok* 74,
77, 108, 109
second 둘째 *tool-tze* 217; **~ class** (train)
일반실 *eelban-seel* 74; **~-hand** 중고
choonggaw
secretary 비서 *peeso*
sedative 진정제 *cheenjongje*
see, to 보다 *pawda* 24, 93; **see you**
soon! 안녕히 가십시오
an-nyong-ee kaseep-seeaw 126

self-employed, to be 자영업자이다 cha-yong-op ja-eeda 116

self-service 셀프서비스 selpu-sobeesu 87, 133

send, to 보내다 pawneda 155

senior citizen 노인 naw-een 74, 100

separated, to be 별거하다 pyol-go hada 120

separately 따로 daraw 42

September 구월 koo-wol 218

serious 진지한 cheenjeehan; **seriously** 심하게 seemhage 162

served, to be (meal) 주어지다 choo-o-jeeda

service (religious) 예배 yebe 105

set menu 세트 메뉴 setu me-nyoo 37

seven 칠(일곱) cheel(eelgawp) 216

seventeen 십칠(열일곱) seep-cheel(yol-eelgawp) 216

seventy 칠십(일흔) cheel-seep (eerun) 216

sex (act) 성교하다 songgyohada

shade 색조 sekchaw 143

shady 그늘진 kunul-jeen 31

shallow 얕은 yatun

shampoo 샴푸 syam-poo 142; **~ and set** 샴푸와 세트 syampoo-wa setu 147

shape 모양 maw-yang 134

share, to (room) 같이 쓰다 kachee ssuda

sharp 날카로운 nalkaraw-oon 69

shaving brush 면도솔 myondawsawl

shaving cream 면도 크림 myondaw kureem

she 그 여자 ku yoja

sheath (contraceptive) 콘돔 kawndawm

sheet 이불 eebool 28

ship 배 pe 81

shirt 와이셔츠 wa-ee-syochu 144

shock (electric) 감전 kamjon

shoes 신발 seenbal 145; **shoe repair** 신발수선 seenbalsoosoon; **shoe store** 신발 가게 seenbal kage 131

shop assistant 점원 chomwon

shopping 쇼핑 syopeeng; **~ area** 상가 sang-ga 99; **~ basket** 바구니 pagoonee; **~ cart [trolley]** 손수레 sawnsoore 158; **~ mall [centre]** 상가 sang-ga 130, 131

short 짧은 zalbun 14, 144, 146

short-sighted 근시 kunsee 167

shorts 반바지 pan-bajee 144

shoulder 어깨 okke 166

show, to 보여주다 pawyo chooda 133; **can you show me?** 보여주시겠습니까? pawyo-jooseege-ssumneekka 106

shower 샤워 syawo 21, 26, 30

shut, to 닫다 tatda 132; **when do you shut?** 언제 문을 닫습니까? onje moo-nul tassumneekka

shut (adj.) 닫힌 tacheen 14

sick: I'm going to be sick 아플 것 같습니다 apul kot kassumneeda

side (of road) 옆 yop 95, 147; **~ order** 반찬 panchan 38; **~ street** 옆길 yop-geel 95

sights 구경거리 koogyong-goree

sightseeing 관광 kwan-gwang; **~ tour** 관광코스 kwan-gwang kawsu 97

sign (road) 도로표지 tawraw-pyojee 95

silk 비단 peedan

silver 은 un 149; **~-plate** 은도금 un-dawgum 149

singer 가수 kasoo 157

single 일인용 ee-reen-nyong 81; 편도 pyon-daw 65; (one-way) 편도 pyon-daw 68, 74; **~ room** 일인용 방 eereen-nyong pang 21; **to be ~** 미혼이다 mee-hawn-eeda 120

sink (washbasin) 세면대 semyon-de 25

sit, to 앉다 anda 36, 77, 125, 126; **sit down, please** 앉으세요 anjuseyo

six 육(여섯) *yook(yosot)* 216; **~pack of beer** 맥주 여섯병짜리 포장 *mekjoo yosot-pyong-zaree pawjang* 160

sixteen 십육(열여섯) *seep-yook (yol-yosot)* 216

sixty 육십(예순) *yook-seep (yesoon)* 216

size 사이즈 *sa-ee-zu* 146; 크기 *kugee* 115

skates 스케이트 *suke-eetu* 117

skis 스키 *sukee* 117; **ski boots** 스키화 *sukee-hwa* 117; **ski school** 스키학교 *sukee hakgyo* 117

skin 피부 *peeboo* 166

skirt 치마 *cheema* 144

sleep, to 자다 *chada* 167; **sleeper** (*sleeping car*) 침대차 *cheemde-cha* 74; **sleeping bag** 침낭 *cheem-nang* 31; **sleeping car** 침대차 *cheemde-cha* 77; **sleeping pill** 수면제 *soomyonje*

sleeve 소매 *sawme* 144

slice 장 *chang* 159

slippers 슬리퍼 *sullee-po* 145

slow 느린 *nureen* 14; **slowly** 천천히 *chon-chonee* 11, 17, 94, 128; **slow down!** 천천히 하세요 *chonchorihee haseyo;* **to be ~** (*clock*) 늦다 *nutda* 221

SLR camera 싱글 렌즈 리플렉스 사진기 *seeng-gul lenju leepul-leksu sajeen-gee* 151

small 작은 *chagun* 14, 24, 40, 41, 117, 134; (*size of drink*) 작은 거 *chagun ko* 110; **~ change** 잔돈 *chan-dawn* 138

smell: there's a bad smell 나쁜 냄새가 납니다 *nappun nemse-ga namneda*

smoke, to 담배 피우다 *tambe pee-ooda* 126

smoking (*adj*) 흡연 *hubyon* 36; (*area*) 흡연석 *hubyon-sok* 69

snack bar 간이식당 *kanee seektang* 73

snacks 간식 *kanseek*

sneakers 운동화 *oondawng-hwa*

snorkel 잠수용 플라스틱관 *chamsooyong pullasuteekkwan*

snow (*n*) 눈 *noon* 117

snow, to 눈이 내리다 *noo-nee nereeda* 122

soap 비누 *peenoo* 142; **~ powder** 세제 *seje*

soccer 축구 *chookgoo* 114

socket 소케트 *sawketu*

socks 양말 *yangmal* 144

soda 사이다 *sa-ee-da* 160

soft drink 청량음료 *chong-nyang um-nyo* 110, 160

solarium 선룸/일광욕실 *son-loom/eel-gwang-yok-seel* 22

sole (*shoes*) 신발창 *seenbalchang*

soloist 독주자 *tawk-zooja* 111

soluble aspirin 물에 녹는 아스리핀 *moo-re nawng-nun asupeereen*

some 약간 *yakkan*

someone 어떤 사람 *otdon saram* 16

something 무언가 *moo-on-ga* 16

sometimes 가끔 *kakgum* 13

son 아들 *adul* 120, 162

soon 곧 *kawt* 13; **as soon as possible** 가능한 한 빨리 *kanung-han han ballee* 161

sore: it's 쓰립니다 *ssureemneeda;* **~ throat** 목 아픈데 *mawk apunde* 141

sorry! 미안합니다! *meean-hamneeda* 10

sort 종류 *chawng-nyoo* 134

sour 신 *seen* 41

south 남쪽 *nam-zawk* 95

South Africa 남아프리카 *namapureeka*

South African (*person*) 남아프리카 (사람) *namapureeka (saram)*

South Korea 한국 *han-gook* 119

South Korean (*person*) 한국 (사람) *han-gook (saram)* 119

A-Z

souvenir 기념품 *kee-nyom-poom* 98, 156; **~ guidebook** 기념품 안내 *kee-nyom-poom anne* 156; **~ store** 기념품 가게 *kee-nyom-poom kage* 131

space 자리 *charee* 30

spare (extra) 여분 *yoboon*

speak, to 얘기하다 *yegee-hada* 41; 말하다 *mal-hada* 11, 67, 128; **do you speak English?** 영어 하세요? *yong-o haseyo* 11; **speak to s.o.** (telephone) 통화하다 *tawng-hwa-hada* 128

special delivery 속달 *sawktal* 155

specialist 전문의 *chon-moon-uee* 164

specimen 검사시료 *komsa-seeryo* 164

spectacles 안경 *an-gyong*

speed, to 과속하다 *kwa-sawk-hada* 93

spend, to 쓰다 *ssuda*

spicy 양념이 강한 *yangnyo-mee kang-han*

sponge 수세미 *soosemee* 148

spoon 숟가락 *sootgarak* 39, 41, 148; **spoon and chopsticks** 수저 *soojo* 29

sport 운동 *oon-dawng* 121; **sporting goods store** 운동구점 *oon-dawn-goo jom* 131; **sports club** 스포츠 클럽 *supaw-chu kullop* 115; **sports ground** 운동장 *oondawng-jang* 96

sprained, to be 삐다 *beeda* 164

spring 봄 *pawm* 219

stadium 경기장 *kyong-gee-jang* 96

stain 얼룩 *ollook*; **~less steel** 스테인레스 *sute-een-lesu* 149

stairs 계단 *kedan* 132

stamps 우표 *oopyo* 150, 154

stand in line, to 줄을 서다 *chool-ul soda* 112

standby ticket 대기표 *tegeepyo*

start, to (car) 시동걸다 *see-dawng-kolda* 88; 떠나다 *donada* 98

starter 전식 *chonseek* 38

statement (legal) 진술서 *cheen-sool-so* 93

station 역 *yok* 96

stationer's 문방구 *moonbanggoo*

statue 동상 *tawng-sang* 99

stay, to 묵다 *mookda* 23, 123; **~ in lane** 차선변경금지 *chason pyon-gyong kumjee* 96

stay (n) 묵음 *moogum* 32

steak house 스테이크 집 *sute-eeku jeep* 35

sterilizing solution 젖병 소독액 *jotbyong sawdawg-ek* 142

stiff neck 목이 뻣뻣한 *maw-gee ppotppot-ham*

still: I'm still waiting 저는 아직 기다리고 있습니다 *cho-nun ajeek keedareegaw eessumneeda*

stockings 스타킹 *suta-keeng* 144

stolen, to be 도난당하다 *tawnan dang-hada* 71

stomach 위 *wee* 166; **~ache** 위통 *wee-tawng* 163

stools 대변 *tebyon* 164

stop (bus/tram) 서다 *soda* 79; (subway/metro) 정거장 *chong-gojang* 80

stop, to 멈추다 *mom-chooda* 98; **~ at** 서다 *soda* 76, 77, 78

stopcock 차단밸브 *chadan-belbu* 28

store 상점 *sang-jom*; **~ guide** 상점 안내판 *sang-jom anne-pan* 132

stormy, to be 천둥이 치다 *chondung-ee cheeda* 122

stove 난로 *nallaw* 29

straight ahead 직진방향에 *cheekzeen bang-hyang-e* 95

strange 이상한 *eesang-han* 101

straw (drinking) 빨대 *ppaltte*

stream 시내 *seene* 107

strong (potent) 강한 *kanghan*

student 학생 *haksaeng* 74, 100, 121
study, to 공부하다 *kawng-boo hada* 121
stunning 멋진 *mozeen* 101
style 양식 *yangseek* 104
subtitled, to be 자막이 있다 *chamagee eet-da*
subway (metro) 지하철 *cheeha-chol* 80; **~ station** 지하철역 *cheeha-chol yok* 80, 96
sugar 설탕 *soltang* 38, 39
suggest, to 제안하다 *chean hada*
suit 양복 *yang-bawk* 144
suitable for 에 적당한 *e chokttang-han*
summer 여름 *yorum* 219
sun block 자외선 차단 크림 *chaweson chadan kureem* 142
sunbathe, to 일광욕하다 *eelgwang-yokhada*
sunburn 일광 화상 *eel-gwang hwa-sang* 141
Sunday 일요일 *eel-yo-eel* 218
sunglasses 선글라스 *son-gullasu*
sunshade 햇빛가리개 *hetbeet karee-ge* 116
sunstroke 일사병 *eelssa-byong* 163
suntan lotion 선탠 크림 *sonten kureem* 142
super (petrol/gas) 고급 *kaw-gup* 87
superb 최고의 *chwe-gaw-uee* 101
supermarket 슈퍼마켓 *soopo-maket* 131
supervision 돌봄 *tawlbawm* 113
supplement 추가요금 *chooga-yogum* 69
suppositories 좌약 *chwa-yak* 165
sure: are you sure? 확실합니까? *hwakseelhamneekka*
surfboard 서핑보드 *sopeeng-bawdu* 116
surname 성 *song*
sweater 스웨터 *suweto* 144

sweatshirt 보온용 스웨터 *paw-awn-nyong suweto* 144
sweet (taste) 단 *tan*
sweets (candy) 사탕 *satang* 150
swim, to 수영하다 *soo-yong-hada* 116
swimming 수영 *soo-yong* 114; **~ pool** 수영장 *sooyong-jang* 22, 26, 116; **~ trunks** 수영팬츠 *sooyong-penchu* 144
swimsuit 수영복 *sooyong-bawk* 144
switch 스위치 *suwee-chee* 25
swollen, to be 부은 *poo-un*
synagogue 유대교회 *yoode gyo-hwe* 105
synthetic 합성섬유 *hapsong somyoo* 145

T **T-shirt** 티셔츠 *tee-syochu* 144, 156
table 테이블 *te-ee-bul* 112; (restaurant) 자리 *charee* 36
tablet 알 *al* 140
take away, to 싸가다 *ssagada* 40
take out, to (tooth) 뽑다 *bawpda* 168
take photographs, to 사진 찍다 *sajeen zeekda* 98
take, to 선택하다 *sontek-hada* 24; (bus) 타다 *tada* 78; (carry) 운반하다 *oonban-hada* 71; (medicine) (약을) 먹다 (yagul) *mokda* 140, 165; (time) 걸리다 *kolleeda* 78; **I'll take it** 이걸로 하겠습니다 *eegol-law hage-ssumneeda* 24, 135; **taken** (occupied) 임자있는 *eemja-eennun* 77
talk, to 얘기하다 *yegeehada*
tall 긴 *keen* 14
tampons 탐폰 *tampawn* 142
tap (n) 수도꼭지 *soodaw gawk-zee* 25
taxi 택시 *teksee* 70, 71, 84; **~ stand** [rank] 택시승차장 *teksee sungcha-jang* 96

tea 차 *cha* 40; **~ bags** 봉지차 *pawng-jee-cha* 160; **~ towel** 티 타월 *tee tawol* 156

teacher 선생님 *sonsengneem*

team 팀 *teem* 114

teaspoon *(measurement)* 스푼 *su-poon* 140

teddy bear 곰인형 *kawm een-hyong* 157

telephone 전화 *chon-hwa* 22, 92; **~ booth** 공중전화 *kawng-joong chonhwa* 127; **~ calls** 전화 통화 *chonhwa tawng-hwa* 32; **~ directory** 전화번호부 *chonhwa-bonhaw-boo* 127; **~ number** 전화번호 *chonhwa-bonhaw* 127

telephone, to 전화를 걸다 *chonhwa-rul kolda* 127

tell, to 말하다 *mal-hada* 18, 79; **tell me** 저에게 말하다 *cho-ege mal-hada* 79

temperature *(body)* 체온 *che-awn* 164

temporarily 임시로 *eemsee-raw* 89, 168

ten 십(열) *seep(yol)* 216

tennis 테니스 *teneesu* 114; **~ court** 테니스 코트 *teneesu kawtu* 115

tent 텐트 *tentu* 30, 31; **~ pegs** 텐트용 쐐기 *tentu-yong sswegee* 31; **~ pole** 텐트용 폴 *tentu-yong pawl* 31

terrible 엉망인 *ong-mang-een* 19

terrific 근사한 *kunsa-han* 19

tetanus 파상풍 *pasang-poong* 164

thank you 감사합니다 *kamsa-hamneeda*

that: that one 그것 *kugot* 16, 134; **that's true** 사실입니다. *saseel-eemneeda* 19; **that's all** 됐습니다 *dwe-ssumneeda* 133

theater 극장 *kukzang* 96, 99, 110

theft 도난 *tawnan* 153

their 그 사람들의 *ku saram-dure* 16

theirs 그 사람들 것 *ku saramdul got* 16

theme park 테마 유원지 *tema yoowonjee*

then *(time)* 그때 *kutde* 13

there 거기 *ko-gee* 12; **there is/are ... ...** 있습니다 *...ee-ssumneeda* 17

thermometer 온도계 *awndawge*

thermos flask 보온병 *paw-awn-pyong*

these 이것들 *eegodul* 134

they 그들 *kutul*

thief 도둑 *tawdook*

thigh 넓적다리 *nobzok-daree*

thin 가는 *kanun*

think: I think 생각하다 *seng-gak hada* 42; **~ about it** 생각해 보다 *seng-gake pawda* 135

third 셋째 *set-ze* 217; **~ party insurance** 책임 보험 *chegeem paw-hom*

third, a 삼분의 일 *samboon-e eel* 217

thirsty: I am thirsty 목이 마릅니다 *maw-gee marumneeda*

thirteen 십삼(열셋) *seep-sam(yol-set)* 216

thirty 삼십(서른) *sam-seep(sorun)* 216

this 이번 *eebon* 218; **~ one** 이것 *eegot* 16, 134

those 그것들 *kugodul* 134

thousand 천 *chon* 216

three 삼(셋) *sam(set)* 216

throat 목구멍 *mawk-goo-mong*

thrombosis 혈전증 *hyoljonzung*

thumb 엄지손가락 *omjee sawn-garak* 166

Thursday 목요일 *mawk-yo-eel* 218

ticket 표 *pyo* 65, 68, 69, 74, 75, 114; **~ office** 매표소 *me-pyo-saw* 73

tie 넥타이 *nek-ta-ee* 144

tray 쟁반 *chengban*

trim 다듬기 *tadum-gee* 147

trip 여행코스 *yoheng-kawsu* 97

trouser press 바지 눌러놓는 기계 *pajee noollonawnnun keege*

trousers 바지 *pajee* 144

truck 대형트럭 *tehyongturok*

true: that's not true 그것은 사실이 아닙니다 *kugo-sun sasee-ree aneemneeda*

try on, to (clothes) 입어 보다 *eebo pawda* 146; (shoes) 신어 보다 *seeno pawda* 146

Tuesday 화요일 *hwa-yo-eel* 218

tumor 종양 *chawng-yang* 165

tunnel 터널 *tonol*

turn, to 회전하다 *hwe-jon hada* 95; ~ **down** (volume, heat) 낮추다 *nachooda*; ~ **off** 끄다 *guda* 25; ~ **on** 켜다 *kyoda* 25; ~ **up, to** (volume, heat) 높이다 *nawpeeda*

TV 텔레비전 *tele-beejon* 22

tweezers 쪽집게 *zawkzeepke*

twelve 십이(열둘) *seep-ee(yol-tool)* 216

twenty 이십(스물) *ee-seep(sumool)* 216

twice 두 번 *too-bon* 217

twin beds 일인용 침대 두개 *eereen-nyong cheemde tooke* 21

twist: I've twisted my ankle 발목을 삐었습니다 *palmaw-gul ppee-ossumneeda*

two 이(둘) *ee(tool)* 216; ~~**-door car** 투도어식 차 *too-daw-o-seek cha* 86

type 종류 *chawng-nyoo* 109; **what type?** 어떤 종류 *otdon chawng-nyoo* 112

typical 대표 *depyo* 37

tyre 타이어 *taeeo* 83

U **ugly** 미운 *mee-oon* 14

ulcer 궤양 *kweyang*

umbrella 햇빛가리개 *hetbeet karee-ge* 116

uncle 삼촌 *sam-chawn* 120

unconscious, to be 의식을 잃다 *ueeseeg-ul eelta* 92

under 아래에 *are-e*; ~**done** 덜 익은 *tol eegun* 41

underground (metro) 지하철 *cheeha-chol* 80; ~ **station** 지하철역 *cheeha-chol yok* 80, 96

underpants 속바지 *sawk-pajee* 144

underpass 지하도 *cheeha-daw* 96

understand, to 알다 *alda* 11; **do you understand?** 아시겠습니까 *aseege-ssumneekka* 11; **I don't understand** 모르겠습니다 *mawruge-ssumneeda* 11

undress, to 벗다 *potda* 164

unemployed 실업자 *seerop-ja* 121

uneven (ground) 울퉁불퉁한 *ooltoong-booltoong-han* 31

unfortunately 불행히도 *poolheng-eedaw* 19

uniform 단체복 *tanchebawk*

United States 미국 *mee-gook*

unleaded petrol 무연 기름 *mooyon keerum*

unlimited mileage 무제한 마일리지 *moojehan maeelleejee*

unlock, to 자물쇠를 열다 *chamoolswe-rul yolda*

unscrew, to 나사를 돌려 빼다 *nasa-rul tawllyo ppeda*

until 까지 *gajee* 221

up to 까지 *gajee* 12

upper (berth) 위칸 *weekan* 74

upset stomach 배탈 *petal* 141

upstairs 위층 *wee-chung*

urgent 응급 *ung-gup* 161

urine 소변 *saw-byon* 164

U.S. 미국 *meegook*

use, to (operate) 사용하다 *sayong-hada* 28, 139

V V-neck 브이 넥 *pu-ee nek* 144
 vacancy 빈 방 *peen pang* 21
vacate, to 비우다 *pee-ooda* 32
vacation, on 휴가로 *hyooga-raw* 66, 123
vaccinated against, to be 예방주사를 맞다 *yebang-joosa-rul matda* 164
vaginal infection 질감염 *cheel-gam-yom* 167
valet service 세탁서비스 *setak sobeesu*
valid 유효한 *yoohyo-han* 75
validate, to 확인하다 *hwageenhada*
valley 계곡 *ke-gawk* 107
valuable 귀중한 *kweejoong-han*
value 가격 *ka-gyok* 155
valve 차단밸브 *chadan-belbu* 28
VAT 부가가치세 *pooga gachee-se* 24;
 ~ receipt 부가가치세 영수증 *pooga gachee-se yongsoojung*
vegan, to be 철저하게 채식하는 *choljohage cheseekhanun*
vegetables 야채 *yache* 38
vegetarian 채식 *cheseek* 35
vehicle registration document 자동차 등록증 *chadawng-cha tung-nawk-zung* 93
vein 정맥 *chong-mek* 166
venereal disease 성병 *song-byong* 165
ventilator 환기장치 *hwan-geejangchee*
video game 비디오 게임 *peedee-aw ke-eem*
video recorder 비디오 *peedee-aw*
view: with a view of the sea 바다가 보이는 *pada-ga paw-eenun*;
 viewpoint 전망대 *chonmang-de* 99, 107
village 마을 *maul* 107
vinaigrette 비너그레트 *beeno-guretu* 38
vineyard 포도밭 *pawdaw-bat* 107
visa 비자 *peeja*

visit (*n*) 방문 *pang-moon* 119;
 visiting hours 방문 시간 *pang-moon seegan*
visit, to 방문하다 *pang-moon hada*
vitamins 비타민 정제 *pee-tameen chong-je* 141
volleyball 배구 *pe-goo* 114
voltage 전압 *chonap*
vomit, to 토하다 *taw-hada* 163

W wait, to 기다리다 *keeda-reeda* 140; **wait for** 기다리다 *keeda-reeda* 76, 89; **wait!** 잠깐 *cham-gan* 98
Waiter! 여보세요! *yobaw-seyo* 37
waiting room 대합실 *tehap-seel* 73
Waitress! 여보세요! *yobaw-seyo* 37
wake someone, to 깨우다 *ge-ooda* 27, 70
wake-up call 웨이크업 콜 *we-eeku-op kawl*
walking route 산책로 *sancheng-naw* 106
walking gear 등산 장비 *tungsan changbee*
wallet 지갑 *chee-gap* 42, 153
want, to 원하다 *won-hada* 18
ward (*hospital*) 병동 *pyong-dawng* 167
washbasin 세면대 *semyonde*
washing: ~ machine 세탁기 *setakgee* 29; **~ powder** 세제 *seje* 148; **~-up liquid** 식기용 세제 *seekgee-yong seje* 148
wasp 말벌 *malbol*
watch 손목시계 *sawn-mawk seege* 149, 153
water 물 *mool* 87; **~ bottle** 물병 *moolppyong*; **~ heater** 온수기 *awnsoo-gee* 28; **~ skis** 수상스키 *soosang-sukee* 116; **~fall** 폭포 *pawk-paw* 107

waterproof 방수 *pang-soo*; ~ **jacket** 방수자켓 *pang-soo-jaket* 145

wave 파도 *padaw*

waxing 피부팩 *peeboo-pek* 147

way (direction) 길 *keel* 94; **I've lost my way** 길을 잃었습니다 *kee-rul eero-ssumneeda* 94; **on the way** 가는 길 *kanun keel* 83

we 우리 *ooree*

wear, to 입다 *eepda* 152

weather 날씨 *nalssee* 122; ~ **forecast** 일기예보 *eel-gee yebaw* 122

wedding 결혼식 *kyolhawnseek*; ~ **ring** 결혼 반지 *kyolhawn panjee*

Wednesday 수요일 *soo-yo-eel* 218

week 주 *choo* 23, 218; 일주일 *eeljoo-eel* 97

weekend 주말 *choomal*; **at the ~** 주말에 *choomal-e* 218; ~ **rate** 주말 요금 *choomal yogum* 86

weight: my weight is ... 제 몸무게는 ... 입니다 *che mawmmooge-nun ... eemneeda*

welcome to ... ...에 오신 걸 환영합니다 *...e awseen kol hwanyong-hamneeda*

well-done (steak) 완전히 익힌 *wanjonee eekeen*

west 서쪽 *so-zawk* 95

wetsuit 잠수복 *chamsoobawk*

what: what do you do? (job) 직업이 무엇입니까? *cheeg-obee moo-o-seemneekka* 121; **what kind of ...?** 어떤 종류 ...? *otdon chawng-nyoo ...* 37; 어떤 *ot-don* 106; **what time?** 몇시에? *myossee-e* 68, 76, 81; **what's the time?** 지금 몇시입니까? *chee-gum myo-ssee eem-neekka* 220

wheelchair 휠체어 *hweelche-o*

when? 언제/몇시에 *onje/myo-ssee-e* 13

where do you come from? 어디서 오셨습니까? *odeeso awsyo-ssumneekka* 119

where? 어디에? *odee-e* 12; **where else** 어디 다른데서 *odee tarun-deso* 135; **where is the ...?** ... 어디 있습니까? *... odee ee-ssumneekka* 99; **where were you born?** 고향이 어디십니까? *kaw-hyang-ee odee-seemneekka* 119

which? 어떤? *otdon* 16; **which stop?** 어느 정거장? *onu chong-gojang* 80

white 흰 *heen* 143; ~ **wine** 화이트 와인 *hwa-eetu waeen* 40

who? 누구? *noo-goo* 16

whose? 누구 것? *noogoo got* 16

why 왜 *we* 15

wide 넓은 *nolbun* 14

wife 아내 *ane* 120, 162

wildlife 야생 *yaseng*

windbreaker 방풍자켓 *pang-poong-jaket* 16

window 창문 *chang-moon* 25, 77; (shop) 진열대 *cheen-yol-de* 149; ~ **seat** 창쪽 자리 *chang-zawk charee* 69, 74

windshield [windscreen] 차앞유리 *cha-amnyooree*

windy, to be 바람이 불다 *paramee poolda* 122

wine 포도주 *pawdaw-joo* 40; ~ **list** 포도주 리스트 *pawdaw-joo leesutu* 37

winter 겨울 *kyo-ool* 219

withdraw, to (돈을) 찾다 (*taw-nul*) *chatda* 139

within (time) 안에 *ane* 13

witness 목격자 *mawk-gyok-za* 93

Won 원 *won* 67

wood 숲 *soop* 107

wool 모 *maw* 145

work, to 작동하다 chakdawng-hada
83; **it doesn't work** 고장나다
kawjang-nada 25; **work for**
에서 일하다 -eso eel-hada 121

worst 최악의 chwe-age

write, to 쓰다 ssuda 11; **~ down** 쓰다
ssuda 136

writing pad 편지지 pyon-jee-jee 150

wrong 잘못된 chal-mawtdwen 136;
틀린 tulleen 14; **wrong number** 틀린
번호 tulleen ponhaw

X Y Z **X-ray** 엑스레이 ekssu-re-ee 164
yacht 요트 yotu

year 해 he 218

yellow 노란 nawran 143

yes 네 ne 10

yesterday 어제 oje 218

yield 양보 yang-paw 96

yogurt 요구르트 yogoorutu

you (singular) 선생님 sonsengneem;
(plural) 선생님들 sonsengneemdul;
you are here 현재위치 hyonje wee-
chee 96

young 젊은 cholmun 14

your 당신의 tangseen-e 16

yours 당신 것 tangseen got 16; **it's ~**
그것은 선생님 것입니다 kugo-sun
sonsengneem koseemneeda

zebra crossing 횡단보도 hwengdan-
bawdaw

zero 영(공) yong(kawng)

zip(per) 지퍼 cheepo

zoo 동물원 tawng-mool-won 113

Glossary
Korean-English

This Korean-English Glossary covers all the areas where you may need to decode written Korean: hotels, public buildings, restaurants, stores, ticket offices, transportation, etc. The Korean is written in large type to help you identify the words from the signs you see around you.

General 일반사항

Korean	Romanization	English
좌, 왼쪽	*chwa, wenzawk*	LEFT
우, 오른쪽	*oo, awrunzawk*	RIGHT
입구	*eepkoo*	ENTRANCE
출구	*choolgoo*	EXIT
화장실	*hwa-jangseel*	TOILETS
신사, 남자	*seensa, namja*	MEN (TOILETS)
숙녀, 여자	*soong-nyo, yoja*	WOMEN (TOILETS)
사용중	*sayongjoong*	OCCUPIED
금연	*kumyon*	NO SMOKING
위험	*weehom*	DANGER
출입금지	*chooreep-kumjee*	NO ENTRY
주의	*choo-ee*	CAUTION {DANGER OF DEATH}
당기세요/ 미세요	*tang-geeseyo/ meeseyo*	PULL/PUSH

분실물	poonseel-mool	LOST PROPERTY
수영금지, 수영엄금	sooyong-gumjee, sooyong-omgum	NO SWIMMING
들어가지 마시오	turogajee maseeaw	KEEP OUT
식수	seeksoo	DRINKING WATER
관계자외 출입금지	kwonkeja-we chooreep-kumjee	PRIVATE
쓰레기를 버리지 마시오	ssuregee-rul poreejee maseeaw	NO LITTER
지하도	cheehadaw	UNDERPASS/ SUBWAY
계단 조심	kedan chawseem	MIND THE STEP
칠 주의	cheel choo-ee	WET PAINT
특실	tukseel	FIRST CLASS *(train)*
일반	eelban	SECOND CLASS *(train)*

Road Signs 도로표지

Korean	Romanization	English
정지, 멈춤	chong-jee, momchoom	STOP
우측통행	oochuk tawng-heng	KEEP RIGHT
좌측통행	chachuk tawng-heng	KEEP LEFT
일방통행	eelbang-tawng-heng	ONE WAY
추월 금지	choo-wol kumjee	NO OVERTAKING
주차 금지	choocha kumjee	NO PARKING
고속도로	kawsawk-tawraw	FREEWAY [MOTORWAY]
톨게이트	tawl-ge-eetu	TOLL
(교통)신호등	(kyotawng) seenhaw-dung	TRAFFIC LIGHTS
경고	kyong-gaw	WARNING
교차로	kyocharaw	JUNCTION
인터체인지	eentoche-eenjee	JUNCTION (on freeways)

Airport/Station 공항/기차역

안내	anne	INFORMATION
일번 플랫폼	eelbon pullet-pawm	PLATFORM 1
일번 게이트	eelbon ge-eetu	GATE 1
세관	se-gwan	CUSTOMS
입국	eepkook	IMMIGRATION
도착	tawchak	ARRIVALS
출발	choolbal	DEPARTURES
짐보관함	cheem-baw-gawn-ham	LUGGAGE LOCKERS
짐 찾는 곳	cheem channun kawt	LUGGAGE RECLAIM
버스/기차	posu/keecha	BUS/TRAIN
렌트카	lentuka	CAR RENTAL
연착	yonchak	DELAYED
지하철	cheehachol	SUBWAY [METRO]

Hotel/Restaurant
호텔/레스토랑

Korean	Romanization	English
안내	*anne*	INFORMATION
프론트	*purawntu*	RECEPTION
예약석	*yeyasok*	RESERVED
비상구	*peesang-goo*	EMERGENCY/ FIRE EXIT
온수	*awnsoo, to-oonmool*	HOT (WATER)
냉수	*nengsoo, chanmool*	COLD (WATER)
직원용	*cheegwonyong*	STAFF ONLY
휴대품 보관	*hyoodepoom paw-gwan*	CLOAKROOM
테라스/정원	*terasu/chong-won*	TERRACE/GARDEN
금연석	*kumyon-sok*	NO SMOKING
바	*pa*	BAR
욕실	*yokseel*	BATH

Stores 상점

영업중, 영업합니다	*yong-op-joong,* *yong-op-hamneeda*	OPEN
영업 안합니다	*yong-op* *anhamneeda*	CLOSED
점심식사 중	*chomseem-seeksa* *choong*	LUNCH
부	*poo*	DEPARTMENT
층	*chung*	FLOOR
지하	*cheeha*	BASEMENT
엘리베이터	*ellee-be-eeto*	ELEVATOR [LIFT]
에스컬레이터	*esukolle-eeto*	ESCALATOR
계산대	*kesande*	CASHIER
세일	*se-eel*	SALE

Sightseeing 관광

Korean	Romanization	English
무료입장	mooryo-eepchang	ADMISSION FREE
성인, 어른	song-een, orun	ADULTS
어린이	oreenee	CHILDREN
학생할인/ 경로할인	hakseng-hareen/ kyong-naw-hareen	CONCESSIONS (students/pensioners)
기념품	keenyopoom	SOUVENIRS
음료수	umnyosoo	REFRESHMENTS
만지지 마시오	manjeejee maseeaw	DO NOT TOUCH
사진촬영 금지	sajeen-chwaryong	NO PHOTOS
정숙	chong-sook	SILENCE
접근 금지	chopkun kumjee	NO ACCESS

Public Buildings 공공건물

병원	pyong-won	HOSPITAL
의사	ueesa	DOCTOR
치과의사	cheekkwa-ueesa	DENTIST
경찰서	kyongchalso	POLICE
은행	unheng	BANK
우체국	oo-chegook	POST OFFICE
수영장	sooyongjang	SWIMMING POOL
시청	seechong	TOWN HALL
택시승차장	teksee-sungchajang	TAXI STAND
약국	yakook	PHARMACY
공중목욕탕	kawng-joong-mawgyok-tang	PUBLIC BATH
박물관	pang-moolgwan	MUSEUM

Numbers

GRAMMAR

In Korean the number system is complex and uses two different sets of numbers. The "general numbers system" (**eel, ee, sam**, etc.) is used for talking about sums of money, telephone numbers, etc. In addition, there is a system for combining a number with an *object-specific counter*. This system groups objects into types according to their shape and size. When a number is combined with an *object-specific counter*, the numbers used are those given in parentheses below (**hana, tool, set**, etc.). Using the "general number system" it is straightforward to build up large numbers – once you have learned 1 to 10, twenty is just 'two-ten', 30 'three-ten', etc.

0 영 (공) *yong (kawng)*
1 일 (하나) *eel (hana)*
2 이 (둘) *ee (tool)*
3 삼 (셋) *sam (set)*
4 사 (넷) *sa (net)*
5 오 (다섯) *aw (tasot)*
6 육 (여섯) *yook (yosot)*
7 칠 (일곱) *cheel (eelgawp)*
8 팔 (여덟) *pal (yodol)*
9 구 (아홉) *koo (ahawp)*
10 십 (열) *seep (yol)*
11 십일 (열하나)
   seep-eel (yolhana)
12 십이 (열둘)
   seep-ee (yol-tool)
13 십삼 (열셋)
   seep-sam (yol-set)
14 십사 (열넷)
   seep-sa (yol-let)

15 십오 (열다섯)
   seep-aw (yol-tasot)
16 십육 (열여섯)
   seep-yook (yol-yosot)
17 십칠 (열일곱)
   seep-cheel (yol-eelgawp)
18 십팔 (열여덟)
   seep-pal (yol-yodol)
19 십구 (열아홉)
   seep-koo (yol-ahawp)
20 이십 (스물)
   eeseep (sumool)
21 이십일 (스물하나)
   eeseep-eel (sumool-hana)
22 이십이 (스물둘)
   eeseep-ee (sumool-tool)
23 이십삼 (스물셋)
   eeseep-sam (sumool-set)
24 이십사 (스물넷)
   eeseep-sa (sumool-net)

25	이십오 (스물다섯) *eeseep-aw (sumool-tasot)*	1,000,000	백만 *beng-man*
26	이십육 (스물여섯) *eeseem-nyook (sumool-yosot)*	first	첫째 *chot-ze*
27	이십칠 (스물일곱) *eeseep-cheel (sumoo-reelgawp)*	second	둘째 *tool-ze*
28	이십팔 (스물여덟) *eeseep-pal (sumool-yodol)*	third	셋째 *set-ze*
29	이십구 (스물아홉) *eeseep-koo (sumool-ahawp)*	fourth	넷째 *net-ze*
30	삼십 (서른) *samseep (sorun)*	fifth	다섯째 *tasot-ze*
31	삼십일 (서른하나) *samseebeel (sorun-hana)*	once	한 번 *han-bon*
32	삼십이 (서른둘) *samseebee (sorun-dool)*	twice	두 번 *too-bon*
40	사십 (마흔) *saseep (mahun)*	three times	세 번 *se-bon*
50	오십 (쉰) *awseep(sween)*	a half	반 *pan*
60	육십 (예순) *yook-seep(yesoon)*	half an hour	반 시간 *pan seegan*
70	칠십 (일흔) *cheel-seep(eerun)*	half a tank	반 탱크 *pan teng-ku*
80	팔십 (여든) *pal-seep(yodun)*	half eaten	반 쯤 먹은 *pan zum mogun*
90	구십 (아흔) *kooseep(ahun)*	a quarter	사분의 일 *saboon-e eel*
100	백 *pek*	a third	삼분의 일 *samboon-e eel*
101	백일 *pek-eel*	a pair of …	… 한 벌 … *han pol*
102	백이 *pek-ee*	a dozen …	… 한 타스 … *han-tasu*
200	이백 *eebek*	1999	천구백구십구 *chon-goobek-gooseep-koo*
500	오백 *awbek*	2001	이천일 *eechon-eel*
1,000	천 *chon*	the 1990s	천구백구십년대 *chon-goobek-gooseem-nyon-de*
10,000	만 *man*		

Days 요일

Monday	월요일 wol-yo-eel
Tuesday	화요일 hwa-yo-eel
Wednesday	수요일 soo-yo-eel
Thursday	목요일 mawk-yo-eel
Friday	금요일 kum-yo-eel
Saturday	토요일 taw-yo-eel
Sunday	일요일 eel-yo-eel

Months 월

January	일월 eel-wol
February	이월 ee-wol
March	삼월 sam-wol
April	사월 sa-wol
May	오월 aw-wol
June	유월 yoo-wol
July	칠월 cheel-wol
August	팔월 pal-wol
September	구월 koo-wol
October	시월 see-wol
November	십일월 seep-eel-wol
December	십이월 seep-ee-wol

Dates 날짜

It's ...	... 입니다. ... eem-needa
July 10	칠월 십일 cheel-wol seep-eel
March 1	삼월 일일 sam-wol eel-eel
yesterday	어제 oje
today	오늘 aw-nul
tomorrow	내일 ne-eel
this .../last ...	이번 .../지난 ... eebon .../chee-nan ...
next week	다음 주 ta-um choo
every month/year	매달/매해 me-dal/me-he
on the weekend	주말에 choomal-e

218

Seasons 계절

spring	봄 *pawm*
summer	여름 *yorum*
fall [autumn]	가을 *ka-ul*
winter	겨울 *kyo-ool*
in spring	봄에 *pawm-e*
during the summer	여름동안 *yorum-tawng-an*

Greetings 인사말

Happy birthday!
생일 축하합니다!
seng-eel chooka ham-needa

Merry Christmas!
메리 크리스마스! *meree kureesumasu*

Happy New Year!
새해 복많이 받으세요!
sehe pawng-manee padu-seyo

Congratulations!
축하합니다! *chooka ham-needa*

Good luck!/All the best!
행운을 빕니다! *heng-oonul peem-needa*

Public holidays

January 1/2 (*S. Korea*)	New Year
March 1 (*S. Korea*)	Independence Movement Day
February 16 (*N. Korea*)	Kim Jong Il's Birthday
April 5 (*S. Korea*)	Arbor Day
April 15 (*N. Korea*)	Kim Il Sung's Birthday
April 25 (*N. Korea*)	Armed Forces Day
May 1 (*N. Korea/S. Korea*)	May Day
May 5 (*S. Korea*)	Children's Day
June 6 (*S. Korea*)	Memorial Day
July 17 (*S. Korea*)	Constitution Day
August 15 (*S. Korea*)	Liberation Day
September 9 (*N. Korea*)	National Foundation Day
October 3 (*S. Korea*)	National Foundation Day
October 10 (*N. Korea*)	Korean Workers' Party Foundation Day
December 25 (*S. Korea*)	Christmas

There are also three public holidays in South Korea which are based on the lunar calendar and so fall on different days every year: Lunar New Year (Jan./Feb.), Buddha's Birthday (May) and the Harvest Moon Festival (Sep./Oct.).

Time 시간

Korean expresses the time in terms of minutes *after* the hour. So one o'clock is **han see**, quarter past one is **han see awboon** ("one fifteen"), twenty to two is **han see saseep boon**, ("one forty"), etc.

Excuse me, can you tell me the time?	실례합니다, 지금 몇시입니까? *seelle-hamneeda, chee-gum myo-ssee eem-neekka*
It's ...	... 입니다. *... eem-needa*
five past one	한시 오분 *han see awboon*
ten past two	두시 십분 *too see seepboon*
a quarter past three	세시 십오분 *se see seep awboon*
twenty past four	네시 이십분 *ne see eeseep boon*
twenty-five past five	다섯시 이십오분 *taso-ssee eeseep awboon*
half past six	여섯시 반 *yoso ssee pan*
twenty-five to seven	여섯시 삼십오분 *yosotsee samseep awboon*
twenty to eight	일곱시 사십분 *eelgawpsee saseep boon*
a quarter to nine	여덟시 사십오분 *yodolsee saseep awboon*
ten to ten	아홉시 오십분 *ahawpsee awseep boon*
five to eleven	열시 오십오분 *yolsee awseep awboon*
twelve o'clock (noon/midnight)	열두시 (정오/자정) *yol-doo see (chong-aw/chajong)*

at dawn	새벽에 *sebyog-e*
in the morning	아침에 *acheem-e*
during the day	낮에 *naje*
before lunch	점심 전에 *chomseem jone*
after lunch	점심 후에 *chomseem hoo-e*
in the afternoon	오후에 *awhoo-e*
in the evening	저녁에 *cho-nyog-e*
at night	밤에 *pame*
I'll be ready in five minutes.	오분이면 다 됩니다. *awboon eemyon ta dwem-needa*
He'll be back in 15 minutes.	그 사람 십오분 후에 돌아옵니다. *ku saram seep-awboon hoo-e tawra awm-mneeda*
She arrived half an hour ago.	그 여자는 반시간 전에 도착했습니다. *ku yoja-nun pan-seegan jone tawchak he-ssumneeda*
The train leaves at …	그 기차는 … 에 떠납니다. *ku keecha-nun … e donam-needa*
13:04	한시 사분 *han-see saboon*
0:40	밤 열두시 사십분 *pam yol-doo-see saseep-boon*
10 minutes late/early	십분 늦게/일찍 *seepboon nutge/eelzeek*
5 minutes fast/slow	오분 빠른/늦은 *awboon barun/nujun*
from 9:00 to 5:00	아홉시부터 다섯시까지 *ahawp-see-booto taso-ssee-gajee*
between 8:00 and 2:00	여덟시에서 두시 사이에 *yodol-see-eso too-see saee-e*
I'll be leaving by …	저는 … 에 떠납니다. *cho-nun … e donam-needa*
Will you be back before …?	… 전에 돌아 오십니까? *… jone tawra awseem-neekka*
We'll be here until …	여기에 … 까지 있겠습니다. *yogee-e … gajee eetge-ssumneeda*